WILDLY SUCCESSFUL

NORTHERN CALIFORNIA

Pam Peirce   *Photographs by* David Goldberg

SASQUATCH BOOKS
SEATTLE

For Heidi & Craig, our buddies in Boston
& for Aisha, who loves to be in a garden

◆

Printed in Singapore by Star Standard Industries Pte Ltd.
Published by Sasquatch Books
Distributed by Publishers Group West
10 09 08 07 06 05 04   6 5 4 3 2 1

Cover photographs: David Goldberg
Cover and interior design: Kate Basart
Interior photographs: David Goldberg

Library of Congress Cataloging in Publication Data

Peirce, Pam
Wildly successful plants : northern California gardens / by Pam Peirce ;
photographs by David Goldberg.
p.   cm.
Includes bibliographical references and index.
ISBN 1-57061-358-3
1. Landscape plants—California, Northern. 2. Landscape gardening—
California, Northern. I. Title.

SB407.P42 2004
6335.9'09794—dc22
2003058975

SASQUATCH BOOKS
119 South Main Street, Suite 400 ▪ Seattle, WA 98104 ▪ 206/467-4300
www.sasquatchbooks.com ▪ custserv@sasquatchbooks.com

CONTENTS

ACKNOWLEDGMENTS

I appreciate the time and energy others have contributed to the making of this book, and want to thank all who helped. My first step was creation of a formal book proposal. Special thanks for reviewing that proposal, and encouraging me to continue, go to Shelley Moore, Craig Bystrynski, and Jennie McDonald.

For kind and expert help in the Helen Crocker Russell Library of San Francisco's Strybing Arboretum Society, thanks to librarians Barbara Pitschel and Kathleen Fisher.

Thanks for generously sharing time and expertise, including reviews of the herbarium record of several plants, to Dr. Frank Almeda of the Botany Department of California Academy of Science.

Callie McRosky and Gus Broucaret, both fellow instructors at City College of San Francisco as well as professional maintenance gardeners, shared their years of firsthand experience with care, maintenance, and removal of the fifty plants. Malcolm Hillan, also an instructor at City College of San Francisco, advised on the introduction to the shrubs chapter.

For help with matters of classical history, special thanks to two people: Colomba Ghigliotti at The Frank V. DeBellis Collection of the California State University System at San Francisco State University, and Bill Thayer, whose website and links on ancient Rome are useful and fun.

Ellen M. Zagory, U.C. Davis Arboretum, reviewed the plant list and indicated which plants would succeed in the Central Valley.

Christy Smith, of Stanford University, answered my questions about the history of Stanford's landscaping and about Arizona gardens.

Thanks for help and information on wildland weed issues to Chris Carmichael of the U.C. Botanical Garden, Frank Starkey of the Catalina Island Conservancy, Doug Johnson, Director of CalEPPC, Peter Warner and other CalEPPC board members.

I had many questions about individual plants, and am grateful to all who answered them, beginning with members of the Mediterranean Plant Society all around the world who shared their experiences with the featured plants. In addition, thanks to the following individuals: Bonnie

Gray-green rosettes of the Echeveria elegans *spill through the garden of the late designer Harland Hand. Other plants include a* Dasylirion, *several aloes, a yellow-variegated* Phormium, *and a blooming wisteria.*

Marquardt of American Takii Seed Company, who inquired of Japanese plant breeders about paludosum daisy and translated the answers, and Robert Leykam, who translated information on that plant from a German journal. Sarah Fitzgerald of Manderville Gardens and garden writer Hazel White told me about English daisy and centranthus in England. Professor John S. Parker, Director of Cambridge University Botanic Garden, sent information and literature about bergenia. David Herndon of the California Poppy Project, and Harold Wood of the Sierra Club helped with questions about the history of and laws concerning California poppies. Dr. John F. Pruski, Missouri Botanic Garden, answered my questions about Mexican daisy. Dr. Peter C. Hoch, Missouri Botanical Garden, helped me locate the home ground of *Impatiens balfourii*. Robin Parer of Geraniaceae Nursery in Kentfield answered many questions about pelargoniums, Marilyn Holt of Holt Geraniums in Vancouver, B.C., helped identify old geraniums, and Doris Brown, a docent at Alcatraz, identified others. Dr. Peter Goldblatt, Missouri Botanical Garden, helped extensively with the botany and range of indigenous South African bulbs.

My understanding of the world of cacti and succulents was fostered by Brian Kemble, Curator of the Ruth Bancroft Garden, Herman Schwartz of Strawberry Press and the Marin/ Bolinas Botanical Garden, Ernst van Jaarsveld of the National Botanical Institute of South Africa, Myron Kimnach, and Mary Irish, co-author of *Agaves, Yuccas, and Related Plants*. For help with fuchsias, both old and new, thanks to Dr. Peter Baye, who has bred several mite-resistant cultivars. Ian Wilson of the British garden design firm Natural Gardens gave me invaluable information about *Hedera helix* in its native British habitats and gardens. Roy Gereau of the Missouri Botanical Garden provided much information about *Impatiens sodenii*. Finally, thanks to Dr. Don Mahoney, Horticulture Manager of Strybing Arboretum, for responding to a number of queries.

Several people read part or all of the manuscript. Thanks to Steve Schoenig, Senior Environmental Research Scientist for the California Department of Food and Agriculture, for reading the manuscript and commenting on weed-related issues; to Dr. Roy L. Taylor, for checking it for botanical or nomenclatural errors; to Richard G. Turner, Jr., editor of *Pacific Horticulture*, for reviewing Chapter 1; and thanks to Craig Bystrynski for checking the Introduction, Chapter 1, and Chapter 2 with his editorial eagle eye. Finally, thanks to David Goldberg, who, in addition to shooting beautiful photos for the book, read each and every word more than once, and often inspired me to write more clearly. Thanks to New Lab Film processing for being there, and Lynn Fulk, Bill Purcell, and Hugh Helm for their cheerful support.

Thanks for advice and help with props for the cut flower assemblage on the frontispiece to Holly Money-Collins, City College of San Francisco Floristry Department. For help growing some of the plants photographed, thanks to volunteers at the Elizabeth F. Gamble Garden in Palo Alto (especially Rotraut Walther). A number of gardeners helped us seek plants to photograph or gave us access to their private homes and gardens for photographs, including the following: Janet Anderson, Katie and Kurt Braun, Lala Corran, Rochelle Ford, Joan Gavernick and Sandra Orr, Michelle Hunziker, Dennis and Marsha Johnson, Rupert Jenkins and Harriet Traureg, Peggy Jones, Kay Kimpton, Mark Lampert, Jennifer Merrill, Bill Milligan, Shelly Moore, Ann Nichols, Michell Schaal, Stuart Sidler, and Walter Teague. Thanks to you all.

Finally, thanks to Pat Morgan, City College of San Francisco Nursery Specialist, for her insights and for being a very good listener.

INTRODUCTION

✻

This book probably became inevitable in the spring of 1968, when I took a long walk through San Francisco's southwest quarter. I had recently arrived from the Midwest, land of big lawns that might, at most, be formally edged with restrained flower borders. By comparison, the gardens I saw on that day were straight out of *Alice in Wonderland*. White daisies dotted small emerald green lawns, while purple daisies peeked out from boxwood hedges. Stately white calla lilies mingled with the voluptuous lavender bells of foxgloves. Dangling fuchsia flowers displayed forms so fantastic that it was hard to believe they were real. Fat-leaved jade plants, which I only knew as house plants, grew several feet tall here and might be draped with vivid orange and yellow nasturtiums. This had to be garden heaven.

As I continued my explorations in Northern California, I learned about many more garden dazzlers, both common and rare, and saw them in wonderful gardens that bloomed nearly all year long. I learned the names and needs of both the common and the rare, and I came to understand the climate that allowed this beauty.

The years that followed brought droughts, with their water restrictions, and freezes that left gardeners gnashing their teeth. As time passed, I came to perceive a certain set of plants, including many I saw on that first walk, as regional garden survivors. These tough, beautiful plants persisted in gardens large and small despite neglect, drought, or frost (though drought or frost could

Typical of many local gardens, this one mingles several of the plants featured in this book, including (roughly left to right) Aeonium harwarthii, nasturtium, out of bloom chasmanthe, and jade plant.

Purple cineraria daisies bloom between a variegated holly and a neatly sheared boxwood hedge.

certainly set them back a bit). They made up a large portion of the plants that decorated untended gardens, casually planted dooryards, vacant lots, and cracks in the sidewalk. In fact, it is rare to walk a city block, especially in the region's older neighborhoods, without passing a few of these plants. They are the ones you wonder about in the front garden of the house by the bus stop and will be among the only survivors in the neglected garden of a home you rent or buy. Plants from this group will pop up unexpectedly in gardens you are tending. If you admire them over the garden fence, your neighbors will gladly offer you cuttings, divisions, or seeds.

In selecting fifty plants to feature in this book, I started with those that are the most common and the easiest to grow, especially ones that are likely to naturalize in gardens, meaning that they return year after year without replanting or survive without supplemental water. I also gave preference to ones that are more familiar to Northern California gardeners than to gardeners in the rest of the United States and to those that have been growing in our gardens for a century or longer. I weighted the list toward annual and perennial flowers. These are the plants we are most often starting, removing, multiplying, and admiring in our gardens within the framework of the more permanent trees and shrubs. I know the list overlooks a number of popular garden flowers, but the plants in this book are all too often given short shrift, and they need their due.

It is true that the ability of these plants to survive and thrive in adverse conditions has led, in some cases, to their overuse. And it is also true that while they survive without care, they may not look their best when they are neglected. In truth, these plants are so successful that they sometimes even survive where they are not wanted. But with good use and good care, they can be beautiful and kept in bounds.

Just because they are common and easy to grow doesn't mean that the fifty featured plants don't have plenty to offer to gardeners. These are great ornamental plants. They offer varied plant shapes and leaf forms. They include flowers that bloom in every season and color, and many of the blossoms are fragrant. Quite a few can be used as long-lasting cut flowers. A number of these plants attract hummingbirds, and some bring beneficial insects to your garden. They are also tough. Most are, by necessity, drought-tolerant; otherwise they would not survive neglect as well as they do. For the same reason, most have few pests, and the ones they have generally do not destroy the plants. In particular, deer, while notorious for eating almost anything if hungry enough, show little interest in the majority of these plants.

My neighbor, who is in his eighties and counts on daily walks to keep him agile, tells me he has "the true lily, the white one, which is so lovely," and that "once you have it, you don't have to worry; it'll bloom every year." He's talking about calla lilies. One day, a moving man, bringing new neighbors to the house across the street, ran over to ask the name of a flower in my front yard. It wasn't any of the fine rare specimens in the garden that had caught his eye. It was the bright tumble of common orange nasturtiums.

As I traveled about observing these plants and looking for examples of them used well in gardens, I heard other praises: "I love four o'clocks because they're easy and bright. And the hummingbirds come for them every evening." "I didn't plant the crocosmias. They were there when we came here. It's been thirty years." "I don't know what those flowers are, but they grow themselves. My kinda plant." "We're about to trim the aeoniums. Would you like a start? It's a wonderful plant."

Professional gardeners often think of these plants as "the free stuff" because they are among the best plants for growing from cuttings and divisions. They are also such reliable performers that they are often used to fill in spaces where a less well-adapted plant has died.

These plants are indeed the free stuff, the easy and tough stuff. If you are a beginning gardener, these are great learning plants, ones that will forgive much as you learn the basics of plant care. Whatever your skill level, though, you will find that these plants fit into many garden themes. May you create *Alice in Wonderland* gardens, tropical paradises, mediterranean gardens, naturalistic gardens, cozy cottage gardens, or elegant Victorian gardens, and may your greater understanding of these plants help you to use them to better advantage in whatever gardens you choose to create.

Chapter One

GETTING TO KNOW THE PLANTS

ome of the plants featured in this book are ones humans have grown for many centuries. The peoples of the ancient Mediterranean and Near East planted gardens that included herbs, flowers, and purely decorative plants. They used flowers as offerings to gods and to make crowns and garlands for many kinds of celebrations and ceremonies. Plants from our list of fifty that appeared in these ancient gardens include ivy, periwinkle, acanthus, viola, centranthus, rose campion, calendula, and borage. North Africans introduced Greeks and Romans to the succulent *Aeonium arboreum*, which they used, along with another North African plant, *Aloe vera*, to treat skin ailments. Among the plants from our list of fifty that are native to northern Europe and the British Isles are ivy, Johnny-jump up, forget-me-not, English daisy, columbine, and foxglove. These were first gathered in the wild and later, by the medieval period, were grown in gardens. The Romans brought a number of plants northward as their empire expanded across Europe, including acanthus, centranthus, rose campion, calendula, and borage.

Orange nasturtiums perfectly accent a mediterranean-style fountain at Allied Arts of Menlo Park.

South African Chasmanthe aethiopica *shares a garden with the North African succulent* Aeonium arborescens.

Long before Europeans reached Mexico and the American Southwest, century plant and other agaves were being used for food and for making the alcoholic beverage pulque, while prickly pear cacti of several species were used for food and to enclose gardens. Aztec flower gardens included dahlias, zinnias, and, from our list, four o'clocks. In South Africa, white calla lily and agapanthus were used as medicinal herbs, and tree aloe was used to fence out wild animals.

Of the rest of the plants of our featured fifty, some may have been used as herbs gathered from the wild, but most had not been brought into gardens anywhere by the beginning of the 1500s. This was soon to change. The many European sea voyages for purposes of exploration and conquest brought most of the rest of the featured plants to Europe. Plant collecting began with economic goals, but as the Age of Enlightenment took hold, the goal became simply to know all of the world's plants. Once carried to Europe, plants were described, named, classified, tested in gardens, and later intentionally bred into more gardenworthy subjects. That is why so many of our fifty plants, as well as many others from around the world, came to California gardens by way of Europe.

The first European ships to reach the Americas sailed under the Spanish flag, and among the first plants they carried home with them, early in the 1500s, were prickly pear cactus, century plant, four o'clock, and nasturtium. Prickly pear began as a curiosity of the Spanish court but soon established itself throughout the Mediterranean and Near East. The last two were soon grown as annual flowers in gardens all over Europe.

The Dutch, who made a big splash in the European gardening world in the 1600s by importing tulips from Turkey, also traveled to other lands. They started a settlement in South Africa in 1652 and carried many plants back to Holland, including aloes, naked ladies, and several species of pelargoniums.

Once plants or seeds arrived in any European country, they soon would be grown in others, especially in England. This English enthusiasm for plants and gardens led to some of the first expeditions undertaken solely for the purpose of plant collecting, sponsored by the newly commissioned Kew Gardens of London. The first director of the garden,

Joseph Banks, sent Francis Masson on several trips to South Africa, starting in 1772, and then to the Canary Islands, the West Indies, and several other places. Many other collectors were at work in the service of England at this time, including colonial residents such as John Bartram of Pennsylvania, who, as the king's botanist in America, sent American plants to England until the American Revolution interrupted such trade.

The last decades of the 1700s found European nations competing fiercely to gather the largest plant collections. Botanic gardens, such as Kew in England and the Jardin des Plantes in Paris, also collected pressed, dried plant specimens, called herbarium sheets, from which living plants could be identified. Illustrators drew plants, and these drawings were published with descriptions in what were some of the first "floras," or compendia, of all the plants that grew in specific parts of the world.

Along with its preeminence in plant collecting, Europe also became the center for breeding plants to produce prettier garden flowers. The knowledge that permitted artificial pollination, used by the ancient Assyrians and Babylonians to breed dates, was lost after those kingdoms declined. Still, over the centuries many unusual flowers were accidentally discovered and propagated in gardens. By the Elizabethan period, for example, English and European gardens included double-flowered English daisies in several colors, red and white rose campion, and single and double columbines in blue, purple, white, rose, and red-purple.

Plant sexuality was rediscovered in Holland by the botanist Rudolph Camerarius in 1694. Botanists of the time found it rather embarrassing at first, but in 1719 an English nurseryman, Thomas Fairchild, put this new knowledge to good use. He artificially pollinated some pinks (*Dianthus* species) to make a hybrid. The news spread, and soon European nurserymen and gardeners were actively breeding plants for gardens. Among the centers of plant breeding were France, Belgium, Germany, and especially England. Even our own California poppy, now the state flower, was exported to England, along with a number of other pretty California natives. There they were cherished and hybridized, and plants of new colors and forms were sent back for our gardens. It is only in the past century that new garden plants have begun to arrive in California directly from non-European nations where they grow wild.

Ornamental gardening is an art of prosperity and peace. As the middle classes grew in Europe, flower gardens became more widespread. These new markets encouraged more hybridizing of garden flowers through the early twentieth century, until the two world wars turned European energies to survival. During the wars, gardeners focused on food crops, and many ornamental specialties, especially those that needed greenhouses to survive in Europe, suffered setbacks. Plant breeding stopped, and many lovely garden varieties were lost. Plants from our list that suffered this fate include pelargoniums, fuchsias, and crocosmias.

Garden history is also affected by styles and pests. Plants that are out of style disappear from nurseries, only to be rediscovered years later in old gardens. Other plants that were once pest-free become susceptible to diseases and insects and so become less popular. Fuchsias illustrate both factors. When the fuchsia gall mite devastated California fuchsias, the plant became understandably less popular in the state. Now older fuchsia species and varieties that had fallen out of fashion are becoming more popular because they resist the mite.

CALIFORNIA GARDEN HISTORY

Many of our fifty plants have figured prominently in the relatively short history of ornamental gardening in California, though most were not present in the earliest years. Indeed, the first four Old World plants to enter California were food or medicinal crops: castor bean, date palm, wheat, and grapes. They were all carried by Father Junipero Serra as he walked from Mexico City to San Diego to start the first mission in 1769.

Spanish mission and pueblo gardens featured patios with a fountain or well, similar to those in Spanish gardens that had a Moorish influence. Modern attempts at restoring mission patios often include many flowers, but, in truth, when the missions were active, the patio had few plants, primarily functioning as a work area. Food crops, herbs, and any flowers to decorate altars were grown in separate irrigated gardens surrounded by walls or prickly pear hedges. When they were first established, the missions had few flowers anywhere, but the Spanish colonists soon imported many kinds, including daffodils, violets, carnations, roses, and, from our list, nasturtiums, four o'clocks, and calla lilies.

By the time of the secularization of the missions after the independence of Mexico from Spain in 1822, Mexican Californians, the Californios, kept an extensive list of flowers with meanings for lovers. Nasturtium, when worn, meant, "I want to be a nun," a severe message indeed to send a would-be suitor!

Once Americans began to arrive in California, the influx of nonnative ornamental plants was surprisingly rapid. The first nursery in California opened in Sacramento in 1849, a year before California became a state. During the next twenty years, nurseries in the Bay Area imported many plants from all over the world. Professionally designed gardens of wealthier Californians were heavily influenced by European ideas, and gardens were built to represent various European themes.

Most settlers' gardens had no unified theme and often reflected the cottage garden tradition. In such a garden, the main design elements are the plants. These may include fruits, vegetables, and herbs, but also include many flowers; all are allowed to grow together with abandon. Quite a few of the plants featured in this book are traditional European cottage

The Gardens of Alcatraz

Over half of the fifty plants featured in this book are found growing on Alcatraz Island, survivors of gardens once planted there. In the second half of the 1800s, when Alcatraz was a military base, the island's landscaping included gardens where officer's wives could feel at home. Then, from 1933 to 1963, when the island was a federal penitentiary, both wardens and prisoners planted gardens. It has become a sort of museum of garden plants that naturalize and survive without human intervention in the near-coastal part of Northern California. These plants, now being inventoried and studied by the National Park Service, include succulents, bulbs, and old varieties of regal geraniums and fuchsias. There are also a number of historic rose varieties on the island. To learn more about the history and plants of the island, see *The Gardens of Alcatraz* in Suggested Reading on page 295.

garden favorites, and many of these arrived with the European settlers. They include columbine, foxglove, rose campion, forget-me-not, English daisy hybrids, feverfew, sweet alyssum, and love-in-a-mist.

As Europe entered the Victorian era, the style of garden we call Victorian took hold, and it became popular among Californians. Important to this style was the lawn. In addition, Victorian gardeners were thrilled by the exotic new plants that were entering Europe through plant explorations, and they wanted to have as many of them as possible in their gardens. Thus, gardens became plant collections.

Another feature of Victorian gardens, though more popular in Europe than California, was "carpet bedding," colorful arrangements of low plants that were meant to be viewed from above. These might include foliage plants such as coleus, fancy-leaf pelargoniums, and golden feverfew; low succulents such as hen and chicks; and many kinds of annual flowers that had been bred to form short, ball-shaped plants. (We owe to this formal Victorian gardening fashion the many short, squat annuals still sold in modern nurseries. See page 65 for more on these plants and the difficulties they present to gardeners who prefer a less formal garden design.)

Other plants Victorians often used were baby's tears, nasturtium, calendula, fancy varieties of English daisy, and bulbs such as watsonia, agapanthus, and crocosmia. Mirror plant, with its shiny green leaves, and the then–newly hybridized fuchsias were among their favorite shrubs. Remember that many of these plants, though familiar to us, were quite unusual and were grown as novelties. Victorians were fond of variegated leaves, so they would have loved the multicolored leaves of the newer mirror plant and the stellar pelargonium varieties.

Like the Californios of Mexican California, Victorians had an extensive list of flower meanings. To the Victorians, nasturtiums meant "patriotism" or "victory in battle"—just one example of how people see things differently in different cultures.

For a century after the Spanish and Mexican era, most California gardeners planted gardens that would have been at home in a wet-summer part of Europe or the eastern United States. These gardens were heavily dependent on plants that require moist soil, such as lawns, rhododendrons, camellias, and roses. Lawns continued to be an important feature in the mid-twentieth-century garden design philosophy called modernism. Gardens in this style depended on simple lines and foliage as the main design elements. Lawns were often important features, as were large plantings of ground cover junipers, bergenias, or ivy, along with paved areas.

There were a few exceptions to the general trend of high-water-use gardens. Stanford University opened in 1891 with a landscape of drought-tolerant plants chosen by landscape architect Frederick Law Olmsted to complement the mission-style architecture of the campus. There were also a few "Arizona gardens," consisting mainly of cacti hauled in from the Arizona desert, often with additional succulent plants. In 1882, the garden designer Rudolf Ulrich planted one of these gardens at Stanford and another in Monterey. (The Stanford garden was renovated in 2002 and is open to the public, but the one in Monterey is on the grounds of a military establishment that is not open to public view.) The remnants of another Arizona garden can be seen on an embankment just east of the Conservatory of Flowers in San Francisco's Golden Gate Park.

At the beginning of the twentieth century, the collection and distribution systems that bring water to California, such as Hetch Hetchy Reservoir, were newly built. The California population was much smaller then, and people thought we would have plenty of water for any imaginable use in perpetuity. However, as the century passed and the population of California grew, we saw that this was not the case. The first water restrictions, during drought years in the 1970s, warned us that we could no longer count on endless water and led to the introduction of the concept of xeriscaping, or designing a garden to reduce its use of water. Drought tolerance has remained an underlying theme of modern California garden designs.

California Gardens Today

California gardeners often achieve a cottage garden look with plants that need only moderate water. Featured here are purple linaria, centranthus, and airy Mexican daisies.

The first Spanish settlers, having come from a land of dry summers, brought plants to California that thrived in these conditions. We have come back full circle to their awareness, though with many more plants to choose from.

Gardeners have become increasingly interested in using California native plants, either in plantings that imitate wild habitats or to fill the roles of nonnative plants in more traditional garden designs. One of the advantages of doing this is that most native plants are well adapted to

California gardeners often achieve a cottage garden look with plants that need only moderate water. Featured here are purple linaria, centranthus, and airy Mexican daisies.

dry summers. Although our fifty plants include just one California native, a number of natives are beautiful, easy choices that are ready to fill roles in our gardens (see also pages 55 and 265).

Quite a few of the plants from our list of fifty fit well into a modern Spanish or Mediterranean-style garden, especially drought-tolerant plants such as prickly pear cactus, tree aloe, century plant, Mexican sage, Mexican daisy, pelargonium, chasmanthe, crocosmia, aeonium, jade plant, yellow sedum, and echium. However, we can also include small areas of flowers that require more water, working them into the design more prominently than did the mission gardeners.

Cottage gardens are also still popular. Although traditional cottage gardens depended on high water use, a number of traditional garden plants survive well with moderate summer water, and other relatively drought-tolerant plants can be used to re-create the feel of such a garden. Using drought-tolerant shrubs to back up smaller beds of annuals and perennials can further reduce water use. For spring bloom, with help from winter rains, choices include foxglove, forget-me-not, sweet alyssum, Johnny-jump-up, calendula, paludosum daisy, English daisy, purple cineraria, and love-in-a-mist. For bloom through summer with moderate water, consider rose campion, centranthus, Mexican daisy, Mexican sage, pelargonium, four o'clock, nasturtium, purple linaria, feverfew, agapanthus, and naked ladies.

Another recent trend in California gardening has been a tropical look that, in its display of gaudy plant forms and colors, echoes the tastes of Victorians. Although plants growing in the tropics can depend on heavy rainfall, a tropical look can be achieved with plants that are relatively drought tolerant. Calla lily, aeonium, acanthus, chasmanthe, and watsonia are among those in the fifty that offer bold, tropical-looking foliage, and the showy flowers of pelargonium, purple cineraria, and nasturtium can be made to fit the theme ably.

The Mediterranean Climate

Because they survive with little or no care in Northern California, the fifty plants described in these pages are obviously well adapted to growing here. And yet all but one of them evolved and spent most of their history growing in other parts of the world. What is it about our climate and the climates of the places these plants evolved that made the plants such good fits for our gardens?

Much of Northern California (except for high mountains) has what is known as a mediterranean climate. This is described as a mild temperate or subtropical climate because, though the average temperature of the winter months is cool, it is above freezing. In fact, while inland areas may have a few frosts every winter, near the coast frost is rare. Another defining feature of this climate is that it has rainy winters and dry summers.

The mediterranean climate is named for the area around the Mediterranean Sea, sometimes called the Mediterranean Basin. It is found in the areas from 30 to 40 degrees north and south of the equator, on the west sides of continents; it makes up only 5 percent of the earth's land surface. Besides Northern California and, of course, the Mediterranean Basin itself, this climate exists in three other regions: the central coast of Chile, southwestern Australia, and the western side of the tip of South Africa, which is known as the Western Cape region.

While the summers in mediterranean climates are always dry, they can be either hot or cool. The areas with cooler summers are the ones nearest the coast in California, central Chile, and South Africa. The cold oceans in these areas create a cool, foggy summer, but inland, and in other regions with a mediterranean climate, summer temperatures can soar. On summer days that aren't foggy, these places have skies of a bright, cloudless blue—the famous Mediterranean light.

In Northern California, the rainy season begins in October or November and is over by the end of April. Average annual rainfall varies from 15 to more than 40 inches per year. The amount that falls varies from place to place, with more rain in the north and in the foothills of the Sierra and less in the Sacramento Valley; local rainfall is also affected by the particular patterns of hills and valleys. Throughout Northern California, rainfall varies from year to year, with greater variation in the areas that have the lowest average yearly rainfall. This unreliable rainfall pattern results in years in which plant growth is unusually lush and ones when the region is unusually stressed for water.

Because the mediterranean climates found throughout the world are similar, plants that grow in one of these regions will generally do well in another. But there are subtle differences. These differences interest gardeners because they may affect how well plants from one region will adapt to a garden in another. While more rain always falls in the colder part of the year, the rainiest months vary, and some mediterranean areas have significant summer rainfall. Summers are hotter along the Mediterranean Sea than along other coastal areas with this climate, since the sea is warmer than the earth's oceans. Also, winters in the mediterranean regions of Australia and South Africa are, on average, a bit milder than in the other regions, since these continents do not extend quite as far from the equator.

Climate and Plant Sources

Not surprisingly, a number of the plants on our list of fifty, and many other nonnative plants that thrive in Northern California, are originally from one of the earth's mediterranean climate regions. In these regions, all of the plants that grow wild, either in natural areas or in untended gardens, must be able to withstand summers with little or no rainfall. Plants from these regions have met this requirement in several different ways. One is that seeds of annual plants germinate in soil moistened by the autumn rains. The resulting plants grow all through the mild, wet winter, bloom, drop their seeds, and die by the time the rains end in spring. Examples are sweet alyssum and paludosum daisy. Mediterranean plants that live from year to year often become dormant in the

Red-flowered 'Mrs. Taylor' scented geranium brightens this tropical-style planting. Also shown are Melianthus major, Alpinia zerumbet *'Variegata', and* Phormium *'Guardsman'.*

dry summer. Woody plants may lose their leaves, and other plants survive the summer as underground structures, such as bulbs or thickened roots, in which water and food are stored, as is the case for naked lady or California poppy. Still other mediterranean plants have leaves that resist water loss. They may be small, tough leaves, like those of our native California lilac (*Ceanothus* species); thickened, succulent leaves, like those of the North African aeonium; or leaves with white hairs, like those of the echiums.

These mechanisms for water storage or the prevention of water loss also help mediterranean plants survive in years when rainfall is unusually light. In addition, the seeds of mediterranean annuals, which provide the only way these plants can survive from year to year, do not all germinate in the year after they were formed. Thus, if a year is very dry, a supply of seeds will survive to try in other years.

While a majority of the fifty naturalizing and gardenworthy plants described in this book are from regions with a mediterranean climate, a sizeable minority are not. Several of these plants are from the Himalayan Mountains. We often think of the Himalayas as being high and cold, and indeed the highest peaks are under snow all year. However, these mountains are between 26 and 34 degrees latitude, at roughly the same distance from the equator as the American Deep South, so the lower slopes and valleys have mild winters. Two of the fifty plants, bergenia and *Persicaria capitata,* are native to the slopes of the Himalayas, from the mild lower elevations to well above the snow line.

In addition, quite a number of the featured plants are from tropical mountain regions. One, poor man's rhododendron, is from the mountains of Kenya and Tanzania, just south of the equator. Several others are from the American Cordillera, a ridge of mountains that runs through Mexico and into South America. Botanists tell us that for a plant from tropical mountains to grow well in the Bay Area, it needs to be from above 5,000 feet in elevation, and this bears out for all of the tropical mountain plants on the list. This makes sense simply from the fact that the tropical lowlands never experience frost or even temperatures approaching freezing, whereas the tropical uplands do have a colder winter season. In fact, the highest elevations have snowy winters. It is typically at around 5,000 feet that the winter temperature drops to near or just below freezing. Mountain climates also differ from tropical lowlands in being much cooler at night than during the day, which also prepares plants for our cool nights and winters. And tropical highlands have frequent mists and clouds alternating with intense sunlight, not unlike conditions in a near-coastal California summer.

It turns out, in fact, that tropical mountains are like islands. They are populated with plants that are more closely related to plants from far-away mountain habitats than to the tropical flora at their feet. The plants move from mountain to mountain by wind or bird-distributed seeds. So in a sense, tropical mountains are islands of temperate plants in a tropical sea.

True islands, the ones surrounded by water, contribute quite a few of our fifty plants. Specifically, a number of the plants are native to oceanic islands at mediterranean latitudes. Why are plants from these islands so well represented? There are two main reasons for this. First, such islands have mild winters not unlike ours. And although summer temperatures, exact rain pattern, and amount of rain vary from island to island and on different sides of each island, their climates are similar to mainland mediterranean climates. Second, islands turn out to be rich troves for those seeking interesting garden plants. While there are only a couple of *Echium* species in Europe and a couple of *Aeonium* species in North Africa, there are many of each to choose from on nearby Mediterranean islands.

This variety results from two factors. One is that few species reach an island from the mainland, and so each one evolves into a number of species and varieties to fill the many ecological niches the island offers. The second is that we know from the mainland fossil record that ancient ice ages killed many mainland relatives of the island plants. Because of their much milder winters, the islands served as refuges for a number of these plants. Our purple daisy, the cineraria, was bred from species that survived ice ages only on the Canary Islands, and a number of other common Northern California plants are native only to the Canaries.

Examples are the palm *Phoenix canariensis* and the pine *Pinus canariensis*. Among our fifty, baby's tears waited out the ice ages on the island of Corsica, and mirror plant is one of many species of *Coprosma* found only on New Zealand and other, smaller Pacific Islands.

PLANT ADAPTABILITY

Knowing the climate of a plant's place of origin and its habitat in that place can tell us a great deal about what it needs in order to grow. It suggests the best pattern of annual rainfall, the amount of cold the plant can take, how much shade it can tolerate, and so on. Some plants can adapt to a wider range of conditions than others. In some cases, we can see this from their behavior in the places where they are native. White calla lily, for example, grows all across near-coastal South Africa, in full sun or shade, from the western area of dry summers through the central year-round rain region and across the eastern dry-winter area, in both drier uplands and boggy lowlands. On the other hand, baby's tears is strictly limited to shady places in upland parts of the island of Corsica that are cool and humid in summer. The island's lowlands, which have hot, dry summers, are devoid of the plant.

Sometimes knowing the native habitat of a plant won't tell the whole story, because some plants can survive conditions that are different from those in which they are now growing wild. This could well be due to climate changes to which the plant has been able to adapt. Although the soil may have become wetter or the summers hotter, for example, a plant may still carry the genes that allow it to survive in drier soil or cooler summers. An example of such wider adaptability is mirror plant, which evolved in New Zealand, where rain is possible on any day of the year. Yet the plant survives in near-coastal Northern California with no summer water. Another is echeveria, which evolved in the dry-winter parts of Mexico but can adapt to our wetter winters if the soil is well drained. While knowing the climate that a plant expects may not tell us the whole story, it can often lead us toward changes that will make the plant more attractive and healthier—such as moving it to a shadier place or a sunnier place, watering it more, or giving it better drainage.

Many of the plants on the featured list of fifty can survive less-than-ideal conditions, which is why they get by with little or no attention, but many of them look better with a bit more care. Hence, you will often find

More or less sun? Summer or winter rain? White calla lily, Zantedeschia aethiopica, *adapts readily to different conditions.*

that the care sections of plant entries include several "but" or "however" sentences—for example, that a plant can tolerate X conditions, but will look better with Y conditions. This phrasing may begin to seem repetitive, but it bears reiterating in order to increase the beauty of these plants.

Rocky Places

Quite a few of our fifty plants originally grew in rocky places. Echeverias inhabit shallow depressions in the rock in Mexican mountain pine forests. Echiums cling to steep, rocky cliffs on the island of Madeira. Kenilworth ivy climbs castle walls in England while centranthus and feverfew scamper across the rocky wastelands of southeastern Europe. Aeoniums survive grazing by goats by growing on inaccessible rocky Moroccan hillsides, while aloes hang from rock crevices in the South African highlands and shrub impatiens nestle in rocky niches behind waterfalls in the Kenyan highlands. Bergenias colonize the shady, rocky glens of the Himalayan Mountains and mirror plants lay low amid the rocks on the windy coast of New Zealand's northern island. Why this preponderance of rock dwellers? My first thought was that an urban environment must be, to a plant, a rocky place—in part due to natural rocks and in part due to human endeavor. We have made places full of craggy stone walls and narrow concrete crevices.

After further study I have decided that there are other factors at work. A starting point is that when a place is mostly rock, it has thin soil. This soil is likely to be poor, since there are few plants to decay and enrich it. Because there is little soil to hold moisture, the plants that can grow in such places have to be able to handle drought. The plants that can survive these conditions are ones that can enter a poor, dry, harsh environment and thrive in it. Therefore, such plants are well prepared to handle our relatively infertile, often shallow and compacted urban soils that are, in addition, dry during half of the year.

In the science of ecology, these clingers to rocks and dwellers in cracks are called pioneer plants. That is, they can grow under harsh conditions, and by doing so they prepare the way for other plants that can't take these conditions. These plants may break up rocks with their roots or trap windblown dust in their leaves so that it falls into a fissure, or they may fertilize a soil pocket when they die. Pioneer plants are brash and tough, tending toward the weedy, and this is a perfect description of most of these plants.

PLANT SCIENTIFIC NAMES

The question of when to list plants by scientific name and when to use common names plagues garden writers, and whatever we do is certain to leave some readers unhappy. On the one hand, if we use only common names, we actually run the risk that many people will not know which plants we are talking about. A "dusty miller" to you may be an entirely different plant than it is to me. At least eight plants go by that common name, and while they share the trait of whitish leaves, they are otherwise quite different. One of them is a plant from our list, *Lychnis coronaria*, but it also has other common names, which include crown lychnis, rose campion, and bachelor's buttons. If, on the other hand, a writer chooses to use the scientific names, giving scant attention to common names, readers who don't know or don't want to know the scientific names will feel overwhelmed by all the unfamiliar Latin.

I have alphabetized the plants by their scientific name in the chapters, but I have made it easy to find them by their common names as well. These follow the scientific names in each entry, and all plants are in the index under both common and scientific names. In addition, the photos will help you locate plants by sight. At the end of each plant entry, a section called "The Name" tells you something of the history and translation of the scientific name and describes how to pronounce it.

Gardeners don't really have to memorize scientific names or be able to pronounce them, but there are two very practical reasons to know what they are. The first is positive identification. Once you have the correct scientific name of your plant, you can find out more about it from books or other sources of information. Also, if you want to buy a particular plant, knowing the scientific name is the key to finding the exact plant you want to grow. The second reason is that the scientific names tell you how plants are related to one another, and knowing this can give you clues about how to care for a plant. Plants in the same species generally have the same, or almost the same, needs and pests as other plants in that species. Plants in the same genus (group of related species) also typically have similar needs and similar pests.

Modern plant scientific names are made up of two Latin words. You may think this is quite enough Latin, but prior to the work of Carl Linnaeus (1707–1778), botanists often used many more Latin words to indicate a particular plant. Carnation, for example, might have been written as *Dianthus floribus solitaries, squamis calycinis subovatis brevissimis, corollas crenatis*. Add to these long names the fact that there was no one method of classifying plants at the time, and you can imagine that it would have been relatively difficult to make your way through botanical reference books even if you had studied Latin.

We have Linnaeus to thank for seeing that the description and the name were two different things, and that the name could be reduced to as few as two words that would distinguish a plant from all other plants. He also did the best job to date of using names to show relationships among plants. These innovations brought the ability to learn to use scientific names into the realm of the nonbotanist.

In using Latin, or Latinized words from other languages, for his plant names, Linnaeus was following the custom of the time. Latin had been the common language of European religious and university scholars for many centuries, allowing them to communicate with one another. While most of us don't learn Latin anymore, that ancient southern European language has passed many decipherable words or parts of words into what are known as the "romance languages," which include French, Spanish, and Italian. Because of this the Latin names of plants are still reasonably translatable to the many people who know any of these languages, at least more so than if Linnaeus had named plants in his native Swedish.

In the modern plant scientific name, the first word represents the genus (plural: genera). A genus is a group of plants that are closely related, though they generally are unable to interbreed or, if they do, don't produce viable seeds.

The second word in a scientific name indicates the particular species within that genus. A species is a group of plants that are very similar and can interbreed and produce seeds that will grow. This second word, called the "specific epithet," is generally an adjective describing a special characteristic that makes this species different from others in the genus.

In the name *Calendula officinalis,* for example, the first word represents the genus. The second word, *officinalis,* indicates which member of the genus is being described. The word officinalis indicates that this was the member of the genus that was used in medieval pharmacies. Other members of the genus *Calendula* have other specific epithets. *Calendula arvensis* has smaller flowers than *Calendula officinalis* and is more often considered a weed. The specific epithet *arvensis* means that this is the *Calendula* that grows in fields.

In the mid-1700s Carl Linnaeus set about giving every plant he could find a two-word name, and then he published books with the names, drawings, and descriptions. A number of our fifty plants were known and named by Linnaeus. (In books that include plant name authorship, Linnaeus is indicated by an "L." following the scientific name. Other botanists have standard abbreviations as well.) In searching about for names, Linnaeus rummaged through old Roman books, such as *Pliny the Elder's Natural History.* This means that some of the plants have ancient Roman names, such as *Calendula, Lychnis,* and *Viola.* However, the plants Linnaeus was naming may or may not have been the ones the ancients were writing about. One problem is that old drawings of plants were not very accurate. Another is that ancient cultures may have had a somewhat broader definition of a plant than do modern botanists. For example, to the Romans, violas included not only the plants we call by that name, but also ones we know as stock *(Matthiola incana)* and wallflower *(Erysimum cheiri).*

Linnaeus, as well as later botanists, also often named plants after other botanists or scholars. When they did this they Latinized the name—for example, *Soleirolia* (after Joseph Francois Soleirol). Other common sources of names are the place or habitat where the plant was found and some detail of its appearance. Although we know the meaning of most scientific names, in some cases we do not. There is no rule that the names have to mean something, and some botanists have chosen words with personal meanings that they have chosen not to share.

While the goal of botanists is to have one two-word scientific name for every plant species, the names do, unfortunately, get changed once in a while. One reason is that a plant may be reclassified when it is studied more closely. It may have to be moved to another genus, for example. You can read about one example of this in the entry on *Cymbalaria muralis* on page 131.

A scientific name can also change when it is discovered that a different botanist has previously published a description of a plant under a different name. In this case the one published first takes precedence. Until recently, poor man's rhododendron was known as *Impatiens oliveri,* but then an older published description was discovered under the name *Impatiens sodenii.* An International Botanical Congress decides these matters, and it is bound by its rules to decide for the older name.

When a plant name has been changed, any former names are printed after it in parentheses—for example *Cymbalaria muralis (Linaria cymbalaria, Antirrhinum cymbalaria).* Knowing these former names may help you find the plants in books that were written before the name was changed or help you communicate with gardeners who blinked when the name change occurred.

Finally, you should know that a plant name can sometimes have more than two words. The additional words are used when describing a variation within a species. The general term for such a variation is "variety."

Deer-resistant?

The expression "deer resistant," as used in this book, means that Northern California deer are less likely to eat a particular plant than they are to eat other plants. While deer rarely eat some of the plants that have been given this designation, a deer will eat almost anything when it is really hungry, so "deer resistant" rarely means "deer proof." Deer-proof fencing provides the only guarantee that deer will leave your garden alone.

When a particular variety is found only in a certain part of the native range of a plant, it is called a "subspecies." A plant that is different from the species in only minor ways is called a "forma." While these differences within a species could disappear if the different plants were allowed to breed freely, gardeners often maintain them for their appearance. An example of a subspecies is *Watsonia borbonica* subspecies *ardernei*. The species has only pink flowers. The subspecies *ardernei*, which is found in only a small area, can have white or pink flowers, and its petals are shorter than those of the species. In a scientific name, variety can be abbreviated "var." and subspecies shortened to "subsp." So, for example, you may see the above name written *Watsonia borbonica* subsp. *ardernei*.

Plant breeders have also created many varieties of our garden plants. These are called cultivars, short for "cultivated varieties." The cultivar name also follows the two-word species name, but it is written differently than the name of a naturally occurring variety. It is capitalized, not in italics, and surrounded by single quote marks—for example, *Linaria purpurea* 'Canon J. Went'. If the parentage of the cultivar is hopelessly confused, the genus name may be used alone, as in *Fuchsia* 'Rose of Castile Improved'. In common use, people often say "Canon J. Went linaria" or "Rose of Castile improved fuchsia." Cultivar names are usually in the language of the nation in which the plant is being sold, though a few are sold in the United States under Latin or Japanese names that slipped by before the rules for naming them had been clarified.

Two more terms you will encounter when buying plants or seeds are "series" and "mix." A series is a group of very similar cultivars, usually differing only in flower color, that are given related names. The Miss Jekyll series of love-in-a-mist *(Nigella damascena)* cultivars includes 'Miss Jekyll Blue' and 'Miss Jekyll Indigo'. When seeds of cultivars that differ only in minor ways such as flower color are mixed together, they are sold as a "mix."

Genetic engineering, which goes beyond traditional plant breeding, is another matter. As far as I know, none of our fifty plants has yet come to the attention of genetic engineers.

If you do choose to memorize some scientific names, hooray for you! Take one at a time, and repeat the name to yourself as you look at or visualize the plant. It gets easier after the first few. Whether you choose to learn scientific names or not, I hope you will enjoy learning more about their history and meaning. In doing so, you'll not only learn something about the plants but will also often gain insights into how other people have seen them.

Caring for Plants

Having a "green thumb" is nothing more than knowing basic plant needs and acting at the right time to help meet those needs. Later in this book, you will find specific information that will help you do this. Chapter introductions give advice on growing each type of plant in Northern California, and each plant entry explains the particular needs of the plant. However, some information is general to growing any plant. In the rest of this chapter you, will find the basic knowledge you need to grow a beautiful garden, such as soil care, watering, dealing with microclimates, grooming, and reproducing your plants. The section "Maintaining a Wildish Garden" (page 38) will help you garden attractively with plants that have a tendency to multiply or spread in a garden.

Soil in the Garden

Most plants require at least a bit of soil, and soil has three properties that we, as gardeners, are most concerned with, because they determine what can grow in it. We ask if it is fertile enough—whether it contains enough of the mineral elements plants need to grow. Then we ask if it will be able to absorb and retain enough water, since plant roots need a steady supply. Finally, we ask whether the water can drain out reasonably well, since plant roots also need air and can get it only when some of the water has left the soil.

First we will consider fertility. Northern California's soils vary greatly, but most are only moderately fertile. In particular, they are usually rather low in the plant nutrient nitrogen. Plants native to California have adapted to this situation, and any nonnative plants that thrive here without care are probably from places where soil conditions are similar or are less fertile. Some plants from South Africa's Western Cape Province, for example, have adapted to the much less fertile soils of that region. And a number of the plants are from particularly infertile places in the lands around the Mediterranean Sea.

The individual entries for the plants tell you whether they require fertile soil or can thrive in soil of poor or moderate fertility. While some fertilizer might improve the performance of the ones that survive in poor soil, it is not necessarily a kindness to grow such plants in highly fertile soil. Gardeners who grow California native plants have learned that if the garden is heavily fertilized, these plants may grow large and lush but will also tend to die long before they would in the wild. And some of the plants on our list, such as calendula and nasturtium, bloom most profusely in relatively infertile soil.

The second and third concerns gardeners have about soil are how well it can hold water and how well it can provide air to plant roots. Northern California soils tend to be either very sandy (made up of relatively large rock particles) or very high in clay (made up of quite tiny rock particles). They also tend to be relatively low in organic matter.

If your soil is very sandy, water will drain out quickly, so that plants will become stressed sooner when a garden is not watered or rain doesn't fall. Plants depending only on rainfall will become dormant earlier in spring than those growing in a more water-retentive soil, and ones you are watering will need water more often. In such soils, if the amount of rainfall or watering by a gardener is inadequate, especially where summers are hot, plants may not survive.

Soil that consists largely of clay particles presents the opposite problem. When clay soil gets soaked, it stays wet for a longer time, so it takes longer for air to return to the spaces between the particles. Most plant roots need ample air, so they can drown in too-soggy soil. You will notice the specification "well-drained" for just about all of the featured plants.

Fortunately, there is a solution for both of our common soil extremes. If you add organic matter to either kind of soil, it will have a better balance of water and air. In sand, organic matter acts as a sponge, holding water so that it can't drain out so fast. In clay, organic matter pushes the tiny particles apart, so that air can return to the spaces between them. Most of the plants in this book do not need a richly organic soil. Vegetables thrive in such soil, and certain of the featured plants, including *Impatiens balfourii* and *Viola tricolor*, prefer it, but for most, adding just a little organic matter once or twice a year will pay off in healthier plants. Organic matter fertilizes soil as well and is probably all the fertilizer that most of these plants require.

When adding organic matter, use homemade compost or choose purchased aged manure, leaf mold, or a product that is labeled "compost" or "soil amendment." Avoid fresh wood products, such as fresh sawdust, which can rob the soil of nitrogen as they break down. (Sawdust and bark products are okay if they have been aged or are mixed with a substance that contains organic matter higher in nitrogen, such as manure or leaf mold.) Spread an inch or two of the organic amendment on the

The succulent Echeveria x imbricata (center) is from the mountains of Mexico, which are dry in winter and wet in summer, but can tolerate winter rain if the soil is well-drained.

soil surface and dig it in before planting, work it into the soil surface between established plants, or just use it as a mulch between plants.

Adding organic matter to clay soil can be particularly helpful for plants that will get more water than they actually need for all or part of the year. This is because the improved drainage reduces the likelihood that their roots will decay when the soil is wetter than it would be in their native habitat. Plants that will benefit include ones that are accustomed to a dry winter, such as tree aloe or *Echeveria*. Plants that are used to dry summers will also appreciate the better drainage if they will be sharing beds with plants you are watering in the summer. These include naked lady, aeonium, California poppy, and many others (see specific entries). To further aid such plants if your soil is clay or otherwise drains poorly, consider growing them in raised beds.

Water

Most of our fifty plants survive in unwatered Northern California gardens. Some are perennials that can get by on winter rainfall, becoming dormant in the summer. Others are cool-season annuals, meaning that they grow in fall and winter, form seed, and then die in the spring when the rains end each year. A few are adapted to desert conditions, with little rain at any time of year, but can survive the amount of rain we get in our winters. But while many of these plants survive without watering, some are more attractive with supplemental water, and a few thrive only in gardens that are watered in the summer. In order to provide them the best conditions possible without wasting water, you will want to know the best way to water plants.

When you water plants, you should give the soil a thorough soaking, then wait until the soil at the surface has dried before watering thoroughly again. This lets air return to the soil and encourages roots to go deep. If you have only a short time each day to water, concentrate on soaking a small area each day rather than on sprinkling the entire garden lightly. For a plant that needs "ample" water and is growing in clay soil or well-amended soil that is sandy or clay, don't water again until the top inch is dry. For a plant that needs "moderate" water, let about the top 2 inches dry. If a plant needs "little" water, let the soil dry to a depth of 3 to 4 inches. If your soil is very sandy and you have added little or no organic matter, let it dry out only half as deep, since surface dryness in sandy soil indicates drier soil below than in other soils. The actual number of days between waterings will vary, since soil moisture is affected by the soil type, temperature, and windiness, and by whether the area is in sun or in shade. You might need to water every few days to provide ample water in a hot, sunny area, or only every 2 weeks where it is cool or shady.

How do you know how deeply the soil has dried or whether you have watered long enough? Longtime gardeners develop a sense of this, but beginners can find out by digging a small hole and looking at or feeling the soil as they dig into it, or by using an inexpensive water meter. As you insert a water meter into the soil, it will tell you the moisture content at each depth.

In drought years, plants that grow most actively in winter can become stunted. Remember, though, that soil dries more slowly in the shorter, cooler days of winter, so the same period of dry weather makes less difference than it would in summer. But if rains fail for several weeks or more, test how deeply dry the soil is, and water it using the guidelines just described for summer. Of course some plants, those that came from dry-winter native habitats, are fine with scant winter water, so these you should leave alone.

Another special case occurs when you are trying to keep winter-into-spring bloomers growing and blooming longer than the natural rainfall would allow. If you want cool-season annuals such as forget-me-nots and sweet alyssum, or perennials such as California poppies and acanthus to have continued bloom and attractive foliage, you have to keep the soil moist as rain tapers off in March and April. Pay attention, since once roots have dried, the plants will be damaged. (*Sunset* magazine says that this period, just as the rains are ending, is the one in which California gardeners are most likely to water their gardens too little.)

Many gardeners water their gardens by holding a hose. It is easy to get bored while doing this and thus not water long enough. Using a sprinkler or special soaker hose lets you do something else while the water spends 10 or 20 minutes going deeper into the soil. However, leaving the water on unattended can create a different problem: forgetting to turn it off. Because this is a waste of water, it is a good idea to get a simple timer. Set it for, say, 20 minutes, and then move the water to a new place. Some timers can be attached at the hose faucet and will actually turn the water off when the time is up. Drip irrigation systems can also be a big help. It is ideal to set them up so that beds with different watering needs can be put on different timers. Another helpful feature in a drip system is a rain sensor that reduces the water released when the soil is already moist.

In order to give plants the best conditions, group them roughly by the amount and annual pattern of water they will need. For example, you won't want to put plants that can't tolerate constantly wet summer soil in the same bed with ones that need constantly wet summer soil. Note, however, that many plants can tolerate a range of soil moisture levels. The entry for each of the fifty plants will tell you what the plant needs or tolerates and will alert you to any possible difficulties.

Whenever you dig an amendment or fertilizer into the soil, or you dig to plant seeds or transplants, your soil should be, ideally, moist but not wet. During the dry season, from May to October, soil that you have not been watering will become deeply dry. Before you dig it, soak this dry soil with a sprinkler for several hours and then leave it to dry for a day to several days, until it is moist but not soggy. If you are planning to dig during the rainy season, from October to April, moisture levels will vary, depending on rainfall. The first few rains, especially if they are not close together, may still leave your soil rather dry. Dig into it or test it with a moisture meter. If the soil is not deeply moist, water and wait before planting, as you would in the summer. Later, frequent rains with short, cool days may result in soil that is too soggy to work in.

To test soil moisture, dig up a handful, squeeze it in your fist, and then open your hand and prod the soil with a finger from the other hand. If it crumbles, the soil is not too wet. If you can't break up the clod with gentle prodding, wait for a day when the soil is drier before you dig.

If the soil is too wet to work during the rainy season and rain continues to fall, you can sometimes solve the problem with a tarp. When it is about to rain, put a tarp over the area you want to plant. Put an overturned plastic bucket under the center and weight the edges with bricks. Whenever there is a break in the rain of a day or more, remove the tarp so the soil can continue to dry.

Sunlight and Shadow

Each entry in this book describes the ideal amount of sunlight and shadow for the plant. In a garden, the term "full sun" means that the sun, if it is not behind clouds or fog, will strike a plant all day or very nearly so. This occurs in garden spots that are either on the south side of objects that cast shadows (such as your house or a tree) or far enough from any shade-producing object to be outside of its shadow. "Partial shade" occurs in places that sunlight can strike only part of the day, which is basically on the east and west of shade-producing objects.

The USDA Hardiness Zone Map indicates average minimum temperatures.

"Light shade" is a special sort of shade produced by being under an open-branched tree or under a lath structure—one covered with north-south strips of wood that have spaces between. It can also be approximated by planting in a spot that has morning sun but afternoon shade. "Full shade" is under a dense tree or on the north side of a shade-producing object.

In urban settings, the many nearby fences and buildings can create especially shady gardens. Shadows are longer in winter than in summer, so plants that require full sun in winter need to be carefully placed. While some plants need more sun than others, only a few can perform in deep shade. If plants are not getting enough sunlight, they tend to have greater distances between the leaves on their stems and fewer flowers. They also lean

ZONE 5	ZONE 6	ZONE 7	ZONE 8	ZONE 9	ZONE 10
–10 to –20°F	0 to –10°F	10 to 0°F	20 to 10°F	30 to 20°F	40 to 30°F

toward the direction of more light. Conversely, if a plant that is adapted to growing in shade is planted in a sunny location, it may develop yellow or white sunburned areas on its leaves and may wilt easily in warm, sunny weather.

In Northern California, many plants that can grow in full sun near the coast require light shade or afternoon shade inland. This is because cooler temperatures and frequent fog moderate coastal conditions, rarely allowing the long periods of heat and bright sun that are common inland. However, brief periods of hot, sunny weather near the coast can wipe out plants accustomed to cooler days, especially if there is a hot wind and the soil is on the dry side. Every summer, some coastal gardeners lose plants during hot spells because they forget to water.

Cold Temperatures

Hardiness indicates how much cold a plant can survive. Cold-hardiness ratings are based most often on the U.S. Department of Agriculture (USDA) Cold Hardiness Map. On this map, numbers indicate the coldest temperatures that occur in different locations. The average minimum temperature of each zone is 10 degrees F colder than that of the next mildest zone. Each zone is also divided into "a" and "b," with 5-degree separations. For example, the coldest temperature in Zone 10a averages 30 to 35 degrees, while that of Zone 10b ranges from 35 to 40 degrees.

Once you have learned your garden's USDA zone, you can predict which plants are likely to survive your winter, though since these are average temperatures, it may get a few degrees colder than the map indicates. In addition, microclimates within a zone, or even within a garden, may be slightly different than in the overall zone.

The mildest zone in Northern California is Zone 10, which has an average lowest temperature of 30 to 40 degrees F. Up to a few miles from the coast, some winters may pass without a frost. When a frost occurs near the coast, it is carried on a wind from the colder inland area, since wind from the ocean at this latitude never bears frosty air. This mild coastal climate is more similar to the one 200 miles north or south than it is to the climate only 20 miles inland, where frosts may occur several times in a

winter. Winter cold also increases in higher elevations of the foothills and into the Sierra Nevada. A few of the fifty plants are damaged by any frost, but many can take temperatures into the 20s or lower.

If you do grow plants that are only borderline hardy in your zone, plant them in your most protected sites. These include beds next to garden or house walls, especially ones that have overhangs, or under broad trees, which offer some protection since they will block some of the falling cold air. Waiting until frost danger is past to cut overwintering plants back also helps, because the uncut stems and leaves offer some protection from cold air. Place borderline plants out of the winter winds and on the south or west side of structures. (The east side is risky, since morning sun hitting frosted plants increases damage.) Or grow them in containers, so they can be moved under overhanging structures or inside in cold weather.

If you are growing a plant in the ground that is usually hardy in your zone and an unusually cold night is predicted, it is probably worth the trouble to cover the plant. You can guess that a night may be frosty when the temperature is below 45 degrees F at 10 P.M., there is no cloud cover, and the air is still and dry. On these nights, cover borderline frost-hardy plants with cardboard boxes, sheets, or tarps held away from the plants by plant stakes. If frost damage does occur, do not immediately prune your plants. Wait a few weeks, or even until growth begins again, so you will be able to tell which parts are really dead.

Staking

While many plants stay nicely upright or lean attractively when left on their own, in some cases stakes are needed to prevent them from falling over or from leaning in unattractive ways. Seasonal winds can knock plants over. They also may lean when they aren't getting quite enough light. Especially keep an eye on tall stems, such as those of foxglove or watsonia, and be ready with stakes and ties as soon as an unattractive leaning begins. Otherwise, the leaning stems will develop bends as they turn upward toward the light. These bent stems won't look right even after they are staked.

Grooming

Plant grooming includes minor changes such as pruning to remove unattractive parts or to shape the plants and moving flexible stems to change the direction in which they grow. A plant that is growing in a container by your front door is likely to get perfect grooming—removal of every leaf that turns yellow or has a blemish, cutting of every flower as soon as it finishes blooming, tucking or trimming of creepers in new directions if they

When you are dead-heading a flower stem that rises above leafy growth, as on Mexican sage, cut low enough to hide the cut among the leaves, so you won't see cut stems sticking up from the plant.

head the wrong way. Plants that are less closely watched—for example, those in a bed that is usually viewed at a bit of a distance—are likely to be groomed a little less carefully. You will set standards for your own plants depending on your available time and how closely they will be viewed.

Part of grooming is the removal of faded flowers, or deadheading. If the plant is soft, you can do this by pinching them off by hand, but it is often best done with flower shears or small pruning shears. The best way to deadhead depends on the architecture of the plant. In some cases, you cut the stems of individual spent flowers all over the plant, and new buds open to replace them. This is true, for example, on calendula and rose campion. Other plants have flowering spikes. The flowers open at the bottom first and then work their way up the stem, so you don't remove the stem until new flowers stop opening at the top and lower flowers become unattractive. Examples of this type of plant are acanthus and foxglove. In yet other plants, side spikes of flowers may follow a central spike, as in the case of watsonia or purple linaria. In these cases, cut out the spent top spikes and let flowers on the side stems open. When appropriate, specific deadheading directions are included in the entry for each plant.

Cutting California poppies back when they stop blooming in late spring often leads to regrowth and reblooming from shoots that form near the ground.

Deadheading isn't possible or required for all flowering plants. We can't really cut the many small spent flowers from borage or four o'clock, so we just enjoy the plants until they begin to look mussy and then pull or cut them. In some cases, the petals of spent flowers drop off and the seedpods that follow them are not noticeable, so we don't have to remove them. Such is the case for poor man's rhododendron and periwinkle. In other cases, we enjoy looking at attractive seedpods, as in the case of love-in-a-mist.

When you are deadheading, follow the first rule of good pruning, which is to cut a stem to a leaf node or to the next lower joint with another stem. But more than that, notice what you have left on the plant. If you have deadheaded so that little bare flower stems stick up on the plant, you have not cut off enough of the stems. Cut spent flower spikes such as those of Mexican sage down into the leafy part of a stem so stubs won't be visible.

While deadheading is often done to make a plant look better, there are other reasons to remove spent flowers. One is to encourage the formation of new flowers or even of entire new flower stems. After a flower has bloomed, it makes seeds. This process requires energy, so removing flowers before seeds can form allows the plant more energy for new flowers. Some plants, if cut back to healthy leaves near the ground when they seem bloomed out, will actually regrow and form new leafy and flowering stems. Examples are forget-me-not, sweet alyssum, and California poppy. These plants will rebloom once or even twice if the weather remains relatively cool and the soil is kept moist. Still another reason to deadhead is that it is one line of defense against having too many seedlings next year. When deadheading isn't possible, as in the case of borage or four o'clock, you can prevent excessive seeding by pulling the plants or cutting them back as soon as they begin to seem bloomed out, rather than letting them stand while their seeds ripen and fall or blow away. To prevent seeding in plants like English or Algerian ivy, which form flowers only on mature branches, prune them to maintain the plant in its juvenile, nonflowering state.

Reproducing Plants

One of the charms of the fifty plants featured in this book is the ease with which they can be started from seeds or cuttings. While most of these plants are among the easiest to propagate by one or both of these methods, a little background information will help ensure your success.

Starting from Seed

When you want to save seed, of course, you should leave the spent flowers on the plant until the seeds ripen. Then you can decide whether you want to let them fall in place or collect them. Seeds need to ripen on the intact plant, so when you do want to collect them, you have to know when they are ripe. Ripe seeds are usually hard and dry. Soft, green seeds are generally immature and won't grow. Directions in the plant entries will tell you if there is anything special you should know about harvesting the seeds. While a few kinds of seeds need to be replanted immediately, most can be stored to plant later. To keep seeds for later, harvest the seeds or the pods containing ripe seeds, then spread them in a tray

To save seed, harvest pods of love-in-a-mist as soon as they are dry and you can hear seeds rattling inside. Hold pods upright as you cut them so seeds won't fall out.

or wide, shallow box. Keep in a dry, warm place out of direct sunlight for several weeks. If you harvested entire pods, remove the seeds when the pods are quite dry. Store the dry seeds in a closed jar or plastic container in a cool place until you are ready to plant them. Most last at least 2 years.

Seeds can be started outdoors when temperatures are mild. When the soil is still too cold outside, gardeners sometimes start seeds indoors in small containers placed in a bright window. Some seeds grow best on the soil surface; others do better when they are tucked into the soil. In either case, pat the soil down lightly and water the seedbed with a gentle sprinkling. Water it lightly whenever the surface is dry. Once the seedlings are well up, water less often. When seed is a practical way to start a featured plant, instructions are included in the entry, although in many cases there are faster ways to get the plants to reproduce, such as by separating bulbs, creating divisions, or growing from cuttings, as described in the individual entries. (More information about dividing plants is also included in the introduction to the chapter on perennials.)

Growing Plants from Cuttings

A stem cutting is a section of stem with some leaves that, if inserted into soil or a good cutting medium, will form roots and grow into a new plant. The easiest are generally tip cuttings, which are taken from the ends of branches. Sections of stems without the tip may also be fine. Cuttings from some plants root readily, while others root less reliably or more slowly. Plants vary in the time of year at which cuttings are most likely to root and in the degree of maturity that the cut stem should have

Bloom Times

In this book, whenever there are references to the times that plants bloom, the seasons used are astronomical seasons. That is, the first days of the four seasons are December 21 (winter), March 21 (spring), July 21 (summer), and September 21 (fall). While the seasons are standard, they are so mild in Northern California that many plants occasionally bloom at unexpected times. Therefore, information about season of bloom can only be approximate.

attained before you attempt to root them, and this information is given in individual listings. Cuttings of plants that root at every leaf node as they creep along the ground, such as English ivy and *Persicaria capitata,* almost always root. A number of other perennials and shrubs root relatively easily. Some perennials root best from cuttings that include the heel, the curved bottom part of the stem. Succulents often root from the base of single leaves, but the process of growing a new plant will be much faster if you use a stem tip with leaves.

This is a big subject, and if you want to increase your success rate, you can find books that give many more details. However, armed with the following basic principles, you will have a good chance for success with many kinds of plants.

1. Take cuttings of healthy stems that include 5 or 6 leaf nodes (places where leaves are attached to the stems). If you have to carry cuttings home before you can prepare them for rooting, keep them in a cool place, out of the sun, in a plastic bag with a moist paper towel. Refrigerate them if you can't finish the job the minute you get them home.

2. Fill clean containers 3 to 4 inches deep with purchased cutting mix or plain perlite. Make sure the containers have drainage holes in their bottoms.

3. Remove any flowers, as well as all leaves on the bottom third of the stem, or at least two lower leaf nodes. (Be sure the cutting is right side up as it grew.)

4. Use a sharp knife or pruning shears to trim the cutting to just below the bottom node—about $\frac{1}{8}$ inch below it.

5. If you are going to use a purchased rooting hormone, apply it to the bottom of the cutting now. Cuttings often root nicely without it, but using it can improve your chance for success.

6. Bury the bottom third of the cutting, the part from which you removed the leaves, in the cutting mix or perlite.

7. Water the containers well and let them drain until the dripping stops.

8. Cover the containers with a plastic bag that is held away from the cuttings with small stakes.

9. Keep them in an area that gets light but not direct sunlight. If the weather is moderate, this could be outside in shade. Otherwise, keep them indoors.

Your goals from now on are to keep the cutting mix and the air around the cuttings moist enough that they don't wilt but dry enough that they don't rot. Beyond this, success is a matter of time and chance. The plastic cover will keep the air moist, and water will condense and drip into the cutting mix. Nevertheless, check once in a while to be sure the cutting mix is still moist. If the cuttings wilt despite the moist air and mix, they may have been too young and tender, or decay may have set in. Decay will be encouraged if the air and cutting mix are too moist. Combat this by opening the cover for a few minutes a day or by providing a means to let some air in, such as propping up the cover a bit or cutting small slits in the plastic bag.

Rooting of cuttings takes from several weeks for many perennials to several months for woody plants. Plants have rooted when they begin to show new growth. To check before that, you can tug at the cutting ever so gently to see if roots give resistance, but of course you won't want to subject plants to this too often or too roughly.

When rooting has begun, give the plants more air by removing the cover for part of the day (but return it if they wilt). When they do not wilt without a cover, they can be uncovered and gradually moved to a brighter position.

Most of the plants among the featured fifty that can be grown from cuttings are rather easy to grow this way, but even with the easiest species it is common for some cuttings to fail. That is why gardeners usually try to root five or ten cuttings at once. If they all succeed, you can share. If your cuttings do fail, check to be sure you took them at the right time of year, try ones that are a bit firmer, try using rooting hormone, and take greater care with the moisture balance. References that explain how to grow plants from cuttings in greater detail are listed in Suggested Reading (page 295).

Maintaining a Wildish Garden

Plants growing in cheerful profusion appear to be so peaceful, and yet gardeners soon learn that these plants are often jostling for space, trying to mug each other to get more access to the sunlight and the soil. That is especially true of a number of our fifty plants. Not only do they not necessarily stay in bounds, but many of them also produce volunteer seedlings, popping up where they would like to grow. Some gardeners hate this. They want to be able to arrange plants in a certain pattern and have them stay put. Others like the serendipity of garden plants that are capable of changing their location by creeping or self-sowing.

As I got to know the gardens of Northern California, I saw that many of them, including the ones that so charmed me on my first walks in San Francisco, were products of a certain amount of serendipity. The effects that I found so engaging were often the result of putting in certain plants and then letting them wander a bit, or of accepting plants that appeared unbidden in gardens.

But even if you like rambunctious plants, you soon learn that you can't just let them spread or come up anywhere they will. Plants that spread need to be kept in bounds, and seedlings that volunteer need to be thinned or transplanted. If left alone, they often will be too crowded to grow well or will grow in patterns that are jumbled and unattractive. You need to edit the choices your plants make to create a design that suits you.

To use self-seeders well, you need to know whether the seedlings can be transplanted successfully and, if so, the largest size at which they can still survive transplanting. If the seedlings don't transplant well, your choices are limited to deciding which seedlings to leave and which to pull out. If they can be transplanted, you have the added choice of moving seedlings to a new location.

To transplant volunteer seedlings, wait until they have several true leaves, then dig them out with a trowel, rather than pulling them, to avoid damage to the roots. Insert the trowel straight down, so you won't cut roots under the seedling, and pry gently on one or more sides until the seedling comes free. Try to keep soil on the roots, if possible, but if seedlings are growing close together, carefully separate their roots so that you will be planting individual plants. (If you have many seedlings, save only the biggest and healthiest.) Set the rootball in a hole as deep as the roots, or if the soil has fallen off, hold the seedling by the stem over a hole that is as deep as the seedling's roots are long. Fill in soil around the roots until the ground under the seedling is level. Pat the soil down gently and water thoroughly.

Learning the eventual size of the plant will help you decide how close seedlings can be allowed to grow to one another or to other plants. Becoming familiar with particular plants in your own garden will hone your imagination. For example, you may read that California poppy plants grow 1 to 3 feet wide, but it may take seeing a huge poppy plant shade out a Pacific coast iris to drive the point home. You will realize then that the tiny seedlings that seem so thin and harmless are forces that cannot be ignored.

Although you don't want plants to crowd each other out, you do want them to be close enough when they are mature that the leaves touch or even intermingle just a bit. This creates a fuller, more luxuriant garden. On a practical note, it also shades the ground, which reduces water loss and discourages the germination of weed seeds.

When plants self-sow too thickly, you will need to pull out or transplant seedlings to give them the space to mature. Seedlings in this photo include nasturtium, California poppy, love-in-a-mist, honeywort (Cerinthe major), and one foxglove.

To keep the task of organizing your wildish garden from seeming overwhelming, change back and forth between a narrow focus and a broader one. Start by focusing narrowly. For example, start by reviewing the volunteer seedlings in a few square feet and deciding what is to be pulled, spared, or moved. Or review the occurrence of a particular kind of plant in the entire garden and decide how much you of it want and in what general areas you want to grow or remove it. Then look up from your small plot to review the whole garden, or shift from a single kind of plant to consider its relationship to the overall design.

Sometimes the irregular patterns in which seedlings volunteer themselves will be charming, and you will want to keep this randomness while thinning or transplanting them to a more reasonable density. (If you are replanting bulbs, try scattering them in a bed and then planting them in the informal arrangement that results.) Other times, you will decide that a straight or curved row of plants, or maybe a geometrically shaped bed, will add just the degree of order that the otherwise exuberantly informal garden needs to give it definition.

In our mediterranean climate, much of your thinning and replanting will occur in the fall, as the rains start and the temperature begins to drop, since cool-season plants start to grow at this time. But there will be other flushes of seedlings in late winter and into the spring, as seeds that need different conditions begin to grow. It is best to study and edit your garden several times a year, with special attention to fall and late winter.

Besides the crowding that can result from too many germinating seeds, some plants tend to grow beyond the space allotted, even into each other, if not restrained. Even if you've given plants the recommended amount of room, you sometimes will be pruning branches or even single leaves to prevent them from crowding or shading out neighbors. Many times I have cut back an extending nasturtium branch or cut off particular leaves for this reason. And while there may be recommended times for pruning or cutting back a type of plant, the bottom line is that they have to be cut back when they are threatening to destroy a preferred plant neighbor.

Often the best place to grow an invasive plant is the sort of enclosed hole-in-the-concrete planting areas that abound in urban settings. These act as a container would, limiting the spread of these plants while allowing them to lean out a bit over the edge to give a more informal impression. Most of the low spreaders are good in such a setting, as are upright plants like calla lily, acanthus, four o'clock, jade plant, and mirror plant.

You may also want to confine some of these plants to actual containers. If so, make sure the container is comfortably large for the plant roots. You might grow a columbine in a 10- to 12-inch-diameter pot or a white calla lily in a 15-inch pot, for example. Or get really large containers and plant several kinds of plants together in them. An investment in a few handsome, well-made containers is always money well spent, since they will ornament your garden and can be replanted with different plants from year to year.

Gardens can be designed in ways that limit the spread of invasive plants. You can limit acanthus or crocosmia, among others, by planting them next to a mowed lawn, because mowing kills the seedlings or

Confined to a container, English ivy can be enjoyed but prevented from running rampant in the garden.

These small calla lily plants grew from overlooked rhizomes. A little more digging revealed a number of rhizome fragments (upper right) that hadn't grown shoots yet.

plants growing from runners. Baby's tears will not extend outside of an area of reliable shade, especially in combination with regular foot traffic in the sunnier area. A thick organic mulch will reduce seeding of plants such as columbine or Mexican daisy.

If you are growing a plant that reproduces from underground structures, such as bulbs, corms, or rhizomes (or if you have weeds that do this), it is important to learn to recognize these structures. Often even the little ones or the broken pieces of such propagules will grow. If there is any chance of overlooking them in your soil, you should avoid moving soil from a location where such plants grow to one where they do not. In my yard, I do not put backyard soil in the front, to avoid spreading the weedy Bermuda buttercup and wild onion. I do not move soil from the front to the back, to avoid spreading stray calla lily rhizome fragments. And I would never, ever bring soil from my community garden plot to any other place, because it may contain stray bits of bindweed root! You should also pay attention when you decide to transplant a plant from an area infested by a pest plant to one that is not—or when you accept a gift plant from another garden. Weedy plants could grow from propagules hiding among the roots of desirable plants. If its roots are sturdy, you can look through them, but if they are fragile, it is better to quarantine the plant for a while. Put it in a container and watch out for growing pest plants. That way you can pull them or pry them out before you transplant to a final location.

Maintaining or Refreshing a Gene Pool

A number of the plants discussed in this book are available in different varieties, the most common difference being that the flowers differ in color. In some cases, your goal will be to keep the flowers all one color, which requires pulling out plants with flowers of other colors. Sometimes you can tell what color the flowers will be before a plant blooms by the color of its

stems or other clues. This is true of foxglove, in which the stems of plants with purple flowers are flushed purple. Other times, you will need to wait until a plant blooms before you know its flower color. I have, for example, maintained only yellow calendula in my garden by removing any plants with orange flowers before the seed could fall.

In some cases, your goal will be to increase variety by introducing plants with interesting colors different from the ones you have. Some plants will decrease in variety of flower color as they naturalize in a garden. For example, nasturtium will eventually bloom in mainly orange, yellow, and an orange and yellow bicolor. If you want to add scarlet, pale yellow, variegated leaves ('Alaska'), or other variations, plant some seed of these types every couple of years.

To save bulb or perennial plants with a particular flower color, such as these yellow chasmanthes, tie tags on the stems so you can identify them when they are dormant.

Chapter Two

WILDISH VS. WEEDY

[decorative flower icon]

*T*here is much to be said, particularly in an urban environment, for plants that offer beauty while surviving neglect; rough treatment; poor, compacted soil; pollution; and other urban hazards. The plants featured in this book will do this, but the traits that make them tough, easy garden plants are often ones that they share with weeds. Are they weeds? Professional gardeners often say of one of our fifty featured plants, "Oh, that's a weed," and though their words sound damning, their tone often suggests approval of or even respect for the ability of the plant to decorate gardens while requiring little care. But it is unavoidably true that some people consider some of the plants in this book to be real weeds. The same willingness to grow that is part of their charm for some is evidence of their weedy nature to others.

Naturalized Chasmanthe floribunda *and winter leaves of naked lady give this abandoned garden a wild beauty.*

These four o'clocks have to be pruned to keep the mailbox accessible in summer.

ARE THEY WEEDS?

The most common gardener's definition of a weed is a flower in the wrong place. This definition assumes that a plant that is considered a weed in one part of the garden might be wanted in another part of the garden, or in someone else's garden. Another way of defining a weed is as something that the gardener didn't intend to grow. If it turns out to be nice, we can call it a volunteer and decide to accept its offer to grow in our garden. Both of these definitions assume that a weed might be a desirable plant in some cases.

Still another way to define a weed is that it is a plant that prevents a piece of land from producing the value we want from it: a pretty garden, a vegetable crop, or a pasture, for example. This concept says nothing about the value of the weed elsewhere, just that we don't want it here, thank you, because we have other plans for this place.

There is, however, a group of plants that appear without being invited and are rarely considered anything but weeds. We would be hard pressed, for example, to choose any right place for bindweed or quack grass. These plants, which have no virtues at all from the viewpoint of a gardener or a farmer, would blanket our gardens if given half a chance.

Weed scientists have long been aware that certain weedy plants follow humans around. These plants are particularly well adapted to our fields and gardens. They grow best in what is known as disturbed soil—soil that has been dug up for planting or overgrazed by livestock. Weeds

A weathered paint job acquires an air of "shabby chic" when ornamented by a self-sown centranthus plant.

that flourish here include bindweed, quack grass, thistle, wild mustard, crab grass, and many others. Like the lichens and "crack plants" that can establish themselves on bare rock, weeds are also pioneer plants. They are good at colonizing areas where few other plants have gotten a roothold. It is this kind of weed that has been most likely in the past to end up on lists of "noxious" weeds, with laws enacted to help control their spread.

Another trait that can make a plant weedy is invasiveness, meaning that the plants spread quickly over a larger area than expected, either by creeping there or by spreading seeds. A third trait is an excellent ability to compete with other plants, sometimes growing over and crowding out more desirable ones. A fourth is persistence, meaning that the plant is difficult to get rid of. Clearly, some desirable garden plants have these traits to some degree, and whether we tolerate them in our gardens is determined by an equation that includes both their weediness and how much we like to look at them.

Certain plants can be weedier in gardens in one location than in another. Gardeners in the Midwest find nasturtium to be rather difficult to grow successfully, and so they treasure it. In California, it grows and resows so prolifically that some gardeners banish it from their gardens. In hot-summer California locations, pink evening primrose (*Oenothera speciosa* 'Rosea') spreads rampantly, while near the coast, in the sandy soil of my garden, it barely survives from year to year.

Are the fifty plants weeds? They vary considerably in their weediness. Columbine, for example, has only a slight tendency to reseed itself and none to persist if dug out. Jade plant is fairly well behaved, except that rooting fragments sometimes grow beneath it. Algerian ivy, on the other hand, spreads quickly by runners, climbs over other plants, and is devilishly hard to get rid of. Our willingness to accept weediness varies too, so that a plant that pleases me will not please you, and vice versa. I grow columbine, for example, as well as nasturtium, calla lily, and a number of other rather rampant plants, but I avoid Algerian ivy like the plague. However, there are plenty of gardeners who think that Algerian ivy makes a dandy large-scale ground cover.

What Are Wildland Weeds?

Until recently, our judgments about the goodness or badness of a plant were based mainly on whether it interfered with our plans to suit ourselves on a piece of land—whether we intend to grow food, medicinal herbs, food for our domestic animals, timber, or, more recently, ornamental plants. We have not been too concerned with wild places, where we weren't trying to harvest something. But weeds have also been running amok in wild areas for some time, and in the past fifty years or so, with the development of the science of ecology, we have begun to recognize that a mostly new group of weeds is invading areas that have never been gardened, plowed, or grazed.

In each area of the world, plant communities create regionally unique landscapes and also support regional birds and other animals. The plants in these habitats cover the ground thickly and remain relatively stable for centuries. In Northern California, these habitats include our redwood forests, oak savanna, chaparral, tule marsh, and other natural landscape treasures. Wildland weeds can degrade these habitats in various ways. Perhaps most obviously, they change the way the wild area looks and how it feels to walk through it. Thorny gorse shrubs crowd out California lilac and coyote brush in our chaparral-covered hillsides. English ivy festoons redwoods and grows over the wild ginger and redwood sorrel beneath them. It can kill native plants by crowding them out or by changing the water balance or the soil type to create conditions in which the natives can't survive. Some weeds also make our Northern California habitats more vulnerable to fire and make the fires more severe when they do occur. Another problem is that they may hybridize with related native plant species, eventually resulting in the loss of native species through the evolutionary process. They often result in many fewer species of plants in an area, and the loss of native plants results in a loss of native birds and other animals.

It takes a somewhat different set of traits for a weed to be able to invade a stable wild environment than it does for it to invade the relatively unstable environment of a garden. Plants that have windborne or bird-distributed seeds have a better chance of getting into wildlands because of these long-distance dispersal methods. Once there, some wildland weeds need the openings they get when roadcuts or other disturbances clear some ground in native habitats. Others can directly invade mature habitats in which the ground is already covered with plants. Any wildland weed is more likely to survive and spread if it is not a favorite food plant for local animals or susceptible to local diseases. Plants that came from far away have an advantage here, because their foragers and diseases were often left in their homeland when they were exported. Deer-tolerant plants that escape in our deer-filled wildlands get a tremendous advantage over plants that deer like to eat.

Although there are overlaps, many wildland weeds are different from garden weeds, because they are invading different environments. A plant that drives us crazy in a garden often can't get past first base in the wild, and a plant that is ever so well behaved in our gardens may become an absolute thug in the wild. A gardener may say of a plant that is galloping across the wild landscape, "Oh, that's not invasive," because it hasn't multiplied in her garden. But the situations are quite different, and so the plant reacts differently.

As the list of wild and invasive plants gets longer, gardeners are being asked not to grow some ornamental plants that seem harmless in a garden. And plants that we have become accustomed to seeing in parklands near urban centers, such as eucalyptus trees, are suddenly considered enemies to be eradicated. In fact, some observers have become rather fond of their neighborhood wildland weeds and are not happy to see them removed.

One of the factors contributing to the spread of wildland weeds is the movement of plants around the earth by human beings. This has increased slowly over the centuries from a trickle to a broad river. Some of these introductions have been accidental, some intentional. Plants have been introduced by governmental agencies as well as by private businesses and individuals. A significant minority of these intentionally introduced species have escaped into wild habitats and become established there.

A sign of the times, this notice explains to hikers why certain plants are being removed from a wild hill. Listen for more varied bird-songs, it suggests, as native plants bring native wildlife back to the area.

Gardeners have contributed to this problem. They have imported many plants from other continents to increase the variety in their gardens. They have also moved to new continents or to islands, which are even more vulnerable, where they have tried to re-create the garden flora they had before they moved. Governmental agencies and wildland experts, hoping to reduce erosion or create new sources of timber, have played a significant role in the problem, because some of the species they chose to plant in and near wildlands later proved to be invasive.

Plants are most likely to become pests in areas that have climates similar to the ones in which they evolved. In many cases, environmental conditions limit the spread of wildland weeds. For example, the Australian paperbark tree *(Melaleuca quinquinervia)*, which a forester intentionally sowed from an airplane in the Florida Everglades, has become a major pest there but not in drier California, where it is used as a street tree. Even within Northern California, plants can be serious wildland invaders in one region but not in another. Pampas grass *(Cortaderia selloana)*, a tall grass with feathery plumes, seems to require the cooler, moister summer near the coast to be able to grow in wildlands, so it has not spread much to inland habitats. The same is true of English holly, which has begun to appear in coastal wooded areas. And English ivy, which is considered a pest in Northern California, is an even worse pest in the moister climates of Oregon and Washington.

Plants that become rampant wildland invaders where they aren't native may have been much less aggressive in their native environment. At home, they had to compete with other plants that have evolved to fight them for space, with insects and larger animals that have evolved to eat them, and with diseases that periodically mow them down. When humans move a plant to a new place they are usually careful to leave behind the insects and diseases that eat the plant. In a new environment, if they can compete with the other wildland plants and survive larger plant-eating animals, they have the added advantage of being otherwise pest-free. In fact, one solution to a nonnative wildland weed problem is to search the weed's native habitat for an insect or disease that destroys only that particular plant, and then introduce it to the new places where the plant is making a pest of itself. Ecologists are even now seeking such a pest they can import from South Africa to California to limit the spread of Cape ivy *(Delairea odorata)*.

Checking the Weed Lists

Three lists of California weeds are of interest to gardeners. You can find out where to get these lists and learn more about the organizations that maintain the lists in the Resources section of this book on page 299.

1. The California Department of Food and Agriculture (CDFA) Noxious Weeds List includes agricultural weeds as well as some wildland invasive weeds. Each county has an agricultural commissioner charged with preventing the spread of noxious weeds. The list is divided into sublists and laws about particular weeds differ depending on the sublist on which they appear.

2. The California Noxious Weeds Control Project Inventory is maintained by 16 federal and state agencies. It includes all of the plants that are being combated in local eradication projects, and lets you locate information about these projects. This online list can alert you to particular problem plants that might be escaping near where you live. This list proves that local problems can be quite different even statewide problems, in that the list includes a couple of usually desirable agricultural plants, almond and fig, both of which have become pests in some areas.

3. The California Exotic Pest Plants Council (CalEPPC, pronounced cal-ep'-cee) is a California nonprofit organization that maintains a list of wildland invasive plants and works to reduce their occurrence in wildlands. They publish a list called "Invasive Nonnative Plants of Greatest Ecological Concern in California," and update it periodically to keep up with changes in patterns of invasiveness. It is under revision in 2003, and this revision may result in some plants being upgraded or downgraded as threats to wildlife, so you will need to check the CalEPPC website and publications for the most recent information. (I should mention that the word "exotic" in the name of the organization has the modern meaning of "nonnative," rather than the Victorian meaning of the word, which was "excitingly unusual.")

CalEPPC lists, prior to 2004, were divided into the following sublists:

- "A" for the "Most Invasive Wildland Pest Plants," which was subdivided into "A-1" for the most widespread and "A-2" for those that were invasive only in certain regions of the state.
- "B" for plants of lesser invasiveness, meaning that they spread less rapidly and cause a lesser degree of disruption.
- "Red Alert" for plants that have escaped in small or localized areas, but have a potential to spread explosively.
- "Need More Information" for plants being studied to better understand the nature of their threat to wildlands.
- "Considered but Not Listed" for plants studied and determined not to present a threat to wildlands.

In 2004, when the reassessment of plants is completed, the plants on the lists will change. Listed plants will be divided into those with "High," "Medium," or "Low" impact on wildland ecosystems. CalEPPC will also issue special "Alerts" for plants on the "High" or "Medium" sublists that are not presently widespread in wildlands, but are considered to be capable of rapidly invading them. They will also continue to publish a list of plants they evaluated and decided not to put on an invader list, but will combine in it those that, when evaluated, either fell below the threshold for listing or about which too little is known still to list them.

Combating Wildland Weeds

Lists of current wildland weeds can't protect us from plants that no one yet knows will escape into the wild, including both newly introduced plants and garden plants that suddenly become a problem. No one guessed that licorice plant *(Helichrysum petiolare)* would become a wildland invader, but its windblown seeds, carried to wild parts of Mount Tamalpais, have germinated there, and the plant has begun to spread. And California gardeners have long grown several species of the red-berried shrub cotoneaster, but only recently have cotoneaster plants turned up in coastal wildlands. Local birds must have been eating the berries all along, and then depositing seeds in wildlands, so why have the plants only recently appeared in the wild? Ecologists think there are several possible explanations. The wildlands could have become more vulnerable, perhaps through disturbance. Or the number of birds that eat the berries and then fly to wildlands could have increased. Or, perhaps cotoneasters in gardens have cross-pollinated, resulting in many natural hybrids, some of which have the ability to compete in wildlands better than the original species. To avoid further invasions, scientists are trying to learn to identify plants that are likely to become wildland weeds. While they do not have a foolproof system, they are most suspicious of plants that:

✽ Are imported from a different continent;

✽ Have proven invasive to wildlands elsewhere or are closely related to plants that are invasive elsewhere;

✽ Are able to grow in a wide range of conditions;

✽ Produce seeds at an early age;

✽ Have seed that germinates easily, without special needs such as exposure to cold;

✽ Have seed that is dispersed at distances from the parent plants;

✽ Reproduce both by seeds and vegetatively (runners, bulbs, etc.).

Plant importers and botanical garden curators are being asked to consider these factors and, if there is some doubt, to grow a plant for a few years and evaluate it before releasing it to the public. Nurseries are being asked not to sell wildland weeds and to offer alternatives whenever possible. The lists of alternatives to wildland weeds are just being developed, but I have suggested alternatives whenever I am aware of them.

There is even a movement afoot to pass laws to create a "white list" of plants that aren't likely to become wildland weeds and then prohibit the import or growth of all other plants. Some proposals are quite draconian and would vastly reduce plant and seed importation, with penalties for gardeners who grow banned plants. I prefer to think that the problem can be solved through education and self-regulation. Here's what you can do to prevent the spread of wildland weeds:

✻ Do not buy or plant any species that are known to be nearly impossible to prevent from escaping, such as pampas and jubata grass or the various brooms (in the genera *Cytisus, Genista,* and *Spartium*).

✻ Plant alternatives to potential invaders whenever possible, including alternatives that are California natives.

✻ Avoid growing potential invaders where seeds or plant parts could wash into nearby waterways and become established downstream.

✻ Avoid putting plant trimmings from possible wildland invaders, or soil that might contain parts of such plants, into wild areas.

✻ If you live in or next to a wildland area, take more care than if you live in an urban setting, avoiding altogether any plants that could escape and invade the nearby wild habitat.

✻ Take part in volunteer efforts to eradicate wildland weeds from wild areas and to replant native plants there, and support organizations that do this.

✻ Support political efforts to reduce the expansion of housing into wildlands, and instead help promote development plans that result in areas of urban density surrounded by undeveloped wildlands that we all can enjoy.

Growing Native Plants

In the midst of all of this concern about our native habitats, many gardeners wonder whether it would be better to grow only native plants. I encourage you to consider native plants, and I have included some books on growing them in Suggested Reading, which starts on page 295. Many California native plants are quite lovely to look at, and growing them provides more food for native birds, insects, and other creatures. However, having them in your garden will not stop the degradation of wildlands by invasive weeds. This can be done only by removing weeds from wildlands, avoiding or controlling them in gardens, and not introducing more of them.

In fact, some experts point out that native plants closely related to ones in nearby wildlands may interbreed with them. This change in the genetic makeup of the nearby relatives may have unforeseen consequences. In Strybing Arboretum's California native garden, for example, yellow bush lupine *(Lupinus arboreus)*, which is native to the southern half of the state, crosses with a Bay Area regional native blue lupine *(Lupinus variicolor)*, producing seedlings with muddied flower colors and mixed plant forms. Because of this, the arboretum has decided not to grow the yellow bush lupine but rather to grow only the several lovely

California Noxious Weed Control Project Inventory

❋ Six of the fifty plants are, at this writing, the subject of control projects somewhere in the state. They are *Crocosmia x crocosmiiflora, Digitalis purpurea, Hedera helix, Myosotis sylvatica, Tropaeolum majus,* and *Vinca major.* Most of these projects are in partially developed public parklands where intentionally planted species have naturalized and are now being eradicated.

CalEPPC Most Invasive Wildland Pest Plants List

❋ None of the fifty plants are on either the A-1 or the A-2 lists.
❋ Two of the fifty plants are on the B list. They are *Hedera helix* and *Vinca major.*
❋ None of the fifty plants are on the "Red Alert" list.
❋ Two of the fifty plants, and one listed as a similar species, are on the "Need More Information" list. They are *Hedera algeriensis, Echium candicans,* and *Echium pinanana.*
❋ Five of the fifty plants are on the "Considered but Not Listed" list. They are *Centranthus ruber, Coprosma repens, Crocosmia x crocosmiiflora, Digitalis purpurea,* and *Zantedeschia aethiopica.*

Note: Because this list and its sublists are under revision at this writing, I cannot report which plants may be moved to different categories in the revision, but I can report, in the "Control and Removal" sections of the plant entries when I have information to suggest that a change is possible. Check the CalEPPC website and print publications for the most recent information.

regional lupine species. To avoid problems like this, buy native plants from local California Native Plant Society chapter sales (see Resources on page 299) or from nurseries that guarantee locally appropriate native species and varieties.

Another misconception is that California natives will be well adapted to a California garden just because they are natives. The habitats of the state are so varied that native plants have a wide range of needs. You should ask about the needs of each plant and arrange the garden so that ones with compatible needs grow together. Natives can also be mixed with nonnative plants that have similar needs.

Some gardeners hope to reproduce particular wild California habitats in their gardens. This will work best if your garden has conditions similar to those that produce that habitat. You may be able to modify your soil somewhat to imitate the soil of a particular habitat, within certain limits, but microclimate is also important. For example, a beach habitat planting will work better near the ocean than in the foothills, and vice versa. Given appropriate soil and microclimate, you can use plants from a unified habitat to give the impression of that habitat. However, you are not likely to have all of the plants that would grow there in the wild. Some will not be available because they are quite difficult to grow outside of their native location. Others will not be attractive or desirable in a garden. For example, *Toxicodendron diversiloba,* which is more widespread than any other native California shrub and is an important source of food for a number of birds (including our state bird, the California quail), is not ever going to be a favored garden plant—it is poison oak!

Beware of Wildflower Mixes

While we are on the subject of native plants, I must tell you to be wary of wildflower mixes. The term "wildflower" does not necessarily mean "native flower." The plants included could be natives in California or somewhere in the United States, but they also might be from other lands. Wildflower mixes could very well introduce plants you would rather not have in your garden. Buy them only if you can read and assess

the suitability of the species they contain for your location. This is especially true for plantings that are in or that adjoin wildlands, since these mixes can contain flowers that invade certain California wild habitats. Examples are ox-eye daisy *(Leucanthemum vulgare)*, bachelor's buttons *(Centaurea cyanus)*, garland chrysanthemum *(Chrysanthemum coronarium)*, and sweet alyssum *(Lobularia maritima)*. California wildflower mixes generally contain, and in fact are usually dominated by, a large-flowered orange variety of California poppy. Near the coast, the poppy variant that is native is two-tone orange and yellow, so the solid orange one in wildflower mixes won't help re-create coastal habitat.

A second misconception about wildflower mixes is that they can crowd out weeds in your garden, creating a lovely carpet of bloom with little or no care. In truth, if weeds have been growing in your garden for a year or more, they have created underground networks of perennial roots and/or long-lived seed deposits in your soil, and these will compete handily with any seeds that you sow. If you scatter-sow seeds over a large area, it will be difficult to get weeds out without trampling your flower seedlings.

CONTROLLING WEEDS IN YOUR GARDEN

Since some plants are undeniably unwelcome in our gardens, and others that may have been welcome at first later become unwelcome, we need some strategies for controlling unwanted plants. Individual plant listings in later chapters include instructions for getting rid of each of the fifty plants, if that is your wish, and reading these will give you many ideas for weed control in general. Here I will briefly summarize weed control and also explain some specific techniques that can be helpful.

Controlling weeds is basically a process of ungrowing the plants you don't want. Just as it helps to know each garden plant and how it grows, it helps to know the identity of each weed, because you can then read about its life cycle and learn how other gardeners have controlled it. Still, there are many general concepts and practices that will give you considerably greater control, even if you haven't identified each weed.

Weeds, like choice garden plants, may be annuals or perennials. Annual weeds can reproduce only by seed, dying after depositing seed on the soil each year. Perennials may make seed, but they also live from year to year as roots, bulbs, rhizomes, or other underground structures. To get weeds under control, you need to reduce the weed seed bank, as well as destroy any perennial weed reproductive structures in the soil. Your first goal is to prevent fresh seeds from falling. Just as we prevent garden plants from seeding by deadheading and promptly removing plants that have finished bloom, we prevent weeds from seeding by pulling them before seed can form—preferably even before the plant can bloom. In general, Northern California weeds grow most actively in two seasons. Cool-season weeds come up in early to mid fall, with the rains, and then bloom and form seed from late fall to spring. Warm-season weeds, most of which grow only in watered gardens, come up in the spring and seed over the summer and into fall. Control each type by scheduling your weeding when each season's weeds are young, not when they have already dropped more seed into your soil. If you get to weeds while they are still seedlings, many can be killed by scraping them from the soil with a hoe. (An added benefit of getting rid of weeds before they have ripe seeds is that these can be added to any compost pile without fear that they will regrow.)

To make a big difference in the number of weeds that come up from seed in your garden, however, you will have to keep up the pressure year after year. This is because seeds, including or maybe especially weed seeds, don't all germinate in the first year. The old saying "one year's weed, seven years seed" refers to the fact that it is typical for only half of the seed from a given year to germinate the next year. If you do the math, you can see that after seven years, you will be down to a pretty small percentage of the seeds. But if new seeds fall, you'll have to start all over again.

Perennial weeds that form seeds will also be slowed down by well-scheduled hand weeding, but if you just pull off their tops, they will come right back from their underground structures. If you are faced with a weedy plot, you may find that it works best to pull all of the annual weeds but to leave standing any perennials with runners or bulbs. The standing weeds serve as markers to tell you where to dig to remove them thoroughly.

Gardeners can take a few tips in setting priorities from those who are seeking to control weeds in wildlands. They pay close attention to weeds that are new, identifying them and eliminating them as soon as possible. If infestations are large, they work from the edges until they have time to do the whole patch. This prevents weeds from spreading. They also give their attention first to weeds that are growing in sensitive spots, such as next to a particularly treasured native species. (In your garden, this might be the ones crowding out favorite flowers.) If time is limited, another option is to pull only a particular species of weed on a given day—because that species is about to go to seed or because you know it will be difficult to pull if it gets much larger.

When soil is full of weed seeds and reproductive structures of perennial weeds, digging and pulling long enough to eliminate them is hard work. Three techniques that can make your efforts more effective are mulching, presprouting, and solarization.

Mulching around garden plants prevents seeds from germinating and makes any that do sprout easier to pull out. Use a 3-inch-thick mulch of compost, leaf mold, shredded bark, or wood chips, making sure that any wood product has either aged or had a nitrogen source added. Big chunks of bark are less desirable, since they will be slow to decay into the soil, whereas smaller particles become soil amendment in a year or so. Water the soil thoroughly before adding the mulch, or it may prevent water from reaching the soil. Keep the mulch away from plant stems, because it can encourage decay.

In areas between widely spaced plants or areas not yet planted, you can use a smothering mulch. Start with several overlapping layers of cardboard from brown corrugated boxes. Water them down, and then cover them with a thick layer of wood chips. To kill weeds, the mulch must remain there for at least a year. Plastics and weed barrier materials are available for use as smothering mulches but are less desirable because they do not decay into the soil. If you do use a nonorganic substance, get one that lets water pass through, such as weed block cloth (or even perforated plastic). Water entering the soil will increase weed seed germination (and subsequent death) and also allows your garden to absorb rain and add it to the water table.

As you can imagine, mulch reduces seeding by desirable plants as well as weeds, so your garden won't have many self-sown flowers while you are controlling weeds in this way. The truth is, though, a garden with self-sowing flowers isn't as much fun when there are so many weeds, so getting them under control first will make your wildish garden more pleasant later.

When you have an unplanted area that you plan to plant in a month or two, use presprouting. Start by pulling any weeds that are there, and then dig out any lurking perennial roots, rhizomes, and so on. If you are planning to dig amendment or fertilizer into the soil, do it now. Water the soil. Wait. When weed seeds germinate, use a hoe to remove them, lightly scraping the surface. When perennials sprout from underground structures, dig them out, disturbing the soil around them as little as possible. (The reason not to disturb the soil is that there is a reservoir of weed seeds in it, and they will stay dormant only if you don't bring them near the surface.) After you have scraped and dug once or twice, you can plant seeds or transplants, again disturbing the soil only as much as necessary to put them in.

To kill weed seeds and roots deeper in the soil, gardeners in warmer parts of the region have an additional tool. Where summer temperatures are over 85 degrees F for at least six weeks or you have several shorter consecutive periods above this temperature, you can solarize your soil by covering it with clear plastic. The heat generated will kill weeds as well as soil disease organisms several inches deep. To solarize soil, pull and dig weeds in an area at least 6 by 9 feet, and then water the bare soil thoroughly. Cover it with one or, even better, two layers of sturdy clear plastic. If you must piece the plastic together, use transparent tape, duct tape, or waterproof glue. Tuck the edges of the plastic into the soil. Remove the covering in 6 to 8 weeks.

Weed-killing chemicals, known as herbicides, can help in weed control, but they should never be the first line of defense. The smart weeding and weed-control methods described here are better for the environment and can go a long way toward controlling your weed problem. If you decide to use herbicides, save them for situations that can't be resolved by other means—for example, weeds that have deeply and firmly rooted themselves in cracks between manmade structures, such as curbs and sidewalks or timbers in garden beds. Even for these difficult situations, try other methods first, such as hand-pulling or pouring boiling water in the crack. If you do resort to an herbicide, use the least persistent, least toxic one possible, starting with herbicidal soap. If that doesn't work, try glyphosate, which is the active ingredient in such brand-name products as Roundup and Kleenup. Read the label and follow the instructions carefully to avoid harming yourself, your pets, or desirable plants.

Chapter Three

ANNUALS

*A*nnuals are plants that live for less than one year. Although their life span is only a few months, they are likely to bloom gloriously during most of their life. When they die, annuals leave behind many seeds, which, if conditions are favorable, grow and repeat the performance the following year.

Because annuals are fast to bloom but short-lived, gardeners typically use them for temporary effects. The garden that was all orange and yellow annuals in spring can be all pink and blue in summer and can, by fall, present a blank slate for your next ideas. Annuals are also good for planting in containers, or in areas for which you haven't yet chosen more permanent plantings. They combine well with spring bulbs, growing up to cover the dying bulb leaves. Annuals also fill in well between more permanent plants, such as shrubs, perennials, or succulents. And they decorate unused corners of vegetable gardens while the (also annual) vegetable crops shift throughout the year. A food garden is an especially appropriate location for annuals with edible flowers, such as nasturtium, calendula, borage, and Johnny-jump-up.

Gardeners divide annuals into cool-season and warm-season plants. Eight of the nine annuals featured in this chapter are cool-season annuals. Only one of them, poor man's orchid *(Impatiens balfourii)*, is a warm-season annual.

Orange nasturtiums in containers add vivid accents to the entrance of a pale yellow house. The creamy-white rose at right is 'Sally Holmes'.

The white-marbled leaves of 'Alaska' nasturtiums offer a striking variation. Below them is blue-flowered Echium vulgare 'Blue Bedder', an annual echium.

Seeds of cool-season annuals germinate in relatively cool soil, and the plants grow best in cooler weather. They are often able to withstand light frosts, and so are called "half-hardy." When a cool-season annual naturalizes in an unwatered Northern California garden, its seeds germinate as the fall rains begin. The plants grow through the winter and bloom in

the spring. They drop fresh seed and then die by summer. However, if you live near the coast, where summers are cool, you can have cool-season annuals blooming in your garden much of the year. If you keep the garden watered in late spring and early summer, the naturalized over-wintering plants will bloom longer. (For details, see the entries that follow and page 26.) Or you can resow seed in a watered garden in spring and summer for bloom in summer and fall. If cool-season annuals are ones that succeed in the Central Valley, they will be winter and early spring-blooming, often dying in the summer even if watered.

Seed of warm-season annuals, such as poor man's orchid, can germinate only as the weather warms in the spring. Therefore, they will naturalize only in gardens that are watered in spring and summer. Many of them will thrive in both coastal and inland summers, though inland summers may be too hot for some of them, and coastal summers may be too cool for others.

Finding Informal Annual Varieties

Many of the annual plants for sale in nurseries are varieties that have been bred into short, ball-shaped plants, averaging 6 to 8 inches tall and wide. Examples are 'Blue Ball' forget-me-not and 'Calypso' calendula. Victorian gardeners used these in "carpet bedding" schemes, described on page 6. Carpet bedding is still used in the plantings that are used to spell out words in public parks. But ball-shaped plants are much trickier to use in other kinds of gardens because they are too uniform and stiff. In addition, they are not well suited to damp coastal climates, where their closely packed leaves encourage disease and decay.

You may wonder why, if they are such problems, these plants are still sold so commonly. Although the Victorians started the trend of using dwarf bedding plants, the nursery industry ran with these little green balls. Growers love the plants because they bloom while they are still small and easy to handle. They know that you will want to buy plants that already have flowers. However, if you buy compact varieties, you will find that they will never grow tall, never lend their swaying branches to charming drifts of garden color, and never mingle with adjacent plants to create a colorful pastiche. In the case of creepers, compact varieties won't drape casually over embankments or the edges of pots.

For greater garden interest, use mostly varieties that are taller, more open, and irregular in shape. Use compact plants only for accents, edgings at the fronts of borders, or in rather formal container plantings.

The entries for the featured annuals give examples of some shorter or taller varieties, and a little checking of nursery plants and seed packets will help you locate others. Nurseries may not carry bedding plants of taller varieties, but they will carry seed for these varieties, and you can find an even wider selection from mail order specialty nurseries. Many are easy to grow from seed.

When annuals sow themselves, voting with their roots that they should grow in certain places, the gardener will have to make some decisions. Shall we have borage in the garden again this year? Shall we let it grow in the new place where it has sprouted, or would it be better to move it over behind the California poppies, since it will be taller? Or shall we just hoe it all out and grow something else? One thing is certain: If you dig out an annual seedling or, for that matter, a mature annual plant, it will not come back from the roots. Unlike bulbs or many perennial plants, annuals lack underground reproductive structures, depending entirely on seeds for regeneration.

Weedy Annuals

The list of annual plants that have become weeds is a long one, consisting mostly of European weeds that have followed the migration of farmers and gardeners across the Atlantic and westward across the North American continent. From the wickedly spined star thistle to the waving wild oats that cover our hillsides and replace our native bunchgrasses, we are plagued with these plants, both in and out of our gardens.

The annual flowers we grow in gardens are clearly much prettier than the annuals we consider weeds. But some of them do have the same muscular tendency, so we have to be careful to keep them in hand. The nine annuals featured in this chapter are among those most likely to naturalize in gardens. If you like having them there, you will consider this a virtue. On the other hand, if you had quite enough of a particular naturalizing annual last year, you are not going to be pleased when all those seedlings appear this year.

Where a gardener draws the line on self-sowing annuals within the garden is a personal matter. I prefer to weed out herb Robert *(Geranium robertianum)*, a small plant with finely cut leaves, a pungent odor, and small, five-petaled pink flowers. Nor do I grow the self-seeding annuals Bells of Ireland *(Molucella laevis)* and Money plant *(Lunaria annua)*.

Where we all should draw the same line is in preventing the selfseeding annuals that we find charming in our gardens from getting into wild areas. This involves taking precautions, such as not growing these plants adjacent to wild areas they might invade and not dumping plants with seeds in wild areas. See Chapter 2 and the individual entries that follow for advice on preventing the escape of garden annuals.

Borago officinalis

❊ Borage

PLANT TYPE: *Cool-season annual* | HEIGHT AND SPREAD: *2 to 3 feet tall and 1½ to 2 feet wide* | BLOOM TIME: *Spring, summer, fall* | LIGHT NEEDS: *Full sun, partial shade* | SOIL NEEDS: *Poor to fertile soil, well drained* | WATER NEEDS: *Moderate to ample water* | OTHER TOLERANCES: *Clay soil, cool coastal summers, deer resistant* | HARDINESS: *Withstands light frost*

This is a hairy plant, even a bit on the prickly side, though it never causes any real harm. The leaves are hairy, the stems are hairy, and even the sepals that enclose the flower buds are hairy. As an ornamental plant, it offers starry blue flowers and the charming effect of sunlight shining through its little hairs. Because of its hairiness, you may be surprised to know that borage has been, and still is to some

Sunlight shining through the tiny hairs of borage give the plant a soft aura.

Coppery pheasant's tail grass (Stipa arundinacea) provides a nice contrast in color and form to the borage in this informal garden. Also pictured are honeywort (Cerinthe major purpurescens) and tulips.

---

extent, used as a vegetable. It has been more widely used as an herb and an ornamental, bouncing back and forth between the herb garden and the flower garden for centuries. It is probably one of the first European plants to be grown in New World gardens, having been brought to Isabella, on what is now Haiti, the first city established by Spanish explorers.

SOURCE AND USES

Borage is native to rocky places in Europe, including the Mediterranean region. Gardeners familiar with medieval manuscript illumination or later European embroideries often notice borage flowers represented in these art forms. Perhaps its most famous historical herbal use is as an addition to claret, to add a nice flavor and to make the drinker courageous and cheerful (though even historical sources mention that it seems equally possible that the wine did the trick). Most recently the oil, marketed as starflower oil in Europe, has been sold as a treatment for rheumatoid arthritis and dermatitis. Borage was harvested in the wild in Spain for use as a vegetable until the late Middle Ages, when it began to be grown as a farm crop. It is a minor crop in Spain now, where the leaves and leaf stems are eaten raw or cooked.

The plant shares a chemical component with cucumbers and thus has a similar flavor. The least hairy, and so the most palatable, parts of the plant are the first two leaves of the seedling and the flowers. Both are nice in a green salad, and the flowers are decorative on fruit salad or floating in iced tea. Some chop the leaves of young plants finely and add them to salad.

Borage has a place among herbs or vegetables or in sunny, informal flower borders. Try planting it with rose campion *(Lychnis coronaria)* or ornamental grasses. It attracts bees and can be planted near deciduous fruit trees in the fall so that its bloom coincides with theirs in the spring, giving bees more reason to visit and pollinate the trees. Sow seeds for this purpose, or, if you have them, transplant small seedlings from other areas. As the trees leaf out and shade the borage, pull it out.

Care and Reproduction

Borage grows easily from seed. It is probably best grown in place, though the seedlings transplant reasonably well if they are still small when you move them. It tolerates clay or sandy soil but needs good drainage and will grow better if the soil is rich in organic matter. It will survive in relatively dry soil but will grow larger and look better if you keep the soil moist.

After the petals fall, seeds form in groups of four at the base of each flower. You can collect them, but it takes a while to gather many, since they tend to fall off as soon as they are fully ripe.

Pinching young borage plants as they grow will make them bushier, though uncrowded plants do branch naturally. Borage plants bloom for many weeks. As deadheading the many small flowers is impractical, the plants eventually look a little untidy. Another factor in their untidy appearance is that lower leaves often turn brown on older plants. It is best to pull the plants when you see them entering this phase and replace them with something more attractive—and by so doing you will reduce seedfall.

Control and Removal

After you have grown borage, you will have borage seedlings. These will sprout throughout the year in mild weather, especially when you disturb the soil, and they often grow far too densely for all of them to grow up. Seedlings that you don't want are not hard to get rid of. Lightly cultivating the soil surface kills them, and doing this a few times will clear your soil of borage seeds. Mulching will reduce the number of seedlings that germinate.

Varieties and Similar Species

Agriculturists in Europe have bred or selected a white-flowered borage, *Borago officinalis* forma *alba*. They feel that the white-flowered plants are superior as a vegetable crop, but I can't help hoping that this variety is not imported, as I like being able to predict the lovely blue color of the flowers.

Borago pygmaea (B. laxiflora) is native to the Mediterranean islands of Corsica and Sardinia. This perennial, which spreads slowly from rhizomes, is most often grown in rock gardens. *B. pygmaea* is hardy to Zone 5 and will be most successful in a climate that provides a bit of winter frost. The flowers are a lighter blue than, and not quite as large as, those of annual borage.

The Name

The genus name *Borago* (bohr-ah'-go) is thought by some to derive from a Latin word that started out being spelled *burra* and meant "rough hair." But there are also proponents of the theory that it derives from the Arabic words *abu rash,* meaning "father of sweat," referring to one of its old herbal uses—to produce sweat. *Officinalis* (oh-fiss-ih-nah'-liss) means that this plant is found in European herbals. Appearing in an herbal published in 1265, it is one of the earliest plants to be included in such works.

Calendula officinalis

Calendula, pot marigold, marigold

PLANT TYPE: *Cool-season annual* | HEIGHT AND SPREAD: *1 to 2 feet tall and 1 to 2 feet wide* | BLOOM TIME: *Spring through fall in cool weather* | LIGHT NEEDS: *Full sun, partial shade* | SOIL NEEDS: *Moderately fertile, well drained* | WATER NEEDS: *Moderate* | OTHER TOLERANCES: *Poor soil, clay soil, cool coastal summers, deer resistant* | HARDINESS: *Withstands light frost*

The bright flowers of calendula bring a casual cheer to our gardens, and when we sprinkle its ray flowers on our salad, we are continuing a tradition hundreds of years old. New cultivars include shorter plants, more colors, and fancy flower forms. Calendula will resow in gardens, gradually reverting to the original taller plants with nondoubled, bright yellow or orange, daisylike flowers.

This selection from the popular calendula mix 'Touch of Red' shows the red petal edges and undersides that give the mix its name.

Naturalized calendula harmonizes with the tawny color of feather grass (Nassella tenuissima), *and contrasts with the bright blue blossoms of sea lavender* (Limonium perezii).

Source and Uses

Calendula came into American gardens from Europe, where it was a favorite garden plant, valued since the 1200s as a food colorant and as an ingredient in salves and other medicinal preparations, and since at least the 1500s as an ornamental plant. Its flowers have added colorful confetti to salads since the time of Queen Elizabeth I. It has been grown in European gardens for so long that no one knows where it originally grew wild. In fact, it is very uncommon in the wild, but it is believed to be native to the Mediterranean region.

The glory of this plant is in the lustrous 3- to 4-inch flowers. Its drawbacks as an ornamental are two. One is that after the first flush of bloom it must be deadheaded frequently to keep it looking fresh. Another is that it will decline in hot weather, often succumbing to powdery mildew.

Like so many garden annuals, calendula has been bred to make short, rounded plants, useful in mass bedding schemes. This was a particularly poor idea for calendula, since it is quite prone to powdery mildew. Taller, more open varieties are not only less disease prone but better for informal planting designs. Use shorter varieties, the most common types being sold as nursery plants these days, in fall or early spring container plantings. Use taller types, which you may have to start from seed, in informal borders and beds in fall or spring and, near the coast, in summer as well. Calendula lasts well as a cut flower, but its habit of closing at night makes it a poor choice to decorate the table during an evening meal.

Care and Reproduction

Sow calendula's large, curved seeds ¼ inch deep. Germination occurs in 10 to 15 days at 65 degrees F. In mild-winter areas, calendula seeds can be sown outdoors in fall or in late winter for early spring or mid-spring bloom. Where summers are cool, they can also be sown in late spring for summer or early fall bloom. Where winter temperatures are often near or below freezing, sow seed indoors in late winter or early spring, starting 8 weeks before the predicted last frost. The final distance between the plants should be 6 to 10 inches.

In a vegetable garden or other very informal setting, you may choose not to deadhead calendula plants. But where appearances count, you will want to deadhead. Start removing spent flowers when the first ones to bloom start to wither and look untidy, pinching or cutting the stems to just above the next lower flower bud or leaf joint. Continue to do so until the size of the plants makes it too great a task, or until powdery mildew renders the plants unsightly, and then pull them.

Control and Removal

Deadheading plants, and removing them when they are no longer attractive, will, of course, reduce the number of seeds that drop to the ground and later grow. Though overthick self-sowing can occur, the number of seedlings is usually relatively light, even when seed has been allowed to fall freely. If you don't want them, the large seedlings with their straplike leaves are relatively easy to spot and easy to pull or hoe out. Seedlings can be transplanted until they are a few inches tall; larger plants are less likely to transplant well.

Although calendula can become a weed in disturbed areas outside of gardens, such as vacant lots or roadsides, it is not usually found in undisturbed wildlands.

Varieties and Similar Species

Double-flowered calendulas were popular by the end of the 1500s, but the heyday of fancy calendula cultivars was the 1920s and 1930s, with three calendula varieties winning All-American Seed prizes in the 1930s. Some calendula varieties are on the market for only a short time, as it is difficult to maintain them in a pure form. Some of the best tall varieties currently on the market are the Pacific Beauty series (18 inches tall; relatively heat tolerant; double flowers; sold as a mix or in single colors of cream, light yellow, apricot, deep yellow, and deep orange), the Touch of Red Mixed series (18 inches tall; double flowers; orange, yellow, and buff, all with red petal edges and undersides), and the Kablouna series (20 inches tall; mixed or only in apricot, pale yellow, deep yellow, or orange, all with darker pompom centers).

Calendula arvensis is a similar species with yellow flowers up to 1½ inches across on a sprawling plant. It is weedier than *C. officinalis* and not as pretty but is sometimes found in wildflower mixes.

THE NAME

If you think the word *Calendula* (kah-len'-dyu-luh) has a distinctively Roman sound to it, you are right. It is derived from the Latin word *calends*, which means the first day of each month, when Romans had to pay interest on borrowed funds, referring to the fact that as the months passed, calendula remained in bloom. The specific epithet *officinalis* (oh-fiss-in-al'-iss) tells us that this was a plant in the medieval European pharmacopoeia.

Incidentally, this plant was the first to get the common name marigold (or "Mary's gold"). Europeans later gave the same common name to plants in the Mexican genus *Tagetes*. The English sometimes call calendula pot marigold, referring to its traditional use in cooking.

Impatiens balfourii

![flower icon] Poor man's orchid

PLANT TYPE: *Warm-season annual* | HEIGHT AND SPREAD: *2 to 3 feet tall and 1 to 2 feet wide* | BLOOM TIME: *Summer* | LIGHT NEEDS: *Partial shade* | SOIL NEEDS: *Fertile, organic, well drained* | WATER NEEDS: *Moderate* | OTHER TOLERANCES: *Cool coastal conditions, full sun near the coast, full shade inland, deer resistant* | HARDINESS: *Frost-tender annual*

*M*ost reference books say only that this plant is from the western Himalayas, a designation that covers a rather broad area. I discovered that its exact native area straddles the Line of Control between Pakistan and Indian Kashmir. In fact, several Kashmiri villages where it has been collected are sites of past battles as well as recent skirmishes in the struggle over the territory, so the plants have surely been minor casualties in this troublesome conflict. From the Jhelum River

The complexity of the lavender and white flowers, with their touches of bright yellow, earned the plant the common name poor man's orchid.

Impatiens balfourii's lacy appearance adds its delicate charm to this Victorian porch.

Valley in Indian Kashmir, the plant ranges westward through Pakistan-controlled Kashmir and the Pakistani districts of Swat and Hazara, just north of Islamabad.

Source and Uses

This is a plant of the lower mountains, growing at 5,000 to 6,000 feet above sea level. In peaceful times, the relatively cool summers, mild winters, and splendid scenery of this region attract many vacationers. While areas to the south are quite hot in summer, the summers here average in the 70s to the low 80s. And while higher elevations have snowy winters, these lower slopes have average winter temperatures in the 40s to 60s. The summer monsoons during July and August bring over half of the annual rainfall of 30 to 50 inches.

Impatiens balfourii was not known in Europe or America until after about 1900, when British plant explorers brought seeds home to England. The plant was first recorded in Bay Area gardens by the mid-1930s, and it soon became a favorite of gardeners on the San Francisco peninsula. In recent years plants have been available in local nurseries. The delicate, airy plants, with hooded and spurred lavender and white flowers, are charming in woodsy settings, cottage gardens, containers, or mixed borders.

Care and Reproduction

Impatiens balfourii is well adapted to coastal and near coastal California, since the temperature range is similar to that of its land of origin. However, because it depends on occasional rain to start growing and has monsoon rain during its bloom, it will thrive in our gardens only with late spring and summer irrigation. Where conditions are to its liking, the plant reseeds prolifically. In poor, sandy soil, or without adequate water, it grows poorly and isn't likely to naturalize.

Plant *Impatiens balfourii* nursery starts 9 to 12 inches apart in mid to late spring. Like all impatiens flowers, this plant forms seedpods that split open violently at the slightest touch, shooting seed forth. To collect the seed, you need to learn to recognize pods that contain ripe seed (the ones with visible seed bulges lower on the flower stems), and cup your hand quickly around them so that the seeds shoot into your palm. Dry these seeds well before storing them, so they won't rot from residual moisture. In nature, cold temperatures help break the seeds' dormancy, and our winter temperatures are sufficient, but if you plan to save seed indoors to sow in spring, keep it at 40 to 50 degrees F for a couple of months before you grow it. Press seed into the surface of prepared soil in mid to late spring, or sow it indoors on the surface of fine seeding mix with clear plastic film stretched over the container until the seed germinates, which should occur in about 10 days at 65 to 75 degrees F.

CONTROL AND REMOVAL

When you recognize the self-sown seedlings, which are narrow stemmed with simple, alternately arranged leaves, you can thin or transplant them or, if you don't want to grow the plant again, pull all of them out before they can form seeds. This plant has escaped to some extent in southern Europe and is recorded as a naturalized plant in areas of California and Wisconsin. It is probably best not to grow it near creeks, which could carry seed downstream to moist creekside wildlands.

VARIETIES AND SIMILAR SPECIES

Impatiens species from several corners of the world are common in our gardens, and others show promise as garden plants. The most common, busy Lizzie *(Impatiens walleriana)*, is America's most popular annual. *I. sodenii*, a shrubby perennial impatiens from East Africa, is discussed on page 291.

There are many other pretty *Impatiens* to discover, but do grow them with caution, since some could become wildland invasives. A case in point is *Impatiens glandulifera*, sold as "policeman's helmet." This plant, also a native of the Himalayas, reaches 7 feet tall, with white or pink hooded flowers similar to those of *I. balfourii*. It has galloped across Great Britain, Europe, parts of coastal eastern Canada and the north central United States, and Washington State. Although you can purchase seed and even plants of this species, I think it is a poor idea to grow it in Northern California, since in the areas where it escapes it tends to dominate the vegetation. In Europe, it competes so successfully for the attention of bumblebees that it reduces the seed set of nearby native plants.

The Name

Various *Impatiens* species, including busy Lizzie *(I. walleriana)* and the American Midwestern native jewelweed *(I. pallida)* are sometimes called touch-me-not, referring to the way the seeds leap from the seedpods at the lightest touch. The genus name *Impatiens* also refers to this feature, it being the Latin word meaning "impatient." The specific epithet *balfourii* (bal-four'-ee-eye) is in honor of Sir Isaac Bayley Balfour (1853–1922), who was a director of the Royal Botanic Garden in Edinburgh, Scotland.

Caution

While sap of the Eastern U.S. natives *Impatiens pallida* and *I. capensis* is said to soothe irritation from poison ivy and nettles, use of other *Impatiens* species, including *I. balfourii*, for such purposes should be considered experimental.

Lobularia maritima *(Alyssum maritimum)*

Sweet alyssum

PLANT TYPE: *Cool-season annual* | HEIGHT AND SPREAD: *2 to 12 inches tall and 8 to 24 inches wide* | BLOOM TIME: *Any time, mainly spring and summer* | LIGHT NEEDS: *Full sun, partial shade* | SOIL NEEDS: *Moderately fertile* | WATER NEEDS: *Moderate* | OTHER TOLERANCES: *Poor soil, sandy soil, cool coastal summers, seaside conditions* | HARDINESS: *Tolerates light frost*

*T*he tiny, honey-scented flowers of sweet alyssum billow from bedding-flats in most American nurseries and adorn many a garden. Recently gardeners have become even more interested in alyssum's white, pink, lavender, or purple blossoms, because they may help in our battle with garden pests. Beneficial insects, the ones that eat pest insects, use nectar from small flowers in part of their life cycle. Alyssum flowers are among their favored nectar sources.

Sweet alyssum softens the strong lines of hardscape, such as this metal fence. Also shown are baby's tears and blue-flowered edging lobelia (Lobelia erinus).

A lavender-flowered sweet alyssum draping over the edge of a large container provides a nice contrast to the bolder form of aeoniums.

Source and Uses

Sweet alyssum is native to the near-coastal areas of the Mediterranean region and the Canary Islands, where it grows in disturbed soil and on rocky slopes. In the 1800s, it became a popular plant for use in Victorian bedding designs. Nowadays, it is often used at the front of borders, under spring bulbs, in rock gardens, in pavement cracks, or in containers. The flowers make sweet miniature bouquets with other tiny flowers, such as forget-me-not, Johnny-jump-up, and grape hyacinth. The beneficial insects sweet alyssum attracts include lacewings, hoverflies, tachinid flies, parasitic wasps, spider mite destroyers, and pirate bugs. Butterflies are also attracted to its sweet nectar.

Care and Reproduction

True to its windblown seaside origins, sweet alyssum thrives best in cool weather. It will grow in poor soil, but the garden hybrids look better in fertile soil that is kept moist. You can sow the seeds directly in early spring and again in late summer, or you can start seeds indoors in winter to plant out after frost danger is past. Seedlings are ready to plant out in 6 to 8 weeks. The flowers may begin to bloom as little as 6 weeks after sowing and will continue for many weeks.

The plants eventually become less attractive, though still healthy, because the lengthening stems fall over, revealing the whorls of ripening seedpods. Plants cut back by half about a month after they start to bloom will often grow back rapidly and produce a second flush of flowers. But they will rebloom successfully only if the plants are in good condition; in moist, reasonably fertile soil; and the weather is, on the whole, cool. When the weather turns hot and the soil dries, the plants, cut back or not, will die. They may succumb to powdery mildew, or they may just decline gradually.

Control and Removal

Although this plant will reseed readily, the seedlings may not be as attractive as the plants you started with. Reseeded plants often become more open, which means that you will see more seedy stems and fewer flowers. Also, when the plants self-sow, colored forms, except perhaps for pale lavender, often revert to white. While you may not mind a few reseeded plants, you will probably want to reduce seed drop by cutting the plants back once, enjoying their rebloom, and then pulling them out. The plants are easy to pull, thanks to their shallow roots. Don't discard your cuttings or pulled plants where you don't want sweet alyssum to grow, as they will probably contain ripe seeds.

To eliminate sweet alyssum, watch for the seedlings in your garden and pull them before they can ripen seed. Even if you don't recognize them until they are just beginning to come into flower, it will be several more weeks before ripe seed can fall.

Those who live near the oceanfront or near coastal wild areas may choose not to grow this plant, to discourage its escape into beach and roadside areas. Read carefully the list of species in any erosion prevention or wildflower seed mix you may buy, to be sure it doesn't contain sweet alyssum. For its ability to grow in wild areas at the coast, it is possible that sweet alyssum could earn a rating on a forthcoming CalEPPC list of plants with either "Low" or "Medium" impact on wildland ecosystems.

Varieties and Similar Species

In recent years, many nurseries have carried mainly 'Snow Crystals', which is relatively heat tolerant and has white flowers somewhat larger than those of most varieties. While this is a nice choice, there are many others to try. Available color mixes include shades of pink, lavender, and purple, and sometimes apricot or buff yellow. (For a nice blending of colors, sow 4 to 5 seeds to a six-pack cell or 2-inch pot, and then transplant the groups of seedlings to the garden, unthinned, 8 inches apart.) If it is strong fragrance you are looking for, three of the best varieties are 'Sweet White', 'Oriental Night' (rich purple), and 'Rosie O'Day' (deep rose). If you plan to grow sweet alyssum in a container, choose a trailing type, such as 'Trailing Rosy-red', that will drape nicely over the edge.

While there is nothing quite like sweet alyssum, there are some similar alternatives. *Malcolmia maritima* (Virginia stock) provides a mix of fragrant white, pink, and lavender flowers that make a nice spring bulb cover that often resows. White or lavender-flowered varieties of *Lobelia erinus* (edging lobelia) will substitute for sweet alyssum in containers or edgings. They may reseed, but usually only lightly, and they are not as likely to grow outside of gardens.

THE NAME

The genus name *Lobularia* (lob-you-lahr'-ee-uh) is derived from the Latin word *lobulus*, meaning "small pod." It refers to the small, round seedpods that form on the stems behind the flowers. The specific epithet *maritima* (mar-ih-teem'-uh) is from *mare*, the Latin word for the sea, referring to the plant's origin near seacoasts.

The present common name alyssum was once the genus name of this plant, and you may still find it sold under this name. (Other plants that were once in the genus *Alyssum* are now in the genus *Aurinia*, which includes a number of yellow-flowered species often used in rock gardens.) The word "alyssum" derives from the Greek word *alysson*, which translates as "without madness." The name referred to an ancient and quite unfounded belief that the plant we now know as *Lobularia maritima* could cure rabies.

Mauranthemum paludosum *(Chrysanthemum paludosum)*

✳ Paludosum daisy

PLANT TYPE: *Cool-season annual* | HEIGHT AND SPREAD: *6 to 12 inches tall and 6 to 12 inches wide* | BLOOM TIME: *Fall, early spring, or late spring* | LIGHT NEEDS: *Full sun to light shade* | SOIL NEEDS: *Poor to moderately fertile, well drained* | WATER NEEDS: *Moderate* | OTHER TOLERANCES: *Cool coastal summers, fertile soil* | HARDINESS: *Withstands light frost*

The paludosum daisy is such a simple little flower, and so common in Northern California gardens, and yet it proved one of the most difficult plants to learn more about, since it is relatively new in our gardens and little known in much of the country. In addition, its name has

At the front of a formal garden border, paludosum daisy has been planted to form an undulating line with blue edging lobelia (Lobelia erinus).

Paludosum daisy also works well in informal settings such as this rock garden.

been changed several times quite recently. Tracing it to its current (and hopefully final) scientific name required quite a tromp through the nomenclatural underbrush.

SOURCE AND USES

The paludosum daisy is native to southern Spain and Portugal and the Balearic Islands, which are to the east of Spain in the Mediterranean Sea. In its native range, it inhabits terrain and plant communities much like those of the California poppy in our region—that is, sloping, often rocky land with shrubs, grasses, and spring-blooming flowers. Like our poppy, it blooms in the cool weather of late winter through spring, dying back when winter rains end and the soil dries. It has not been popular in gardens for long, probably less than 50 years, and is little known outside of areas where it is most commonly grown: northern Europe, Japan, Alaska, and Northern California.

A number of plants produce white daisies, so why choose this one? One reason is that it is an annual that can be planted so that it blooms in any relatively cool season. Flowers can be had in the fall, early spring, or late spring, depending on when you start the plants. And when planted en masse, paludosum daisies make a low, nearly level sea of bloom. Another reason is that the flowers and plants are small, in scale with other small flowers, such as violas and forget-me-nots.

The leaves and flowers are miniatures of those of larger cousins such as Shasta daisies. They can be used around shrubs, in borders, as an edging, or in rock gardens, and they are very nice in containers. The flowers are good additions to small-scale bouquets.

CARE AND REPRODUCTION

These plants are truly undemanding, requiring mainly sunlight and moderate water, but they can tolerate more fertile soil or more water if they are growing with other plants that need these conditions. In small-scale plantings, such as in containers, you may wish to deadhead a bit to prolong bloom and maintain appearance. In larger plantings you will probably forgo this nicety, though you may want to cut the plants back by one-third if flowering decreases, to try for a rebloom.

Sow paludosum daisy seed 2½ to 3 months before you want them to begin to bloom. Sow indoors when the soil is cold, outdoors in late spring through early fall. Cover the seeds lightly with soil. They should germinate in 10 to 14 days at 60 to 65 degrees F. Or purchase nursery starts a few weeks before you want blooms. Plant them 8 to 12 inches apart. The bloom period will be longer in cool weather.

CONTROL AND REMOVAL

If plants ripen seed and the seed falls, a few seedlings may grow, but so few that they are rarely problematic. When you see them, you can easily dig them and put them in places where you want them to bloom. The plants that grow from these seedlings are often more open and "branchy" than the ones from purchased seed or nursery starts, giving them a wilder, more natural look. Seedlings often appear in the fall, leading to welcome winter and early spring blooms.

VARIETIES AND SIMILAR SPECIES

Nursery plants are likely to be sold simply as paludosum daisies. The variety 'Snowland' has 1½-inch flowers, while those of 'White Buttons' are about 1 inch across. Nursery labels or seed packets may say that the plants reach 6 to 8 inches tall, but in cooler seasons and microclimates, they often grow taller.

For similar white daisies that are perennial and summer blooming, look for dwarf Shasta daisy *Leucanthemum maximum (Chrysanthemum maximum)* cultivars, such as 'Snow Lady'.

THE NAME

I will list all of the recent scientific names of this plant, because you will probably run into all of them when you read about this plant elsewhere. Its first and longest-standing name was *Chrysanthemum paludosum* (though someone apparently used the genus name *Hymenostemma* to describe it for a while). In 1970 it was reclassified as *Leucanthemum,*

placing it in the same genus as Shasta daisy and ox-eye daisy. Then, in 1993, the plants were reanalyzed and the name was changed to *Leucoglossum paludosum*. In 1995 the name was changed once again, to *Mauranthemum paludosum*. This last name change was required because it was discovered that the name *Leucoglossum* had already been given to a type of fungus, and two creatures can't have the same scientific name.

The newest and hopefully final genus name, *Mauranthemum* (mahr-an'-thuh-mum), is from the Latin word *maurus*, referring to North Africa, and the Greek word *anthos* meaning "flower." This name was chosen because other species in the genus are from North Africa. Judging by the native range of those species—the Mediterranean coast from Morocco to Tunisia—the word root "maur-" relates more to the land or peoples of ancient Mauretania, which was in this area, than to the new (1904) nation of Mauritania, which is farther to the south and west. The specific epithet *paludosum* (pal-yew-doh'-sum) is from the Latin word *paludos* and refers to moist places, though the places our plant grows seem to be moist only during the winter rains.

Incidentally, paludosum daisy has sometimes been confused with *Melampodium paludosum*. That plant is an annual yellow daisy known commonly as black-foot daisy that is native to the United States and thrives in hot summer weather—not our plant at all.

Paludosum daisies run through this exuberant streetside planting, tying the various beds together. Other plants include tulips, purple pansies, white Iceland poppies, red ranunculus, Scotch moss (Sagina subluata), lime thyme (Thymus serphyllum 'Lime'), and golden feverfew.

Myosotis sylvatica

Garden forget-me-not, woodland forget-me-not

PLANT TYPE: *Cool-season annual or biennial* | HEIGHT AND SPREAD: *12 to 18 inches tall and 6 to 12 inches wide* | BLOOM TIME: *Mostly late winter and spring* | LIGHT NEEDS: *Full sun, partial shade* | SOIL NEEDS: *Poor to moderately fertile, organic, well drained* | WATER NEEDS: *Moderate to ample* | OTHER TOLERANCES: *Full shade, wet soil, deer resistant* | HARDINESS: *Withstands light frost*

In spring, this plant produces a cloud of pale to medium-blue flowers, each about ³/₈ inch across, with five rounded petals and a pale yellow eye surrounded by five tiny white rays. To many, it is a garden standby, lending its reliable background charm to garden

Even quite shady spots can be covered with the dainty blue blossoms of garden forget-me-not.

Weaving through a tulip border, forget-me-nots will provide continuity when the tulips are replaced with later spring flowers.

styles from romantic to tropical. Others consider it a weed because of its ability to resow, popping up in unexpected places.

Source and Uses

Garden forget-me-not, which is in the same plant family as borage, is native to Great Britain and mid-latitude Europe as far north as southern Scandinavia, where it grows in damp woodlands and mountain grasslands to about 6,000 feet in altitude. If seed is sown in the fall as spring bulbs are planted, its blooms will conceal their fading leaves in the spring. It is also charming with other spring annuals in this chapter, or growing through ground covers like star jasmine *(Trachelospermum jasminoides)* or yellow archangel *(Lamium galeobdolon)*. Use it in containers or in bouquets with other small spring flowers. For the most attractive bouquets, cut garden forget-me-not before the stems have elongated and formed seedpods.

Care and Reproduction

For early spring to mid-spring bloom, sow seeds outside in late summer, or set out nursery plants in early spring. Near the coast, you can also sow seeds in early spring or set out plants in mid-spring for late spring bloom. Forget-me-not will usually reseed to bloom each spring and, in watered gardens near the coast, some seedlings may also appear in late spring and summer to bloom into fall and winter. Although they do not require rich soil, the plants will grow larger if soil is more fertile. As spring continues, take special care to water the plants between rains, as once the soil dries, especially during a warm spell, they decline quickly. When the weather is steadily warm, they usually succumb to powdery mildew even if watered carefully.

The flowers are borne at the tops of ever-lengthening flower stems, with seeds forming lower on the stems. When the plants have become leggy, with more seedpods than flowers, pull them, or if more cool weather is expected, cut the plants back to basal leaves to encourage a rebloom. When forget-me-nots are growing through a ground cover, cutting back is difficult, so it is better just to pull them out when they become leggy.

Control and Removal

Cutting mature plants back or pulling them out before all of the seeds can ripen will reduce seeding somewhat. If seedlings appear in the wrong places, they are easy to pull or, if they have not yet begun to bloom, easy to transplant.

Be careful when you are working among the plants to wear clothing that is as smooth as possible. The seeds will cling to sweaters, sweat shirts, and even to cloth shoelaces. They are a nuisance to pick off and may fall in places where you do not want them to grow. Dogs or other animals that brush against the plants may also disperse the seeds.

Garden forget-me-not has not been listed as a wildland weed in the past, though it has escaped in some disturbed wild areas such as in the fire-scarred Point Reyes National Seashore and in Muir Woods. Because of this, it may earn a place on one of the California Exotic Pest Plant Council's updated lists. In any case, it is unwise to grow it in locations adjacent to native meadows or woodlands, or by creeks that might carry the seeds downstream to wild areas. Also, do not grow it where dogs will roam in gardens and later carry seeds in their fur into wildlands, and avoid discarding plants or soil under plants that might contain garden forget-me-not seeds in wild areas. Several native and nonnative alternatives offer more easily controlled variations on the theme.

Varieties and Similar Species

The species *Myosotis sylvatica* is open in habit, with widely angling branches, the flower stems reaching 18 inches tall. 'Royal Blue Improved', with somewhat deeper blue flowers, can reach 16 inches with good conditions. Intermediate types such as 'Blue Basket' reach a foot tall, and there are also a number of dwarf, ball-shaped cultivars, including 'Blue Ball' and the Victoria series. Pink and white varieties exist, with perhaps the best pink color in 'Rosylva', a dwarf plant reaching 6 inches tall.

Cynoglossum amabile, known as Chinese forget-me-not, is an annual in the same family that also reseeds, though generally less aggressively. A popular variety, 'Firmament', has flowers of a richer blue than the

Myosotis species, and there are less commonly available varieties in white, pink, and turquoise. It can be sown in fall or early spring, is happy in full sun, and blooms until late spring or until the weather turns warm.

A perennial relative, *Omphalodes cappodocica*, or navelwort (photo on page 267), offers similar blue flowers in spring and attractive foliage in spring through fall. Its leaves will be damaged by frost, but the plant survives to Zone 6. It reseeds little, but it does spread somewhat by underground stems. The cultivar 'Starry Eyes' has white-edged blue petals.

For California native woodland gardens, consider *Cynoglossum grande*, or western hound's tongue, a native perennial plant with leaves to a foot long that unfurl in late winter, followed by blue flowers in March and April. Other California natives even more similar to *Myosotis sylvatica* are the *Hackelia* species, small perennials that are less commonly offered for sale.

THE NAME

When the ancient Greeks looked at little plants with short, pointed, somewhat furry leaves, they thought of mouse ears. They didn't name this particular plant, but Linnaeus borrowed their common name for similar plants when he chose the genus name *Myosotis* (my-uh-so'-tiss), which is from the Greek words *mus* ("mouse") and *otos* ("ear"). The specific epithet, *sylvatica* (syl-vah'-tih-kuh), is from the Latin word *silva* (forest), referring to its most common native habitat.

Nigella damascena

 Love-in-a-mist, devil-in-a-bush

PLANT TYPE: *Cool-season annual* | HEIGHT AND SPREAD: *6 to 18 inches tall and 9 inches wide* | BLOOM TIME: *Spring or summer* | LIGHT NEEDS: *Full sun, partial shade* | SOIL NEEDS: *Fertile, well drained* | WATER NEEDS: *Moderate* | OTHER TOLERANCES: *Cool coastal conditions, deer resistant* | HARDINESS: *Withstands light frost*

These days, people looking at a lacy flower are more likely to think of love than the devil, but we can see from the traditional English common names of *Nigella* that this was not always so. In any case, this flower is complexly constructed, and it develops into a quite attractive seedpod. You may be surprised to know that the colorful petal-like parts of this flower are its sepals, while the small petals are tucked in above them. The feathery green structures that frame the flowers and enlarge to ornament the seedpods are modified leaves, which, together, are

Gardeners enjoy not only the flowers of love-in-a-mist, but also the elegant seedpods.

Dewdrops ornament the intricate form of this love-in-a-mist flower and the lacy green involucre behind it.

called an involucre. The curled horns at the top of the seedpods are the styles (extensions of the ovary).

Source and Uses

Nigella damascena grows wild in lands all around the Mediterranean Sea, though it is possible it was carried to Mediterranean Europe from the Near Eastern part of this range in the 1500s. Its seeds are sometimes used as a spice, though they are not as good as those of *N. sativa*, which is grown for that purpose.

Nigella damascena enjoyed great popularity in the last part of the 1800s as a favorite plant of the garden designer Gertrude Jekyll, and her favorite strains are still available. She loved to use these plants for informal drifts of color in her updated cottage-style gardens. Love-in-a-mist works well in containers and is a pretty addition to the flower border or between more permanent plants in a mediterranean-style garden. If you are cutting love-in-a-mist flowers for a bouquet, choose the ones with the shortest "horns" at the top, as these are the ones that opened most recently and will last longer. The seedpods can be harvested for use in dried flower arrangements when they are fully formed but still green. When first picked, the green pods may be striped with purple; when dry they are a light brown color.

Care and Reproduction

In their native lands, seeds of love-in-a-mist germinate in the late summer or fall and form leaves throughout the winter. In this way, they develop a strong root system that may let them bloom longer than plants from seeds sown in spring. You can imitate nature in Zones 9 or 10 by sowing seed in the fall. The feathery leaves are attractive during the winter months, and the early flowers are welcome. In all zones, you can also plant seed in early or later spring, and the plants that grow from these sowings will bloom in about 3 months. Plants develop best from seed sown in place, as their delicate taproot makes them sensitive to transplanting. Sow them thinly, lightly covering the seeds. When the plants have a few leaves, thin them to 6 to 10 inches apart.

Plant seeds in fertile soil, and be ready to water when the rainy season ends in mid-spring or later. The plants tolerate less fertile or drier soil but will not reach full size in these conditions.

To gather seeds, keep a watch on developing seedpods, and harvest them when they first turn brownish and you can hear the seeds rattling inside. Otherwise, the seeds will fall to the ground and you will be left with empty pods. If you don't harvest the seeds, the plants will probably resow themselves and grow the following autumn or spring.

CONTROL AND REMOVAL

Most gardeners enjoy seeing the decorative seedpods in the garden, so they don't bother to deadhead, and then they deal with the profusion of seedlings from fallen seeds later. If the resulting seedlings are too close together, thin them as you see them emerge in fall and winter, or as the mild days of late winter encourage you to get into the garden again. While the plants will reseed from year to year, they do not compete strongly with other garden plants and weeds and will decrease over time in gardens crowded with other seedlings, or where the ground is thickly mulched or frequently cultivated.

VARIETIES AND SIMILAR SPECIES

The Miss Jekyll varieties have semidouble flowers in various single colors. The most common are 'Miss Jekyll Blue' (mid-blue) and 'Miss Jekyll White', but you may also see 'Miss Jekyll Indigo' (deep blue) or 'Miss Jekyll Rose'. These 18-inch-tall, single color strains are useful in flowerbeds with other flowers of similar height. There are also shorter single-color varieties, such as 'Dwarf Moody Blue' (6 to 9 inches). 'Persian Jewels' blooms in white as well as dark and pastel shades of blue, lavender, and pink, on plants about 15 inches tall.

Gardeners sometimes grow two other *Nigella* species as novelties. *N. orientalis* 'Transformer' has small yellow-green flowers followed by dark, ribbed seedpods that are useful in dried arrangements. *N. hispanica* has large blue flowers with red stamens and also has attractive seedpods.

Nigella sativa, the species grown for its spicy seeds, has 1½-inch blue flowers that lack a lacy involucre. The seeds are used from India to Mediterranean Europe as a seasoning for curries and bread, under the names black cumin or black caraway.

THE NAME

Nigella (ny-jell'-uh), the genus name of this flower, derives from *niger,* which is the Latin word for "black." The "ella" on the end makes the name diminutive, and it refers to the plant's little black seeds. The specific epithet, *damascena* (dah-muh-see'-nuh), refers to the belief that the plant was brought to Europe from Damascus, Syria.

Tropaeolum majus

 Nasturtium

PLANT TYPE: *Cool-season annual, sometimes trailing or climbing* | HEIGHT AND SPREAD: *Bush types: 10 to 12 inches tall and 10 to 12 inches wide; trailing types: to 6 to 12 feet long* | BLOOM TIME: *Mostly spring through fall* | LIGHT NEEDS: *Full sun, light shade* | SOIL NEEDS: *Poor to moderately fertile, well drained* | WATER NEEDS: *Moderate* | OTHER TOLERANCES: *Cool coastal summers* | HARDINESS: *Frost-tender annual*

ew plants are easier to grow from seed, require less soil improvement, or are more willing to cover bare ground quickly than nasturtium—and few flowers are brighter in color. So dazzling are they that Charles Darwin's daughter Elizabeth thought they

One of the survivors of Victorian plant breeding is 'Empress of India' nasturtium, with its blue-green leaves and deep red blossoms.

Naturalized trailing nasturtiums festoon a retaining wall with their casual glory. Trailing varieties can also climb an arbor or provide temporary ground cover.

glowed in the dark and presented a paper before a scientific society to that effect. It may have been deference to her famous father that delayed disproof, but it has become clear that her impression was poetic rather than scientific.

Source and Uses

The modern garden nasturtium, which we call *Tropaeolum majus,* doesn't exist in the wild but is thought to be a hybrid that appeared in a Peruvian garden in the 1600s. It is believed that one parent was *Tropaeolum minor,* a smaller trailing plant with yellow flowers marked with red. These first hybrid plants were larger than *T. minor* and had orange flowers. While we don't know the full parentage of our modern hybrids, we do know that all of their ancestors are from the Andean mountain region of South America, where they grow in the cooler uplands. Thus it is not surprising that they grow best in cool weather.

Europeans welcomed nasturtiums not only because they were pretty, but because their peppery-flavored flowers, leaves, and immature seeds were useful in cooking. Modern cooks agree that the flowers are attractive in a salad, though the practice of pickling immature seeds as a caper substitute is not often repeated in modern kitchens.

In the 1800s, plant breeders had a field day satisfying the desire of Victorian flower gardeners for novelty, creating nasturtiums with flowers from pure white to deep crimson, ones with frilly double flowers, plants with leaves splashed with white, and ball-shaped dwarf plants that are still useful in borders and containers. The older trailing forms can be allowed to creep on the ground, as they do on the gravel walkway at Monet's garden at Giverny, or they can be trained over an arbor or up a fence. The flowers make nice small bouquets, or you can add a trailing branch with leaves and flowers to larger arrangements.

Care and Reproduction

Nasturtiums bloom best in full sun, with moderate water and poor to only moderately fertile soil. Shade, overwatering, or overfertile soil will result in leaves so tall that the flowers barely peek above them. They are not well adapted to hot weather (as in the Central Valley), but they have the best chance to survive heat in shade with regular water.

Remove yellowing or damaged leaves to keep the plants attractive. When the plants have died, pull out the straw-colored dead stems. Plants growing into winter may survive to bloom the following spring, but they will be damaged by even light frost.

If the branch of a trailing type is creeping in a direction you don't want, turn it in another direction, or simply prune it off. If you want trailing nasturtiums to climb, you sometimes have to wrap or even tie them on the supports as they grow, though the leaf stems of some plants will clasp the support.

Nasturtium is practically foolproof when grown from seed sown in place or planted from nursery starts, but seedlings that are growing in the ground do not transplant very well. Plant seed in late winter through mid-spring and, where summers are coolish, into summer as well. Plant them $\frac{1}{2}$ to 1 inch deep, setting the trailing types about a foot apart and dwarf ones 6 inches apart.

If you plan to store garden-gathered seed, dry it well first so it doesn't rot. Seed gathered under the plants may have a different plant form or flower color than the parents. In naturalized populations of the plant, trailing forms with yellow, orange, or red-eyed-yellow flowers eventually predominate.

Control and Removal

Gardeners who lack a cool growing period envy our success with nasturtiums, while we sometimes wish they were a bit less successful. Trailing types seem to grow several feet overnight, and where the stems find bare soil, they will root. After the plants die back, the ground will be covered with the $\frac{1}{4}$-inch buff-colored seeds. If the soil is cleared and dry, I have even used a brush and dustpan to scoop these up, so a too-thick stand of seedlings won't develop. Even if you remove most of the visible seeds, when you turn the soil and water it to plant something new, some of the big, fast-growing seedlings will appear, and you will have to weed them out several times if your plans for that spot do not include nasturtiums. Fortunately, if grasped near their bases, the seedlings pull easily.

Nasturtiums have not appeared on any wildland weed lists, but could earn a listing on the California Exotic Pest Plants Council's upcoming list of plants with "Low" impact on wildlands. To prevent further escape, it is best to avoid planting them, or discarding pulled plants that are blooming, in or adjacent to wild areas. Remember that seeds that may not appear to be ripe may have ripened within their green pods, and once they fall from the plant they can readily roll downhill to a new location.

VARIETIES AND SIMILAR SPECIES

The Victorian pure white nasturtium has been lost, but many old and new types are available. 'Double Gleam Mix' (semitrailing) and 'Whirlybird Mix' (dwarf) both have semidouble flowers. Single colors include 'Moongleam' (pale yellow, trailer), 'Peach Melba' (peach, dwarf), and 'Empress of India' (deep red with blue-green leaves, semitrailing). 'Alaska Mixed' (dwarf) and 'Jewel of Africa' (trailing) have white-variegated leaves—attractive in a garden or a salad. (If variegated-leaf forms self-sow, some of their offspring will also be variegated.)

You might also like to try *Tropaeolum perigrinum*, the canary creeper, another Peruvian mountain plant. It bears small, sunny yellow flowers among rounded, lobed leaves and can reach 8 to 10 feet tall with support.

THE NAME

Tropaeolum minor was the plant that Carl Linnaeus had before him when he created the genus name *Tropaeolum* (trow-pay-ol'-um). It refers to a *trophaeum*, Latin for a pillar hung with the bloody shields and helmets of the vanquished, an image inspired by the round leaves and red-splashed yellow flowers. *Minor* means "smaller," while *majus* (mah'-juss) means "larger." The common name nasturtium tells us something about the first reaction of Europeans to the strongly scented plant. They described it with the existing name of a familiar and similarly spicy plant: watercress (*Nasturtium officinale*). The word "nasturtium" derives from the Latin words *nasus tortus*, meaning "nose-twisting."

Viola tricolor

Johnny-jump-up, heartsease, love-in-idleness

PLANT TYPE: *Cool-season annual* | HEIGHT AND SPREAD: *12 inches tall and 8 inches wide* | BLOOM TIME: *Mainly spring through fall, in cool weather* | LIGHT NEEDS: *Full sun, partial shade* | SOIL NEEDS: *Fertile, organic, well drained* | WATER NEEDS: *Moderate to ample* | OTHER TOLERANCES: *Cool coastal summers* | HARDINESS: *Withstands light frost*

*P*eering at us still, through all the subsequent breeding and crossbreeding that created modern pansies and violas, is the three-colored face of the wild viola known as Johnny-jump-up. Its flowers are rather small, its form is lanky compared to modern plants, and yet it is still grown for

Close examination often reveals that Johnny-jump-up flowers on the same plant have different color patterns.

The loose, scrambling form of Johnny-jump-up lets it climb as well as trail between the rocks in an unmortared retaining wall.

its charm and its readiness to reseed and decorate our gardens without having to be replanted. This is the plant known in medieval England as the pansy, a word derived from the French word *pensée*, which translates as "thought." We hear this connection in Shakespeare's *Hamlet*, when Ophelia says, "And there is pansies, that's for thoughts."

SOURCE AND USES

Viola tricolor grows wild in meadows and often in cultivated fields, from Great Britain across Europe into Siberia and northwestern India. It appears in medieval manuscript illustrations and has been planted in European gardens since at least the 1600s. It has been used as an herb, most recently for some skin disorders, and as an ingredient in a love potion, which may be the source of the English common name heartsease. It wasn't until the early 1800s that two wealthy British estate owners, growing this plant alongside two other viola species, *V. cornuta* (horned violet), from Spain and the Pyrenees, and *V. lutea* (mountain pansy), from western and central Europe, independently discovered natural hybrids in their gardens that began the development of modern pansies *(V. x wittrockiana)* and modern viola cultivars.

While hybrid pansies and violas are certainly charmers, there are still reasons to plant Johnny-jump-ups. They are less prone to rain damage than pansies, and they flower for a longer period. Planted at the fronts of borders, or in front of shrubs, they will clamber among the taller plants with their flowers peeking out as they go. They are nice in containers or in the corners of vegetable gardens. Be sure to enjoy the stipules, which are pairs of baroque wing-shaped structures at the base of each leaf, and the purple or black "whisker" lines that guide insects to the center of the flowers.

Use Johnny-jump-ups in bouquets of small flowers, or serve them atop green or fruit salads. They have a faint wintergreen flavor, which you probably won't notice, but they are wonderfully decorative. (Be sure the Johnny-jump-up flowers are face up on a salad for maximum visual impact.)

CARE AND REPRODUCTION

Sow seed for Johnny-jump-up in fall or in late winter to early spring, 1 inch apart, covering it ¼ inch deep. When the plants have several leaves, thin them to 3 to 5 inches apart. Plants need fertile soil and plenty of water to grow well. If you cut them back when they get leggy, they may rebloom. They will decline in hot weather but may recover to bloom again when nights cool in the fall. When the three-pointed seedpods ripen, they shoot seeds as far as 15 feet away. It is difficult to collect the seeds before this happens, so most gardeners let serendipity take its course and then relocate any seedlings that come up in the wrong places. The reseeding at a distance makes evolutionary sense when you know that violas and pansies often succumb to root diseases when they are grown in the same garden spot for more than a couple of years.

CONTROL AND REMOVAL

Ordinary mulching and weeding of the easy-to-pull seedlings and plants will easily control Johnny-jump-up. You may see a few seedlings where you don't want them, but they are not usually serious pests.

VARIETIES AND SIMILAR SPECIES

There is some variation in color patterns among the flowers of *Viola tricolor*. The flowers from seed in one packet may be slightly different from those in another packet, and flowers on the same plant can even vary somewhat. There are also some named *V. tricolor* varieties, such as 'Helen Mount', with flowers to 1½ inches; 'Bowles Black', which is almost black with a small yellow eye; and 'King Henry' (or 'Baby Lucia'), which is fragrant.

You may want to try other small-flowered viola species and cultivars. They don't reseed as often, but they do offer more colors and heavier flowering, and they often have the "tufted" or spreading plant form that keeps plants low and wide. Among the most commonly available are the Penny series and the Sorbet series. Rotate all violas or pansies so they grow in the same spot only once in four years, to avoid root rots. Note that all viola and pansy flowers are edible, though it is best not to eat flowers from nursery starts for a month after purchase, to be sure any residual pesticides have left the plants.

The Name

The genus name *Viola* is the Latin name for various sweet-scented flowers and is derived from the Greek word for a violet, which was *ion* (the word once had a "v" or "w" at the beginning, which was later lost). *Tricolor*, of course, refers to the typical three colors of the flowers: purple, white, and yellow, although flowers of the species display various combinations of white, yellow, lavender, and purple. The common name Johnny-jump-up refers to the readiness with which the plant self-sows. People have applied this common name to several other members of the genus, including *Viola cornuta; V. rafinesqui*, a wildflower of the eastern United States; and *V. pedunculata*, a native of the Channel Islands and the Santa Cruz Mountains of California.

Chapter Four

PERENNIALS

*A*ny plant that lives for three years or longer is technically a perennial, but gardeners generally limit the category of perennials to those long lived plants that are not trees, shrubs, or woody vines. Gardeners also customarily separate bulbs and succulents from other perennials; hence these plant types have different chapters in this book.

There are perennials to provide flowers and interesting foliage in every season. To get the most use from a perennial, you need to know the following about it: (1) the season or seasons in which it will look its best, (2) how to keep it looking tidy throughout the year, and (3) the kind of care it needs to keep it healthy from year to year.

Although perennials live for many years, many of them do not look their best all year. While some have a long bloom season, others bloom for as little as two weeks. Some may have attractive foliage when they aren't in bloom; others do not, or may even become dormant part of the year. Traditional English and European-style gardens had perennial beds and borders containing many kinds of perennials that bloomed during the same season—say, early spring or late summer. Modern perennial gardeners are more likely to plan a perennial bed so that different perennials, or groups of perennials, reach their peak bloom at different seasons. For even greater seasonal interest, modern

These zonal geraniums in a half-barrel have stood up to the challenge of decorating an urban sidewalk.

Like zonal geraniums, regal geraniums are excellent choices for window boxes or containers.

gardeners plant "mixed borders" combining perennials with shrubs, bulbs, annuals, and even succulents, so that the flowers or foliage of the widely different plants grab the viewer's attention throughout the year.

Cutting back is an important part of care for most perennials. Some just need ongoing removal of dead flower stems and leaves. Others look ratty during part of the year and should be cut back more or less severely at that time, typically after the annual bloom period. Subtropical perennials that bloom most of the year, such as Mexican daisy and Mexican sage, often decline in the winter. Still, they are often left untrimmed until late winter or early spring. This avoids the chance that pruning will stimulate new, tender growth that will be damaged later by frost. In addition, gardeners often prefer a plant that looks a bit untidy in winter to bare stubs of stems.

To divide an overgrown perennial, like this rose campion, cut or pull the clump apart, making sure each section or plantlet has roots.

Perennials do not, on average, need rich soil to grow well. An inch or two of organic amendment dug in at planting time and a nice layer of organic mulch is often all they need for ongoing health. If yours are rather smaller than the expected height and are getting enough water, you may also want to dig in a slow-release fertilizer such as hoof and horn meal, alfalfa pellets, or a commercial slow-release product, following the directions on the package.

Books written for gardeners in places where the soil freezes in winter will tell you to pile organic mulch over winter-dormant perennials. Unless you live in the Sierra foothills or in higher elevations, however, you are unlikely to have frozen soil in your Northern California garden. In the mild-winter parts of the region, use mulch between but not on top of your perennials in winter, because it will cause their roots to rot in winter-wet soil.

Perennials that are native to regions with mediterranean or other dry-summer climates may be subject to decay if you water them too much in the summer. Plan your beds so that plants that thrive with little summer water are separate from ones that require ample summer water. While a number of perennials tolerate a range of soil moisture levels, extreme cases should be planted in different places.

Most perennials benefit from being dug up and divided, or separated into more than one plant, from time to time. Plants that can be divided generally spread into a larger clump, with an increasing number of leaf rosettes that have attached roots, or with rooted runners. When a clump of perennials has taken up more space than you have allotted it, or when it blooms noticeably less, it needs dividing—separation into smaller clumps or individual plantlets with roots. Some short-lived perennials, such as *Digitalis* x *mertonensis*, may live longer if the plants are divided every two years, but in most cases, perennials don't need dividing before they have grown for at least three years. Other means of increasing the number of perennial plants you have are cuttings, ground layering, or seeds. The entries for the featured plants include advice about dividing them or propagating them by other methods.

CHOOSING PERENNIALS FOR NORTHERN CALIFORNIA

A number of perennials that are popular in other parts of the country are not very good choices for Northern California. Some, such as Oriental poppies and herbaceous peonies, need a colder winter than we get in much of the region to perform well. Others suffer from pests or diseases here but not in the East, as is the case with most European and eastern U.S. asters and fleabanes. Hosta, America's favorite perennial, will grow here, but it is a favorite of our voracious slugs and snails. Unless these pests are kept in perfect control, they will eat the leaves to lace and then dig in the ground in winter to eat the dormant buds, killing the plants. We also often find that woodland perennials, such as astilbe, which may die if the gardener forgets to water once, are difficult to nurse through our long, dry summer.

On the other hand, perennials from mediterranean and other sub-tropical climates thrive in Northern California. Unlike perennials from colder climates, which grow in summer and become dormant in winter, these may have green leaves, and may even bloom, during our winter rainy season. Perennials from regions with a mediterranean climate may be dormant in summer or, if not, are able to thrive in relatively dry summer soil. A number of plants that are thought of as annuals in cold-winter areas are really subtropical perennials that live from year to year in local gardens. They include geraniums (*Pelargonium* species), cineraria (*Pericallis* x *hybrida*), California poppy (*Eschscholzia californica*), and four o'clock (*Mirabilis jalapa*).

When you are reading books or nursery catalogs that do not take climates of the western United States into account, you may not be able to trust their use of USDA climate ratings to tell you whether a perennial will naturalize in Northern California. Plants rated only to USDA Zone 8 or 9 may not be adapted to California's Zone 9 or 10 because they need more winter cold. On the other hand, they may be perfectly at home in your California Zone 9 or 10 garden, which has dry summers, but may rot in Zone 9 or 10 in Florida and the Gulf Coast, where summers are rainy and humid. If you are thinking of buying an unfamiliar perennial and are not sure whether it is adapted to your Northern California mild-winter garden, check Western-savvy books or nurseries before you purchase the plant. Zones of adaptation given in this book are for California.

Weedy Perennials

As with all types of plants, there are perennials that make pests of themselves in gardens and in the wild. Gardeners fight a number of perennial grassy weeds, including quack grass, Bermuda grass, and Kikuyu grass, all of which spread fiercely by runners. Among nongrassy perennial weeds, bindweed grows from a network of thin roots and then springs up to twine about and strangle other plants, while dandelions and curly dock have deep taproots that will regrow from fragments left behind.

It must be said that a few of the featured perennials have some weedy tendencies. See the individual plant entries in this chapter, and the section on lists of weedy plants in Chapter 2, for more information about these plants.

Here is a short list of some perennials (not featured in this book) that have escaped from gardens and that wildland stewards now suggest you avoid growing or use great caution in growing:

✳ Pampas grass *(Cortaderia selloana)* and jubata grass *(Cortaderia jubata)*. These plants crowd out native species in coastal dunes and interfere with regeneration of logged redwood forests. Some varieties are still sold, but if seedlings form under the parent plant, it's best to take it, and them, out.

✳ Fountain grass *(Pennisetum setaceum)* in Central California. The red-leaved cultivar 'Purpureum' may not form viable seed, but it bears watching, lest it also escape.

✳ Pennyroyal *(Mentha pulgeum)*. A serious problem in Sonoma County, the Central Valley, and in wetlands everywhere.

✳ Ox-eye daisy *(Leucanthemum vulgare)* in the North Coast Range, and in the northern Sierra Nevada to 7,000 feet.

✳ Purple loosestrife *(Lythrum salicaria)*, a weed of wetlands near the coast and in the northern Sierra foothills.

✳ Capeweed *(Arctotheca calendula)*. This plant is spreading in the Bay Area and along the north and central coast.

✳ Licorice plant *(Helichrysum petiolare)* has escaped by windborne seed to Mount Tamalpais and other wild areas. If its nondescript flowers are pinched off, it can't make seed.

Acanthus mollis

PLANT TYPE: *Perennial* | HEIGHT AND SPREAD: *5 to 8 feet tall and 3 to 4 feet wide* | BLOOM TIME: *Late spring into summer* | LIGHT NEEDS: *Sun to shade* | SOIL NEEDS: *Fertile, well-drained* | WATER NEEDS: *None to moderate* | OTHER TOLERANCES: *Poor soil, cool coastal summers, hot inland summers, deer-resistant* | HARDINESS: *Zones 7 to 11*

The bold form of Acanthus mollis pairs well with other bold plants. Here, its partner is the vine Burmese honeysuckle (Lonicera hildebrandiana), *which has large leaves and 6- to 7-inch long fragrant blossoms.*

*I*n the fifth century B.C. a Greek artist carved elegant leaves in the stone at the top of a column, using a species of acanthus as the model. His design became popular as the Corinthian style of column, and if you peer up at neoclassical columns in modern cities, you will often still see acanthus leaves at the top. The plants themselves are not always as honored in our gardens, often sticking up in odd corners, seemingly unappreciated and untended. But when acanthus is healthy and well placed, it is a strikingly elegant plant.

SOURCE AND USES

Acanthus mollis is native to rocky woods across Europe, from Portugal to Italy, Sicily, the former Yugoslavia, and northwest Africa. The ones in our gardens are mostly *A. mollis* var. *latifolius,* a native of Spain and Portugal with leaves reaching 2 feet across on stems 4 feet tall, the stately flower stalks averaging 5 to 6 feet.

Look closely at acanthus flowers to see the froggy stamens. Under each flower is a lavender-green spiny bract that reminded the Romans of bear's claws.

Traditional outward-curling acanthus leaf motifs are evident in the Corinthian style columns of San Francisco's Palace of Fine Arts.

Acanthus makes a bold statement in a small space or can be splendid in larger spaces with other strongly architectural plants—witness the acanthus with tree ferns across from the Conservatory in San Francisco's Golden Gate Park. The plant is likely to overrun other small plants grown with it, except for similarly aggressive plants such as bergenia or *Nephrolepis cordifolia*.

Acanthus flowers are pollinated by large insects, mainly bumblebees, which are able to force apart the two pairs of sturdy stamens to reach the nectar at their bases. Gardeners often think of the crooked stamens as little frogs inside the flowers. Each flower has four sepals and one spiny bract, all flushed soft purple, and a tubular corolla with a three-lobed lower lip. Though not brightly colored, stems of acanthus flowers are formally handsome. They last well in bouquets and, if cut before the bottom flower fades, preserve well for use in dried arrangements.

CARE AND REPRODUCTION

Acanthus is at its best in partial shade where summers are hot, but full sun is fine in cool-summer areas. It will also survive in deep shade but may flower little there. The plant generally survives with no care, dying back in summer and regrowing in fall. It will look better if grown in fertile soil, and the leaves will stay green through the summer if the soil is kept moist, though the plants may benefit in vigor if their leaves are cut back at summer's end. Check the plants frequently for slugs and snails, and use iron phosphate bait if they are numerous.

Acanthus clumps enlarge slowly. They can be divided by cutting off sections of rootstock with leaf buds in fall or spring and can also be grown from root cuttings taken in late fall or early winter. Plant 3-inch-long root sections vertically in cutting mix.

To germinate ripe acanthus seeds, soak them in water for a day or two, plant them ¼ inch deep in seeding mix, and keep them at 50 to 55 degrees F. They typically sprout in 21 to 25 days. Seedlings will take 2 or more years to reach flowering size.

Control and Removal

Acanthus seeds form in capsules that split open when ripe, expelling the seeds some distance from the plant. It is best to cut the flower stems before the capsules can ripen, to prevent seeding all around the mother plants.

Where acanthus meets a lawn, mowing will stop its spread. To confine it with the greatest certainly, you can plant it in a bed bounded by concrete or confine it using an 8-inch-deep root barrier, such as you would use for bamboo.

The ability of acanthus to grow from small sections of root makes it difficult to eradicate should you wish to grow something else in its place. While it can be done, total removal requires deep digging, and you may have to remove sprouts for two or three more seasons. (Under no circumstance should you rototill the area, because doing so will only increase the number of root fragments from which plants can grow.)

Varieties and Similar Species

Acanthus mollis has leaves only 8 inches across and of a duller green than those of *A. mollis* var. *latifolius*. A common cultivar, 'Hollard's Gold' (also known as 'Fielding's Gold' and 'New Zealand Gold'), has broad, golden green leaves.

The adventurous gardener can find several other species of *Acanthus*. One that is easy to locate and an excellent garden plant is *A. spinosus*. (The variety sold is usually *spinosissimus*). This plant has flower stems to about 4 feet and narrower, more finely divided leaves than *A. mollis*. It grows best in full sun. Some gardeners feel its attractiveness and restrained size more than make up for the rather sharp leaf spines. Because this species is native to the Greek area where the first Corinthian columns were carved, some think it might have been the one that provided a model, though both species were grown in ancient Greek gardens.

The Name

Acanthus (uh-can'-thus) derives from the Greek word *akantha,* which means "thorn" or "prickle"; *mollis* means "soft." While a number of acanthus species are rather prickly, the thorniest part of *Acanthus mollis* is the bract under each flower. It has several moderately firm points and probably also served as the source of the common name, bear's breech. We use this name without thinking much about what part of the plant a bear might wear, but it seems likely that the original name referred to the sharp-pointed bracts, which were seen as little bear paws with claws on them, according to plant name expert William T. Stearn. He thinks the breech part is due to a mishearing of a medieval Latin name *branca ursina,* meaning "bear's claw." Medieval French gardeners may have misheard *branca* as *braca,* or "trousers," a word that later became *braies* and finally breech or "breeches."

Aquilegia (species and hybrids)

Columbine

PLANT TYPE: *Perennial* | HEIGHT AND SPREAD: *1 to 3 feet tall and 1 to 2 feet wide* | BLOOM TIME: *Midspring into summer* | LIGHT NEEDS: *Sun to partial shade* | SOIL NEEDS: *Moderately fertile, organic, well drained* | WATER NEEDS: *Moderate* | OTHER TOLERANCES: *Cool coastal climate, hot inland climate, deer resistant* | HARDINESS: *Zones 3 to 11*

The common name of this flower, columbine, derives from the Latin word for "dove," *columba*, because the upside-down flower reminded some long-ago Europeans of five doves. In the religious art of the early medieval period, the flower symbolized the Holy Spirit. However, it disappeared from such art in the later Middle Ages, and

Long-spurred hybrid columbines bloom in a number of pastel or bright single colors and bicolors. Seedlings often produce new combinations.

Where vivid colors are called for, select a columbine with red sepals and yellow petals, such as this one that is blooming on a terrace.

many historians think this is because, in the popular view, it had come to symbolize quite another bird. The petal spurs reminded people of horns, which symbolized a cuckold. The flowers came to symbolize the cuckoo, a bird that lays its eggs in other birds' nests.

Source and Uses

Though the purple- or white-flowered European *Aquilegia vulgaris* lost its place in European religious art, it remained a popular garden flower. When New World species began to arrive in Europe, starting with the red-and-yellow-flowered *A. canadensis* in 1640, Europeans found that they readily crossed, resulting in hybrids with new flower colors and proportions. Because both of these species had short spurs, the early hybrids were short-spurred as well and were often given the common name "granny's bonnets." By the Victorian era, many more species had been brought to Europe from their habitats all through the nontropical Northern Hemisphere and were being grown as species or used to create new hybrids.

Columbines are attractive in beds and borders or massed informally. They are also often grown in containers. While their bloom period is only a few weeks long, they do attract hummingbirds, and nothing else provides the same fanciful and delicate flower form. In addition, the leaves are attractive when the plant is not in bloom.

Care and Reproduction

Columbine grows best in soil that has had plenty of organic matter worked into it. Poor drainage will often kill columbine, so if your soil is heavy clay, adding organic matter to aerate the soil is particularly important.

Columbine plants are often available in small six-packs, which may not bloom the first year, or in 4-inch pots, which will. Most types should be set 1 to 1½ feet apart. Cut spent flower stems to encourage more to form. Some gardeners treat the plants as annuals, pulling them out at season's end; others cut back dead leaves and wait for the dormant plants to reemerge in the spring.

Columbines often die after only 3 or 4 years. You can prolong their life by dividing the plants every couple of years as they begin to grow in spring. You can also grow new columbines easily from seed collected as soon as you can hear it rattling in the pods. While it can be sown indoors in winter or early spring, it will germinate best if sown in late summer, soon after it is collected.

Leafminers, insect larvae that form trails in leaves, can cause much disfiguring damage. Some gardeners ignore the pest, but you may be able to limit damage by cutting off disfigured leaves as soon as you see the first ones. Summer oil spray combats the pests by smothering the eggs they lay on the leaves.

Control and Removal

Seedlings generally grow near the parent plants, since the seeds fall rather than being blown or carried by animals. You will be able to recognize them by their distinctive leaves, gray-green and cut into leaflets with rounded lobes, and you can then decide whether to pull and discard or dig and replant them. Seedlings in a planting of hybrid columbines are likely to have flowers different from those of the parent plants. Species columbines may cross, producing hybrid offspring, or may breed true.

If you don't want any surprise variations from seedlings, remove the flowers as soon as they fade, so the seed can't ripen. If seedlings do mature, you can pull plants with flower colors and forms you don't like. Create more plants with traits you do like by dividing them. If you allow self-seeding and notice a long-term drift away from flower colors and forms that you like, you can always add a few purchased plants with flowers that you like better, to refresh the gene pool.

Unwanted columbine plants are easy to dig out. They form little thickened roots at the base of leaf sections, which could regrow if missed, but they are so near the surface that you are likely to be able to remove them all easily.

Varieties and Similar Species

Gardeners can now choose short- or long-spurred hybrids in a number of colors, as well as plants with yellow-variegated leaves. There are even doubles, which barely look like columbines. Most hybrids are based on two or more of the following species: *A. vulgaris*, *A. canadensis*, *A. caerulea* (blue and white, long spurred, from the Rocky Mountains), *A. chrysantha* (yellow, long spurred, from the southern United States to northern Mexico), and *A. longissima* (yellow, long-spurred, from the southwestern United States). We can also grow these individual columbine species, as well as many others, including the red-and-yellow-flowered California native *A. formosa*, which hikers, to their delight, often happen upon in the spring.

The Name

Carl Linnaeus named the genus *Aquilegia* (ah-kwih-leh'-jee-uh), from an ancient Latin name for the plant. One expects these fancifully formed flowers to inspire fanciful names, and this seems to be the case, though there is a disagreement as to which fancy inspired the genus name. Many references give as a source the Latin word *aquila* ("eagle"), referring to the five spurs as the five talons of the bird. However, one of the most respected of American botanists and horticulturists, Liberty Hyde Bailey, specifically says that this is not the source of the name, but rather that the name derives from the Latin noun *aqua* ("water") and the verb *lego* ("to gather"). He says it refers to the resemblance of the nectar-bearing petal spurs to ancient jars with pointed ends that were sunk in sand to keep the contained liquid cool.

Bellis perennis

※ English daisy

PLANT TYPE: *Perennial* | HEIGHT AND SPREAD: *2 to 8 inches tall and 3 to 8 inches wide* | BLOOM TIME: *Mostly spring and summer* | LIGHT NEEDS: *Sun or partial shade* | SOIL NEEDS: *Moderately fertile to fertile, well drained* | WATER NEEDS: *Moderate to ample* | OTHER TOLERANCES: *Low fertility, cool coastal climates, some foot traffic, usually deer resistant* | HARDINESS: *Zones 4 to 11*

There are at least three ways to make a daisy chain for a crown or necklace. If you have only a few daisies, you can slit each stem partway down and insert the stem of the next flower into the slit. Or you can tie each stem around the base of the previous

'Aetna', a hybrid English daisy, has double flowers that may be white or red.

The English daisies and fescue in this garden meadow are allowed to grow tall, then mowed once a year, in late spring.

flower in the wreath. But when daisies are plentiful, you can make an elegant braid, starting with three daisies tied together and then braiding the stems, adding flowers as you go.

Source and Uses

Though we know it as English daisy, and it certainly is native to England, *Bellis perennis* also grows wild across much of Europe and into western Asia. Still, it has always been particularly loved in England. There are several old English sayings to the effect that spring has not come until you can cover some number (such as three, nine, or thirteen) of daisies with your foot. Whatever the number, you were sure to find it easily. Wild daisies grew in the hand-scythed meadows of medieval gardens, and fancier varieties have been favorite cottage garden plants for many centuries.

Wild English daisy grows readily in Northern California lawns but has become much less common in recent years. Gardeners in both California and England who are seeking a more formal lawn, perhaps influenced by the pure green expanse of a golf course, now try to eliminate the daisy. Countertrends show that some gardeners welcome it as a feature in a "natural garden" or "ecolawn," and it is also common in California's public lawns where municipal rules forbid pesticide use.

Wild English daisies are occasionally mixed with a grass such as creeping red fescue to make a spring meadow in California gardens. After the daisies have bloomed, the meadow is mowed once and then left until the following spring. In such meadows, wild daisies will have flower stems up to 8 inches tall. Wild English daisies are also attractive between rock or slate stepping-stones, where foot traffic will keep stems short. Both the wild form and fancy domestic varieties are good rock garden plants, and the domestic types are useful in borders, as edging plants, or in containers.

Care and Reproduction

Although English daisy grows best in full sun, it can survive considerable shade, sometimes thriving in shady parts of lawns where the grass is unable to survive. It is well adapted to the high fertility and moisture of a lawn. It can also survive moderate drought where it is well established; however, container plants or recent transplants will wilt alarmingly if they dry out.

Those who still enjoy daisies in lawns can find English daisy in seed mixes for "ecolawns" (an approach that I consider risky, since such seed mixes might easily contain plants you may later regret introducing). If you want only daisies, try scattering seed collected in midsummer from existing lawn plants, but avoid introducing *Bellis perennis* to lawns in or adjacent to wildlands. Central Valley gardeners should be aware, however, that English daisies may be more aggressive spreaders there than near the coast.

English daisy for other uses can also be grown from seed sown indoors in late autumn for spring bloom, or sown outdoors in early summer for bloom the following spring. Cover the seed shallowly. All types also reproduce by forming new plants at the ends of short stolons, or underground stems, and can be divided in early spring or midsummer. This is the only way to propagate certain sterile hybrid cultivars.

CONTROL AND REMOVAL

You may want to deadhead domestic varieties of English daisy to prevent reseeding. They don't seem to reseed heavily, but when they do the offspring will gradually revert to the wild form.

The desire to be rid of lawn daisies may simply reflect the advent of more effective control methods. The availability of purchased turf allows one to skim off the top $1\frac{1}{2}$ inches of soil, rototill, and returf the lawn. "Weed and feed" chemicals, formulations of herbicide with fertilizer, eliminate daisies along with most broadleaf weeds. These all-purpose chemicals are poor choices for constant use, since they often leach chemicals into the groundwater, and therefore into the bay and ocean. If you use an herbicide selective for broadleaf weeds once in spring, and possibly again in 6 weeks, and if you mow the lawn high and often, you can eliminate most broadleaf weeds, including daisies.

Varieties and Similar Species

By the end of the 1500s, gardeners could choose from English daisies that were double (had extra rows of ray florets), red-flowered, or were larger than the wild form, and these have been bred and improved ever since. (There was also a "childling" daisy, one that had a ring of tiny daisies around each larger one, which is still to be found, though it is not common.) Traits valued in modern varieties are bigger flowers, pink or salmon ray florets, and flowers so double that the yellow centers are hidden. Some series that come highly recommended are Carpet (1-inch double flowers), Habanera (1½ to 2 inches, double), and Pomponette (1½ inches, double, quilled or rolled petals).

The Name

The genus name *Bellis* means "pretty" in Latin, and *perennis* means "perennial." Perennial it certainly is, and quite hardy too, but because the hybrid forms are most often treated as annuals, you are likely to find the plant listed in books or seed catalogs as an annual. Old spellings of the name "daisy" were "daeyeseye" or "days eye," referring to the way these flowers open in the morning and close at night. In the day, the flowers reveal the golden eye of the sun, and the pinkish undersides of the closing petals echo the tints of sunset. They were the favorite flower of the English poet Geoffrey Chaucer (1342–1400), who hastened out to see them on spring mornings and evenings.

Bergenia (species and hybrids)

 Bergenia

PLANT TYPE: *Perennial* | HEIGHT AND SPREAD: *1½ feet tall and 1½ feet wide, spreading* | BLOOM TIME: *Late winter, early spring, sometimes into fall* | LIGHT NEEDS: *Sun to shade* | SOIL NEEDS: *Fertile, well drained* | WATER NEEDS: *Moderate* | OTHER TOLERANCES: *Poor soil, clay soil, drought tolerant, cool coastal climate, full sun near the coast, inland climates with light shade, deer resistant* | HARDINESS: *Zones 4 to 11*

*A*fter enjoying great popularity in California gardens of the mid-1900s, bergenia has been out of fashion for some years, misunderstood and neglected. It remains, nevertheless, a tough plant with a striking appearance that is handsome when grown and used well. British and European gardeners have recently

A single bergenia plant can be a bold accent in a small garden. This one is the modern hybrid 'Silberlicht'.

Sturdy and attractive bergenia is useful in large plantings. This is B. x schmidtii, probably the most common type in old Northern California plantings.

taken fresh interest in the plant because of new varieties that are being created there, but there are also reasons to renew our interest in the old bergenia plantings that survive in many regional gardens.

Source and Uses

Eight species of *Bergenia* grow in cold temperate regions of Asia, in mountain meadows, open forests, and among rocks. They are often found on shady, north-facing slopes. *B. crassifolia* and *B. cordifolia* are native to Siberia and Mongolia, while *B. ciliata* ranges from western Pakistan to southwestern Nepal. *B. crassifolia,* first brought to Europe in the 1700s, has naturalized there.

Bergenias form a tight, weed-fighting ground cover with a bold texture that looks good at a distance and can be handsome with other bold plants such as acanthus or with delicate-looking plants like ferns or grasses. The leaves may take on a red tint in winter, and the pink, white, or red flowers are a bonus. Bergenia is most often planted in clumps of at least ten plants, or allowed to fill in larger areas, but with careful siting and care, you can use it as a small but dramatic specimen plant, growing one or a few plants where they can be observed closely. It can also be built into an unmortared stone wall, for a vertical display. Flower arrangers have long valued the bold, sturdy leaves.

Care and Reproduction

Set bergenias 1½ feet apart in spring or early fall. They can grow in full sun where summers are cool, but in hot-summer areas they will need at least light shade. They tolerate full shade but will always bloom more and have better winter leaf color in a brighter place. While bergenia will survive in most soils, it grows best in soil with plenty of organic matter. Water regularly and deeply in the first growing season. After that, the plants can survive with little summer water in cool areas or in shade, but they'll need moderate water in sun or hot weather. They will grow faster with moister soil. Once they are well established, if you clear them of grassy weeds they will keep other weeds out pretty well.

Rake through the plants with your hands as often as once a month to take out dead leaves, which become black and crispy but hang onto the plants. Early removal of spent flower stalks encourages new ones to form. Cut spent flower stalks at their base while they are still green, or pull them out when they have dried up. Use iron phosphate bait to control slugs and snails. Apply beneficial nematodes to the soil if damage from black vine weevils (notched leaf edges) is severe, or handpick the beetles at night in small plantings.

Renew bergenia beds as often as every 2 years, or as rarely as every 5 years, but don't wait longer, or the rhizome mass will be difficult to work on. In spring, when blooming decreases, use a fork to lift all of the rhizomes, cut the rooted tips to several inches behind the last good leaf, removing any damaged leaves, and replant them upright. Increase the size of beds by planting extras when you renew the beds. Be sure the soil is moist but not soggy until the newly set plants have begun to grow.

Control and Removal

When bergenia grows over other plants or leans onto a lawn, cut back individual rhizomes or leaf bases, being careful not to injure the remaining leaves. When you cut the end of a rhizome, a new plant will pop out, so cut to a foot behind the place where you want the new edge of a bed to be.

To remove bergenia, insert a digging fork sideways under the rhizomes and see if you can lift them out. If they are too deep for this method, they were probably started from potted nursery plants and so have deeper roots than ones started from divisions. In this case they will have to be dug out, using the fork. Try not to break up the rhizomes too much, since they may sprout from cut pieces that you miss when you are digging.

Varieties and Similar Species

Early documentation of which bergenias were being grown in gardens was so poor that most old plants have not been properly identified. The most common bergenia from 40 to 100 years ago was probably *Bergenia* x *schmidtii (B. crassifolia* x *B. ciliata)*, with some leaves over 10 inches long and mid-pink flowers in late winter to early spring. These are still common in public and private gardens. (There are identified plants in San Francisco's Strybing Arboretum.) Also common were the very similar, though usually smaller-leaved *B. crassifolia*, *B. cordifolia*, and *B.* x *media (B. crassifolia* x *B. cordifolia)*. One of the main values of the older bergenia plantings in our gardens is that they seem to resist the viruses that may cause streaked leaves or even death in some modern types. However, newer hybrids offer visual charms, from more colorful winter leaves ('Bressingham Ruby') to white flowers ('Silberlicht').

The Name

The genus name *Bergenia* (ber-gen'-ee-uh) honors Karl August von Bergen (1704–1760), who was a professor of botany at Frankfurt an der Oder. The specific epithet *crassifolia* (krass-ih-fohl'-ee-uh) means that the leaves are thickened, from the Latin *crassus* ("thick") and *folia* ("leaf"). The name *schmidtii* (shmit'-ee-eye) honors Ernest Schmidt, a German nurseryman who bred the hybrid *B.* x *schmidtii* in the late 1800s.

Centranthus ruber

PLANT TYPE: *Perennial* | HEIGHT AND SPREAD: *2½ feet tall and 1½ feet wide* | BLOOM TIME: *Bloom possible in any month, main flush in spring* | LIGHT NEEDS: *Full sun, partial shade* | SOIL NEEDS: *Poor to moderately fertile, well drained* | WATER NEEDS: *Little to moderate* | OTHER TOLERANCES: *Clay soil, limy or calcareous soil, drought tolerant, cool coastal climates, hot inland summers, snail resistant, deer resistant* | HARDINESS: *Zones 5 to 11*

*A*n old saying in England is that wherever you find *Centranthus ruber* there once was a Roman encampment. The plants have become so common there that the saying can no longer be true; it is probably true that Romans brought them from the Mediterranean,

This wide skirt of lavender-pink–flowered centranthus spills prettily over the sidewalk from a narrow bed.

Both white and red-flowered centranthus ornament this spring border. The planting also includes, from left to right, bulbous iris, ground morning glory (Convolvulus sabatius), *sea lavender* (Limonium perezii), *and Mexican daisy.*

either accidentally or on purpose, while Great Britain was part of the Roman Empire. The wind-spread seeds did the rest.

Source and Uses

Formerly a wildflower around the edges of the Mediterranean Sea, centranthus became a popular cottage garden flower in Great Britain. It also has become something of a weed, especially in southwestern England, Ireland, and parts of Northern California. Its affinity for alkaline and calcareous soil enables it to grow freely on the famous English "white cliffs of Dover," hiding them every summer under a blanket of its gray-green foliage and masses of tiny rosy blossoms. It is also common in old stone or brick walls, perhaps because it can survive the alkalinity of the decaying mortar. It was grown in eastern U.S. gardens by the beginning of the 1800s and in California by at least mid-twentieth century.

In some urban areas of Northern California, so much centranthus is blooming on rocky embankments and in neglected places that the question is not whether it will escape gardens but whether one wants to allow it in. Still, it can be a handsome plant for a rock garden or cottage garden. Try red-flowered centranthus with the blue-flowered sea lavender *(Limonium perezii)* or ground morning glory *(Convolvulus sabatius)*, and any of the colors with Mexican daisy *(Erigeron karvinskianus)* or with lamb's ears *(Stachys byzantina)*. The masses of tiny flowers have a light scent and make attractive cut flowers.

Care and Reproduction

This easy-to-grow plant will thrive wherever it can get sunshine and a modest amount of water, but it will not mind more fertile soil or more frequent water, as long as the soil is well drained and not too acidic. The biggest flush of flowers is in mid to late spring, but with adequate water and deadheading, they may bloom well into summer.

The plants can look rather mussy after they have bloomed. You can, depending on your needs, cut them back part way, to a pair of leaves below the spent flower head, to give them the best chance to regrow, or cut them back nearly to the ground, assuming that if they die, new seedlings will replace them the following year.

Centranthus grows easily from seed and blooms the first year. Set plants 12 to 15 inches apart. You can also regrow plants from divisions taken in spring or fall, either by cutting the crown apart and separating the fleshy roots or by carefully removing a rooted stem from the outside of the plant in the spring.

Control and Removal

Deadheading as soon as the flowers fade will reduce the number of seeds produced, and therefore the number of seedlings that appear in the following year. If any of the flowers you are deadheading have mature seeds, cut their stems gently with pruning shears and put the spent flowers into a paper bag immediately so fewer seeds will float away and find a place to grow. Centranthus has been classified by the California Exotic Pest Plants Council as "Considered, but not Listed," but it could end up being upgraded to the new "Low" impact list, because of its ability to displace native plants from certain rocky cliff habitats.

Unwanted seedlings are easy to pull or transplant, and mature plants are not difficult to dig out, since the roots are not deep. Be sure that you get all of the crown, since it will regrow if you miss some of it. Plants growing in cracks can be difficult to pull out once they get large, so you'll probably need to apply an herbicide to their cut stems.

Varieties and Similar Species

Although there are about a dozen species in the genus *Centranthus,* the others are not much used in gardens. The three color variants of *C. ruber* have been given the variety names *albus* (white), *coccineus* (red), and *roseus* (lavender-pink). Purchased seeds are often mixes of red- and white-flowered plants, and sometimes lavender-pink as well. Unless you are able to purchase a single-color seed packet or get a plant with a known color of flowers, you have to wait for the first flowers to bloom on young plants and then, if they are not the color you want, remove the plant.

The gene for white flowers is dominant in this plant, so you would expect wild populations to gradually become all white. This doesn't happen for reasons relating both to the plants and their environment. White-flowered centranthus produces somewhat fewer flowers per plant and per flower stem, and the seeds are smaller, so all things being equal, it would reproduce a little more slowly than the other varieties. A further impediment, however, is that pollinators, including butterflies and hummingbirds that visit the pink and red flowers, tend to ignore the white ones. Therefore, despite its genetic advantage, the survival of white-flowered centranthus is largely thanks to gardeners, who often select it in preference to the colored forms.

THE NAME

Centranthus (ken-tran'-thus) means "spur flower," from the Greek words *kentron* ("spur") and *anthos* ("flower"). It is named for the small spur at the base of each flower. The specific epithet *ruber* is the Latin word for "red." The common name red valerian often confuses gardeners who want to learn more about this plant, since other plants, members of the genus *Valeriana*, are also known by the common name of valerian. Both genera do belong to the same plant family, the Valerianaceae, but they are different in many ways.

Cymbalaria muralis

Kenilworth ivy, ivy-leaved toadflax

PLANT TYPE: *Biennial or short-lived perennial* | HEIGHT AND SPREAD: *6 inches tall and up to 3 feet wide* | BLOOM TIME: *Spring, summer into fall* | LIGHT NEEDS: *Shade, partial shade* | SOIL NEEDS: *Moderately fertile, well drained* | WATER NEEDS: *Moderate to moist* | OTHER TOLERANCES: *Full sun near the coast, most soils, cool coastal climates, deer resistant* | HARDINESS: *Zones 3 to 11*

Some gardeners are charmed by Kenilworth ivy, while others consider it weedy for its habit of popping up where it pleases. But if it is a weed, it is a pretty one. This creeper scrambles along the ground and up walls, its tidy scalloped leaves forming a low mat dotted with tiny snapdragon-like blossoms. (If you squeeze the sides of the flowers, they will open and close just like snapdragons,

If lavender isn't in your garden's color scheme, seek out the kenilworth ivy variety 'Alba Compacta'.

Kenilworth ivy appears to tumble down these brick stairs, softening the corners. Though it tends to stay in the corners, a little trimming may be needed to keep it out of the way of foot traffic.

which are in the same plant family.) It is well adapted to living among rocks or bricks. As the flowers bloom, their stems turn toward the light, so they are held above the plant. However, when the flowers are forming seedpods, their stems turn away from the light, depositing the seeds into a moist crack.

Source and Uses

Found originally in the southwestern Alps in Italy, the western Balkans, and Sicily, Kenilworth ivy has crept across Europe and Great Britain, both in gardens and out of them. Its ability to inhabit the cracks of stone, brick, or concrete structures is no doubt the source of the French common name, which translates to "ruin of Rome," and the English-language common name coliseum ivy. It first came to England in the 1600s, some say in marble statues sent to Oxford from Italy. If this is so, it seems likely that the Kenilworth of the common name applies to either the town of Kenilworth or the castle by the same name, since both are located not far from Oxford. The plant was very popular in English gardens from the time of its introduction until the 1800s, when it fell out of favor, but it has survived very well in and out of gardens both there and here. It often appears unbidden in paved-over urban neighborhoods in Northern California and in other parts of the country as well. It is, for example, common in some neighborhoods of Baltimore, Maryland.

This plant is one of the prettiest small-scale creepers for shady garden areas. Grow it on walls, between pavers, along stairs, or in shady rock gardens. It thrives in containers, where it is best grown alone or under single-trunked plants into which it can't tangle.

Care and Reproduction

Kenilworth ivy is usually sold in the ground cover section of nurseries. Set plugs 8 to 12 inches apart in spring. Or collect seed from plants in the summer, probing under them to find the ripe seedpods that release small black seeds when crushed. Sow the seed in the spring, on the surface of soil in a shady, moist place. It is also easy to root cuttings taken in spring or summer.

Once established, Kenilworth ivy often thrives with no care whatsoever. Its main need is not to dry out completely, but if this does happen and the plant dies back, it will probably regrow when moisture returns. It will also go dormant in cold winters but will survive and regrow after surprisingly low temperatures. Whether it has returned after adverse conditions from still-living roots or from seed is not always clear, but the effect is the same.

CONTROL AND REMOVAL

As with any wall or rock creeper, your garden will be more interesting if parts of the wall or rocks are visible along with the plant. This often happens naturally with Kenilworth ivy because it is a rather small plant, but if your garden features do disappear beneath it, it is time to tear or cut a little of it away. Doing so is easy, as the stems are quite fragile. It may look bad for a short while, but the plants will recover quickly.

The plant can be quite a pest if it grows with other plants in containers, tangling itself into them. To remove it, you may need to unpot the plants and extricate them from the Kenilworth ivy stems and roots. If you think Kenilworth ivy seed has formed, remove as much potting mix as you can and repot in fresh mix.

Once established in a garden, Kenilworth ivy tends to be a permanent, though not very aggressive, resident of shady cracks where most other plants wouldn't grow. You can probably get rid of it in particular places by cutting it back and dabbing it with an herbicide, but you will probably need to repeat this as new plants appear from seed.

VARIETIES AND SIMILAR SPECIES

There are several varieties of Kenilworth ivy. Some have hairy leaves, but you will generally see the one with smooth, hairless leaves. Flower color varies from pale to darker lavender, all with small yellow patches. If the color you want isn't in the nursery, you may be able to collect seed or cuttings of the flower color you want in a friend's garden or from a curbside plant. The variety 'Alba Compacta' has white, yellow-marked flowers and is more compact than the species.

Cymbalaria aequitriloba, sometimes seen in nurseries, makes a mat only about an inch tall, with most leaves under ½ inch across. Use it only where it can be viewed at close range.

The Name

Carl Linnaeus classified this plant as *Antirrhinum cymbalaria*, putting it in the same genus as snapdragon. He chose the specific epithet *cymbalaria* (sim-buh-lair'-ee-uh) to mean that the rounded leaves were like little cymbals. A later botanist moved the plant to the genus *Linaria*, making the name *Linaria cymbalaria*, thus grouping it with *Linaria purpurea* (see page 00). Its current name elevates its former specific epithet, *cymbalaria*, to its genus name and adds the specific epithet *muralis*, a word derived from the Latin word *murus*, meaning "wall."

Digitalis purpurea

Foxglove

PLANT TYPE: *Biennial or short-lived perennial* | HEIGHT AND SPREAD: *4 to 8 feet tall and 1 to 2 feet wide* | BLOOM TIME: *Midspring, early summer* | LIGHT NEEDS: *Partial shade, shade* | SOIL NEEDS: *Fertile, neutral to acidic, organic, well drained* | WATER NEEDS: *Moderate to moist* | OTHER TOLERANCES: *Poor soil, cool coastal climates, full sun near the coast, inland climates, rabbit resistant, deer resistant* | HARDINESS: *Zones 3 to 11*

Often, while working in the garden, I have caught a sidewise glimpse of movement and turned to see who was there, only to realize it was just a tall, swaying stem of foxglove flowers. At these times I have understood the sense of wonder that this stately and toxic plant must have created in long-ago people who came upon it in wildwoods and meadows. Several old English names (dead man's bells, bloody fingers,

Foxgloves are great companions for roses of all kinds. These are mingling with a climbing rose on an adjacent fence.

While gardeners often struggle to keep tall plants upright, the combination of upright and leaning flower stems lends an informal beauty to this large planting of foxgloves.

witch's gloves) show an association with magic and death. The name fox-glove may refer to a legend that foxes wore the flowers to avoid leaving footprints when stealing chickens, but it is equally likely to derive from "folks glove"—the gloves of the fairies.

SOURCE AND USES

Foxglove is believed to have originated in the western Mediterranean region and is considered native to Great Britain and much of Europe. It has been grown in cottage gardens since at least the 1400s. It had many herbal uses throughout history, most of them unrelated to the heart-stimulant use that modern medicine recognizes.

Foxglove is a fine plant for the back of a border or the back of a garden. It starts to bloom just before roses begin their spring flush, and its narrow, upright spires provide a nice counterpoint to these bushier, round-flowered plants. Foxglove flowers attract hummingbirds and bees, and they last well in bouquets.

CARE AND REPRODUCTION

Sow the tiny seeds outdoors or in containers indoors, uncovered and ½ inch apart. Transplant container-grown seedlings into individual pots when they have two to three true leaves. Plant them in the garden when they are about 3 inches across. The final distance between plants should be 15 inches. In mild-winter areas, start seed in mid to late summer, or purchase small plants to set out in late summer or early fall for bloom the following spring. Where winters are colder, sow seed in spring or set out transplants by midsummer. In spring, you can purchase bigger (and more expensive) plants that are about to bloom.

If young flower stalks begin to lean unattractively, tie them to stakes. Cutting out the flower stalk as soon as it finishes blooming will often stimulate the formation of one or more shorter flower stalks. If you remove all the flower stalks before seed can form, the plant may survive to bloom again the following spring. Most plants will dry up and die after one season's bloom and can be removed when they finish blooming.

If you want foxglove to sow itself and return each year, you will have to allow some seed to form. Leave the flowering stalks standing until you see that the pods have opened. Seeds usually fall when the stalks sway in the wind, and they will also fall out if you cut the stalk and invert it.

Control and Removal

To reduce reseeding, remove the flower stalks before the seeds ripen. If you find that the pods have already opened, cut the stalks from the standing plants in short sections and hold each section upright as you place it in a paper bag.

When the seeds fall, some, but usually not a huge number, will produce plants by the following spring. When you recognize the whorls of broad, hairy, gray-green leaves where you don't want them, you can either pull and discard them or scoop them out with a trowel and move them to a better location. Foxglove plants, even mature ones, are not difficult to dig from moist soil, and they do not grow back from underground structures.

Digitalis was considered, but not listed as an exotic pest plant, by the California Exotic Pest Plant Council, but it could end up on their new "Low" impact list. It does invade open woodlands, pastures, and roadsides—mainly areas where the soil has been recently disturbed—in coastal counties and in the northern Sierra Nevada foothills under 3,000 feet elevation. Prevent further spread by not growing it adjacent to wildlands, especially where water can disperse the seeds into nearby wild areas, and take care not to dispose of plant debris with ripe seeds that could grow in a wildland area.

Varieties and Similar Species

The flowers of wild plants lean to one side of the stalk and face downward. The variety 'Excelsior' has flowers pointing in all directions around the stalk and facing outward. The recently introduced 'Foxy' is similar, though shorter, and blooms the first season (in about 5 months) from seed sown in spring. Most foxglove varieties bloom in a range of colors that include lavender, pink, white, and sometimes yellow. There are also single-color strains, such as 'Apricot Beauty' or 'Alba' (unspotted white). In a self-seeding population, you can select for colored or white flowers by observing the flower stalks, which will be purplish if the flowers are to be colored.

There are about twenty species of *Digitalis*, most of which are not as ornamental as *D. purpurea*. Perhaps next most popular with gardeners is *Digitalis* x *mertonensis*, the result of a cross between *D. purpurea* and *D. grandiflora* (which has pale yellow flowers). Its showy flowers have a wonderful crushed-strawberry color. The plant is perennial, grows to about 3 feet tall, and comes true from seed, but it doesn't self-sow much. Dividing plants every other year helps maintain their vigor.

The Name

You can see the Latin word *digit* in the genus name *Digitalis* (dij-ih-tahl'-iss), referring to the fingerlike shape of the flowers. The name is a Latinization of an old German common name *fingerhut*, literally "finger hat" or "thimble." The specific epithet *purpurea* (pur-pur'-ee-uh), is Latin for "purple."

Warning

All parts of the foxglove plant are toxic to humans and animals. People sometimes die from drinking tea made from the leaves, having mistaken them for comfrey. Poisoning deaths are common enough that herbal uses of this plant or drugs derived from it are best left to medical professionals.

Erigeron karvinskianus (*E. karvinskianus, E. mucronatus*)

❋ Mexican daisy, Santa Barbara daisy

PLANT TYPE: *Perennial* | HEIGHT AND SPREAD: *1 to 2 feet tall and 3 to 5 feet wide* | BLOOM TIME: *Spring, summer, fall* | LIGHT NEEDS: *Full sun, partial shade* | SOIL NEEDS: *Moderately fertile, well drained* | WATER NEEDS: *Moderate* | OTHER TOLERANCES: *Poor soil, infrequent water, cool coastal summers, seaside conditions, hot inland summers, snail resistant, deer resistant* | HARDINESS: *Zones 9 to 11*

Mexican daisy plants are covered with airy clouds of ¾-inch blossoms, some fresh white, others a soft lavender-pink. The two-tone effect occurs because the flowers are white when they first open but then age to pink. The yellow-centered daisies seem to float among the wiry stems and small, narrow leaves. The lacy mounds more often play supporting roles than garden stars, but their low-key charm fits into many kinds of gardens.

White daisies fade to pink, giving Mexican daisy plants two blossom colors on one plant.

An imposing mound of Mexican daisy punctuates the end of this border in a raised planter. Also shown are centranthus, blue Convolvulus sabatius, and yellow bulbous iris.

Source and Uses

Mexico is indeed one home of this plant, which grows mainly in mountain regions at 4,000 to 11,000 feet above sea level in much of Central America and into South America. Although Mexico is next door to California, it is probable that this plant, like many Mexican plants, arrived in California by way of Europe. For much of the past century it was not available in Northern California nurseries and so was passed from garden to garden. Having recently entered the market again, it has made up for lost time by becoming extremely popular.

Mexican daisy is used as a ground cover, an edging, and in borders. It provides a carpet under street trees, clings to garden walls, and billows out of containers. It enhances various garden styles: naturalistic, mediterranean, romantic, cottage, rock, rose, and even tropical gardens feature Mexican daisy under plants with bold forms such as phormiums or palms.

Care and Reproduction

The mountain origin of this plant prepares it for cool weather, but it also tolerates considerable heat. It will survive some drought and may live through the summer without water, though underwatered plants will lose their fresh green look. Hard frosts will kill it to the ground, but, if the cold is not too prolonged, the plant will regrow in spring.

Gardeners generally cut Mexican daisy back hard at least once a year to encourage fresh new growth. Some cut it to 8 to 10 inches, others to only a couple of inches from the ground. This can be done in early spring, but another option is to cut it back in late summer, by August, so it will regrow before winter. (If you cut Mexican daisies back too late in fall and the bed looks bare during winter, interplant it with some primroses and wait for spring.)

Set nursery plants in gallon containers 14 to 20 inches apart. The plants can also be started in spring from divisions of the plant that include some root. Or store ripe seed in a cool place and sow it in spring, on the surface of a seeding mix, at 70 degrees F. Expect germination in a week or two.

Control and Removal

When you cut Mexican daisy back yearly to keep it looking fresh, you will also be keeping it from getting too big for its site. You may also want to cut it back lightly from time to time during the year to be sure it doesn't overrun small plants nearby.

The species itself will reseed. More seedlings will grow in watered gardens than in dry ones. Deadheading is not practical because there are so many flowers, but the seedlings are not hard to pull out. It is a good idea to check the ground around the edges of Mexican daisy plants for seedlings whenever you are cutting them back. This plant is probably a poor choice for a relatively untended area, where it could easily reseed and take over; however, in a garden with a modicum of care, it is quite possible to keep it in particular areas as a design element.

Digging out unwanted mature plants is not difficult, though you will need to watch nearby areas for seedlings for a couple of years after you do so. Plants growing in unwatered pavement cracks may die as the dry summer progresses, but if they do become large, they will be hard to eliminate and may require use of an herbicide.

Despite its drought tolerance and proclivity for reseeding, Mexican daisy has not been considered a wildland weed in California; however, it could earn a place on the future "Low" impact list being created by the California Exotic Pest Plant Council. We should probably be cautious based on its behavior elsewhere. It has naturalized in various places that have year-round rainfall, including southwestern England, the Channel Islands, and Australia. It is considered a major problem in Hawaii's fragile habitat; and is so weedy in New Zealand that it is illegal to sell it there. To be cautious, avoid planting near wildlands, and select the varieties that are least likely to form seed over the more freely self-seeding species.

Varieties and Similar Species

Seed sold as *Erigeron karvinskianus* 'Profusion' is probably selected from early-blooming plants but is otherwise the same as the species. *E.* x *moerheimii* (which is probably more correctly written as *E. k.* 'Moerheimii') has slightly larger flowers that are pink or lavender-pink from the time of opening. The plant is smaller (1 to 2 feet tall and 2 to 3 feet wide). Gardeners report that it reseeds less than the species, though the variety is not sold with such claims. Venders do claim that a newer cultivar, 'Spindrift' reseeds less profusely. 'Spindrift' has the normal white-to-pink fading blooms of the species and the plant is only 8 to 10 inches tall and 12 inches wide.

Erigeron glaucus (beach aster) is a California native that performs best near the coast. Most *Erigeron* species from Europe and the eastern United States are not well suited to California's climate and suffer disease problems here.

The Name

Carl Linnaeus named the genus *Erigeron* (ehr-ih'-jer-ahn) as part of his vast plant-naming effort in the mid-1700s. The word derived from the Greek roots *eri,* meaning "early" or "spring," and *geron,* which means "old" or "old man." The plant he was looking at would have been a European species, and it must have had either fluffy white seedheads or densely white, hairy buds. Mexican daisy has neither but was later classified in this genus for other identifying traits. The man who handed the five-syllable species name to this New World *Erigeron* was the French botanist Alphonse de Candolle (the same de Candolle who named the succulent genus *Echeveria*). In 1836 he chose the name *karwinskianus* (kar-win-ski-ahn'-us) to honor the botanist Baron von Wilhelm Friedrich Karwinski von Karwin, who collected the plant on his first Mexican collecting trip in 1827 to 1832.

Eschscholzia californica

✳ California poppy

PLANT TYPE: *Perennial* | HEIGHT AND SPREAD: *1 to 1½ feet tall and 1 to 3 feet wide* | BLOOM TIME: *Late winter to midsummer* | LIGHT NEEDS: *Full sun* | SOIL NEEDS: *Poor to moderately fertile, well drained* | WATER NEEDS: *Ample when young, moderate when mature* | OTHER TOLERANCES: *Cool coastal summers, seaside conditions, inland climates, snail resistant, deer resistant* | HARDINESS: *Zones 9 to 11*

The California poppy was declared the official state flower by the California legislature in 1903, after having been so designated by the California State Floral Society in 1890. During this period, California went through a sort of poppy madness. Poppies appeared frequently as a brand name, as motifs in the decorative arts, in poetry, and in song. Much was made of their golden color in relation to the gold that the forty-niners found in the

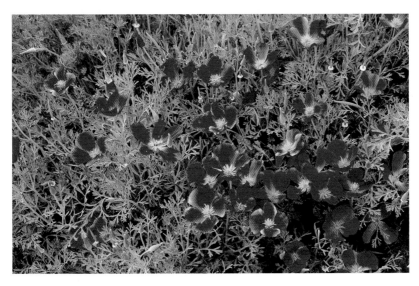

When you are seeking to produce a bright spring show quickly and inexpensively, fall-sown California poppy seed is one of the surest solutions.

'Red Chief' is one of the many cultivars available for those who would like California poppies in colors other than bright orange.

Sierra. Californians still love the poppy. In 1974, April 6 was declared "California Poppy Day," and this day is still celebrated by the state's schoolchildren.

Source and Uses

The species *Eschscholzia californica* subspecies *californica* is native in much of California, as well as into Oregon and Baja California. The first California poppy seeds to germinate in England were collected in Oregon by the plant explorer David Douglas in 1825. California poppies soon became popular in England and are now grown in gardens in many parts of the world.

The plants are dramatic en masse, either alone or with small grasses and other bright flowers and are useful in a rock garden or among succulents and cacti. The satiny blossoms close at night and on foggy or overcast days but open fully during whatever part of a day is sunny.

Care and Reproduction

Full sun and a rather infertile sandy soil will produce the best California poppy plants and the ones most likely to survive for several years. Over-rich soil reduces bloom. For the longest bloom period, you can deadhead often, cutting flower stems to a joint with a bud-bearing stem, but most gardeners wait until the plants are pretty well bloomed out and then cut them back to near the ground. These plants will usually regrow and rebloom a few weeks later in watered gardens, and may do so twice, though the plants that grow back are usually smaller than the ones produced at first.

The plants are best grown from seed. In fact, they are so easy from seed that when California native wildflower mixes contain poppies, they are usually the plant most likely to come up. In mild-winter areas, sow seed in the fall, barely covered. If rains don't do the job, water to keep the soil consistently moist for the first month or so, until seedlings are growing heartily. Seed sown in late winter or early spring may succeed, but avoid overwatering the resulting plants as the weather warms, as they become more susceptible to soil-borne disease in warmer weather. Small plants can be transplanted with some success only if they can be moved without disturbing the soil around the roots. A 2-inch-tall seedling can already have a 4-inch-long taproot, and if it is broken the plant probably won't survive.

Control and Removal

California poppies can reseed rather prolifically in a site they like, and it is easy to overlook the tiny, narrow-leaved, gray-green seedlings, which sprout most of the year in watered areas. Deadheading will reduce seeding somewhat, but some seeds will certainly pop out of their long pods before you can remove them. People sometimes have to overcome residual nervousness about harming Our State Flower to pull out unwanted plants. Just remember that each tiny seedling will form a plant at least a foot in diameter, or as wide as 3 feet in a favorable location. Thin them to at least 8 inches apart. Use a trowel or shovel to remove full-grown plants that you don't want.

Because California poppies are a treasured native species, no attempt is made to avoid their spread from gardens. It is sobering to know, however, that California poppy grows wild in parts of France and is considered a potential problem weed in Hawaii, Alaska, and even in Tennessee.

Varieties and Similar Species

Purchased seed of the orange-flowered species is most likely *Eschscholzia californica* subspecies *californica*, which you can identify by the forked seed leaves. Those of the subspecies *mexicana*, an annual plant that grows mainly in northern Mexico and Arizona, aren't forked. In the wild, the species is actually quite variable, including differences in plant size, leaf form, flower color, and width of the torus, the little red rim at the base of each flower. These variations have given plant breeders material from which to create many hybrids, including ones with white, apricot, red, pink, and burnt orange flowers, double flowers, and ones with fluted petals. Plants of hybrids are often more compact than those of the species, often only 10 to 12 inches tall.

The plants sold as *E. caespitosa* 'Sundew' are really *E. lobbii*, an annual poppy just 6 inches tall with small, pale yellow, scented flowers. It is quite useful with other small annuals.

THE NAME

The name *Eschscholzia californica* (esh-shol'-see-uh cal-ih-for'-nih-cuh) commemorates a friendship. A Russian ship visited San Francisco in October 1816 with a team of naturalists aboard. When botanist and poet Adalbert von Chamisso went plant collecting in the Presidio with his friend, Johann von Eschscholtz, the ship's surgeon, among the plants they found was a very late-blooming California poppy. Chamisso named it *Eschscholzia* after his friend (dropping the "t" in his name). Later, Eschscholtz returned the honor by naming a blue-flowered lupine collected on the trip *Lupinus chamissonis*.

Can You Pick a Poppy?

It is a common belief that there is a California law against picking California poppies, but the only relevant law on the books says it's illegal to pick any plant (that is not a noxious weed) on roadsides, in public parks, or on private property without permission of the owner. In your own garden, you are the boss.

Linaria purpurea

※ Purple toadflax, purple linaria

PLANT TYPE: *Perennial* | HEIGHT AND SPREAD: *2 to 3 feet tall and 1½ to 2 feet wide* | BLOOM TIME: *Late spring into fall* | LIGHT NEEDS: *Full sun, light shade* | SOIL NEEDS: *Any, well drained* | WATER NEEDS: *Moderate* | OTHER TOLERANCES: *Alkaline soil, cool coastal summers, hot inland summers* | HARDINESS: *Zones 5 to 11*

When I first saw the miniature snapdragon blossoms and narrow leaves of *Linaria purpurea*, I thought of the much shorter annual toadflax, *L. maroccana* 'Fairy Bouquet'. The two plants are indeed cousins, but while 'Fairy Bouquet' is fragile, difficult to get started, and

Viewed close up, the similarity of linaria blossoms to snapdragons becomes evident. This is Linaria purpurea *'Springside White'.*

A mutabilis rose and orange oriental lilies are able to peek through this screen of purple linaria. It is typical for a few pink-flowered plants to appear among the purple-flowered ones.

lives only a few months, *L. purpurea* only looks delicate. It is tough and easy to grow and comes back in future years from dormant roots or from seed. It is one of those quiet plants that combines well with showier garden flowers and can even be planted in front of them, since its open, airy growth habit lets other flowers peek through.

Source and Uses

Most of the approximately one hundred species of *Linaria* come from the Mediterranean region. *L. purpurea* is native to central Italy, southern Italy, and Sicily, where it is found on dry, often rocky slopes. It was first grown in British gardens in 1648 and has been a moderately popular cottage garden flower on and off ever since.

Some find the particular purple color of the species difficult to use in gardens. However, I think it works well with many shades of peach, pink, and lavender. Try it with roses, lilies, Mexican daisy, or with the lavender or white forms of centranthus. It can also be stunningly dramatic with orange montbretias. The pale pink–flowered variety of purple toadflax works well with pastels, and white-flowered varieties go with any color. Use purple toadflax alone or with other plants in containers at least 12 inches across and deep, and be sure to include the dainty spires in bouquets of larger flowers.

Care and Reproduction

The tiny seeds of purple toadflax are easy to collect by rolling a stem of ripe (brown) seedpods on a piece of paper. You can sow the seed in place in the fall or chill it for 3 weeks in late winter and then sow it indoors in early spring. You can also start from purchased plants or from rooted divisions of mature clumps, taken in early spring. Set plants, or thin seedlings, about a foot apart. The only problem you may encounter is that the plants like soil on the dry side, and they may succumb to root rot in unamended clay soil or garden locations where soil is constantly wet. The plants thrive and bloom best in soil that isn't very fertile, making them a good choice for starter gardens.

Each spire blooms from the bottom up. When a top spire finishes blooming, deadhead by cutting its stem and enjoy continued bloom from spires on the side stems. Eventually, all the flower spires on a branch will be spent, and you can cut that branch to the ground. Whole branches may sometimes suddenly turn brown during the growing season; cut these out as well. In the fall, when the plant looks bloomed out, cut all the old stems close to the ground leaving new growth.

Control and Removal

If you are trying to prevent reseeding, deadhead regularly so seeds can't form. If the plant does reseed, the small plants, with their whorls of short, narrow, gray-green leaves, are easy to recognize the following spring—as long as you don't plant one of the blue-green leaved flax species where you are trying to get rid of linaria. While purple toadflax isn't known to be a wildland invader, don't discard plant parts with ripe seed where they could germinate in wild places.

Be wary of introducing other plants in this genus, since at least two of them, both plants with mid-green leaves and yellow flowers, have become noxious weeds in parts of the country. *Linaria vulgaris,* often called butter and eggs, and *L. genistifolia* subspecies *dalmatica* are pests in the Northwest, and *L. vulgaris* is also a common weed in the eastern part of the country.

Varieties and Similar Species

Occasional pale pink–flowered plants pop up among plants of the purple-flowered species, and one seed mix, called Canons and Bishops, contains a more balanced proportion of the two colors. To get only plants with soft pink flowers, you need to buy the pink-flowered variety 'Canon J. Went'. (This variety is also a bit less likely to reseed than others.) For only white flowers, purchase 'Springside White' (also sold as 'Radcliffe Innocence') or 'Reverend C. E. Bowring'. A pink or white form will breed true if it is the only kind of purple toadflax present in your garden. If you are collecting seed from a stand that has mixed colors, your seed may produce any of the colors present in the stand.

The Name

Linum, Latin for "flax," is the genus name of the flax plant—the source of linen and linseed oil. *Linaria* (lin-air'-ee-uh) derives from the same Latin word and means that plants in this genus are flaxlike. The similarity is in the leaves. Both genera include species with small, narrow, blue-green leaves. However, *Linum,* which is in a different plant family, has saucer-shaped rather than two-lipped flowers. The common name toadflax means something like "false flax." If you had to weed a flax field, you would definitely need to be able to tell one from the other. The specific epithet *purpurea* (pur-pur'-ee-uh) derives from the Latin word for "purple."

There seems to have been a fashion in England to name *Linaria* varieties after clergy in the Church of England. The identity of 'Reverend C. E. Bowring' has so far proved untraceable, but Canon J. Went was indeed a real person. Canon James Went, a kind-looking man with flowing white sideburns, was the popular headmaster of Wyygeston Hospital Boys' School in Leicester, England from 1877 to 1919.

Lychnis coronaria

Rose campion, crown lychnis, dusty miller

PLANT TYPE: *Short-lived perennial* | HEIGHT AND SPREAD: *2 to 2½ feet tall and ½ to 2 feet wide* | BLOOM TIME: *Late spring into summer* | LIGHT NEEDS: *Full sun, light shade* | SOIL NEEDS: *Moderately fertile, well drained* | WATER NEEDS: *Moderate* | OTHER TOLERANCES: *Relatively infertile soil, sandy soil, limy or calcareous soils, drought tolerant, cool coastal summers, hot inland summers, snail resistant, deer resistant* | HARDINESS: *Zones 5 to 11*

The stems and narrow leaves of this hand-some plant are all covered with soft white hairs, creating a pale, silver-gray accent in the garden. The leaves resemble those of lamb's ears *(Stachys byzantina)* in color and shape, but while lamb's ears leaves feel thick and woolly, those of rose campion are thinner and silky to the touch. The plant has a wide-angled branching pattern,

These white and magenta rose campion blossoms are mingling on adjacent plants.

The bright magenta of rose campion contrasts nicely with the cool gray of its leaves.

with flowers borne singly at the stem tips. Because of this, the flowers never cover the plant densely. Although the magenta or red flowers are vivid, the blooming plant still gives an impression that is as much ice as fire.

Source and Uses

Native to the Mediterranean and eastern Europe, rose campion has ornamented gardens since Ancient Greek and Roman times, when its blooming stems were often used in garlands and wreaths. It was introduced to gardens in other parts of Europe and was first recorded as a garden plant in England in the mid-1300s. By 1597 the white form was being grown. From the early 1600s to the end of the 1700s, double-flowered forms were the most popular. It is thought that "spotted" version available by 1629 may be the one with pink-centered white flowers we still see today. Rose campion arrived in America in the mid-1700s and was grown by Thomas Jefferson at Monticello in 1807.

Try red- or magenta-flowered rose campion with other bright flowers, such as a borage and a yellow-flowered variety of calendula. White-flowered rose campion mixes equally well with brights or pastels, while the form with pink-centered flowers glows among other pastel flowers such as 'Moonshine' yarrow and 'Miss Jekyll' nigella. The plants attract hoverflies and predatory wasps, which will help your garden by eating pest insects. Cut stems for bouquets, in which the flowers will last for several days.

Care and Reproduction

Rose campion will look best if watered regularly, though it can survive drought better than it can overwatering. It is best watered at ground level, keeping moisture off the leaves. Deadheading prolongs bloom somewhat and keeps the plant looking fresh, though it is probably too much work to deadhead large plantings. Be sure you are removing the spent flowers, not the buds, since they look similar. Both are ridged and gray, but the developing seedpods are larger and have browning petals at their tops. Cut the stems of spent flowers to the next lowest flower bud or to the joint between two flower stems. In midsummer the plant will begin to have more seedpods than flowers, at which point most gardeners cut it back to the lower leaves.

Where the ground is not heavily mulched, rose campion seed will germinate to produce seedlings the following spring or summer. You can transplant these plants where you want them to bloom the following year. You can also collect seeds in late summer and press them into the surface of seeding mix indoors. While the seed is said to require a couple of weeks of chill to germinate, I have grown it without such treatment in San Francisco, perhaps because our midsummer nights are so cool. Seed sown in fall or winter may bloom the following spring, while seed sown in spring will take a year to bloom. Plant out homegrown or nursery plants in early spring, setting them 10 inches apart.

Sections of older plants often die at the end of summer, and these dead portions can be removed at this time or in the spring. Rose campion lives only a few years, but dividing large clumps into rooted sections in fall or early spring extends the life of the plants. Reproduction by division also assures that the flower color will be the same as that of the parent plants.

Control and Removal

While this plant does reseed, it generally does not do so heavily. Seedlings are easily identified by their gray-green leaves; remove or transplant them as needed. Reduce reseeding by deadheading and cutting plants back before fall, as well as by mulching the ground around the plants. Established plants are not difficult to remove by digging them out.

Varieties and Similar Species

The white-flowered form of rose campion, known as 'Alba', is as vigorous as the magenta or red-flowered form. Plants with pink-centered white blossoms are sold as 'Angel's Blush' and 'Oculata'. 'Angel's Blush' is sometimes described as having a deeper pink eye, but it is possible that the two names are describing a slight genetic or environmentally caused variation within what is actually one cultivar. The pink centers will be brighter when the weather is cool. A cultivar with double magenta flowers exists but is not common.

Several other *Lychnis* species are grown in gardens. The most common is *L. chalcedonica* (Maltese cross), a species with hairy, dark green leaves and rounded clusters of vivid red-orange flowers. There are also white-, pink-, and peach-flowered varieties for those who prefer less vivid colors. Another species, *L. flos-cuculi*, known as ragged robin, bears stems topped with several feathery pink or white flowers over a long period.

THE NAME

The genus name *Lychnis* (lick'-niss) is derived from the Greek word *lychnos* meaning "lamp." Some think this refers to the brightness of the flowers of some species, while others maintain that the leaves were used as wicks in oil lamps. The specific epithet *coronaria* means "used for coronas," from the Latin word *corona*, meaning "crown." Crowns or wreaths of flowers and leaves were common in ancient cultures of the Mediterranean, used at parties, festivals, and weddings; to crown the dead, and to festoon statues of gods. The Greeks were a bit freer with these decorations than the sober Romans, who forbade the wearing of party crowns in public.

Mirabilis jalapa

Four o'clock, marvel of Peru

PLANT TYPE: *Perennial* | HEIGHT AND SPREAD: *Variable, 2 to 5 feet tall and 3 to 4 feet wide* | BLOOM TIME: *Late spring, summer* | LIGHT NEEDS: *Sun, light shade* | SOIL NEEDS: *Moderately fertile, well drained* | WATER NEEDS: *Moderate* | OTHER TOLERANCES: *Cool coastal climates, hot inland climates, most soils, drought tolerant, deer resistant* | HARDINESS: *Zones 8 to 11*

While their exact hour of opening may vary, four o'clock flowers really really do open in the late afternoon, so that night-flying moths can pollinate them. They remain open for a while in the morning if not pollinated, maybe longer on foggy days, but essentially each flower blooms for a single night. The plant makes up for having short-lived individual blossoms by having many buds in each cluster

Bright four o'clock flowers open in the evening to attract night-flying moths, but they also attract hummingbirds.

Europeans marveled, as the Aztecs did before them, at the ability of four o'clock to bear striped and solid-colored flowers on the same plant.

and by blooming for most of the summer. A relative of bougainvillea, which has brightly colored bracts around small, white, tubular flowers, four o'clock has clusters of green bracts under large, brightly colored tubular flowers.

Source and Uses

From the English name marvel of Peru, you'd assume that this was a South American plant. Actually, it is no longer found in the wild but is thought to be native to Mexico, where it was cultivated for ornamental and medicinal uses long before the Spanish arrived. It is now found in gardens or formerly cultivated areas throughout the former Aztec sphere of influence (including around Aztec ruins) and in all of the towns established by Spain in Mexico. When the Spanish brought *Mirabilis jalapa* seed home from the New World, Europeans were mightily impressed with its fast growth, tropical appearance, and interesting flowering habits, and also by the way that it sometimes bore bicolored and single-colored flowers on the same plant.

Thomas Jefferson first grew four o'clocks in 1767 and later planted them by a window for their sweet scent. The large black seeds were surely carried to California by immigrants from both the eastern United States and Mexico. In fact, the variegated flowers in the photo on page 155 came to Northern California in the pocket of a gardener who emigrated from Mexico. The plant is now a common garden flower in most tropical regions and is grown as an annual in colder areas.

Four o'clocks have been considered old-fashioned for a couple of centuries, but they are worthy of a fresh look in informal tropical-themed or cottage gardens, where they can be striking specimen plants or can create summer hedges. They attract hummingbirds, and they often have a sweet scent that perfumes gardens in the evening.

Care and Reproduction

Four o'clock is easy to grow from seed, but it does need warm soil to germinate and warm weather to grow. Sow seeds outside in May, inside in

March or April. The plants will grow tallest and perform best with regular water and reasonably fertile soil, but they will grow with neither. When the above ground parts die back in the fall, cut and remove them.

Where winters are colder than 10 degrees F, dig the roots and overwinter them in an unheated room, packed in river sand. Fall would also be the best time to dig a dormant root and move it to a new location. Plants grown from seed may differ from the parents in flower color or other traits, while those from overwintering roots will be the same each year.

CONTROL AND REMOVAL

Where four o'clock grows larger than the space intended, it can be cut back as needed to keep it in bounds. Deadheading this plant to prevent seeding is not feasible, since the seeds form continuously during bloom and drop to the ground as soon as they are ripe. They may resow freely, but in truth the plants I have grown have not made many seedlings. The seedlings, which resemble pepper plants, are not difficult to pull when they are small.

To those who want to be rid of mature plants, the only marvel is how difficult it is to eradicate them. Few realize what lurks beneath the ground. The tuberous root, which can be a foot or more long and several inches in diameter, can be difficult to dig from hard soil, and the plant can resprout from parts you miss. Herbicides might be required to kill mature plants growing in pavement cracks.

VARIETIES AND SIMILAR SPECIES

To witness the speckled and streaked flowers that have impressed so many, look for the Broken Colors mix. Also commonly available are mixes that bloom in white, yellow, magenta-red, or pink, and you may also find seed for individual colors, such as 'Tea Time Rose'. Scent seems to be unreliable in modern strains; some plants are fragrant, others are not. Flowers of some varieties may stay open longer than others, but none stay open all day, despite advertising claims (including those of a company that sells *Mirabilis jalapa* roots under the name "Japanese Wonderflowers").

You may also see the species *M. longiflora* (4- to 5-inch-long white flowers, flushed magenta with magenta stamens, strong evening fragrance) or *M. multiflora* (from several southwestern states, bright magenta flowers, with a huge root like *M. jalapa*).

THE NAME

The genus name Linnaeus chose for this plant, *Mirabilis* (mir-uh-bee'-liss), is Latin for "able to cause wonder." It is an echo of the Spanish common name *miravilla*, meaning "miracle."

He chose the specific epithet *jalapa* (jah-lah'-puh) because four o'clock roots were sometimes confused with the roots of *Convolvulus purga*, a morning glory relative that was the source of a drug known as jalap. Both plants did grow in the vicinity of Xalapa or Jalapa, Mexico, but four o'clocks were apparently named after the drug, rather than the town. (True jalap, which is now a discredited drug, was once used as a purgative, a drug that would quickly clear the digestive system. Four o'clock root is poisonous, as is the rest of the plant, though possibly not more so than jalap itself.)

Pelargonium x domesticum

Regal geranium, Martha Washington geranium

PLANT TYPE: *Perennial* | HEIGHT AND SPREAD: *1 to 4 feet tall and 1 to 6 feet wide* | BLOOM TIME: *Mainly late spring into summer* | LIGHT NEEDS: *Full sun or light shade* | SOIL NEEDS: *Moderately fertile, well drained* | WATER NEEDS: *Moderate* | OTHER TOLERANCES: *Cool coastal climates, seaside conditions* | HARDINESS: *Zones 10 to 11*

*R*egal geranium plants, often tall and straggly, topped with their clusters of brilliantly colored 2- to 4-inch flowers, adorn many old Bay Area public and private gardens. Few people remember the names of the varieties or realize how popular they once were in their heyday, from the Victorian era to the middle of the twentieth century. These old-fashioned favorites, several of which survive on Alcatraz Island, are well worth saving for their historic charm and bright flowers.

These are two of the most common heirloom regal geraniums surviving in Northern California gardens. While the exact cultivars are difficult to trace, due to loss of records and possible mutations, they are probably (left) 'Prince Bismarck' and (right) 'Mrs. Langtry'.

Source and Uses

Regals are hybrids among several South African *Pelargonium* species that interbred in the garden of an English estate in the mid-1800s. The flowers are quite similar in form to those of *P. cucculatum*, a species that is common in the coastal Western Cape Province. There are no early records, but it is thought that the parents also include *P. angulosum*, *P. grandiflorum*, *P. fulgidum*, and perhaps others. Regals became popular in English and European gardens by the 1880s. In 1938, the California Cooperative Extension listed 88 regal varieties available here, and when the American Pelargonium Society was founded in Palo Alto in 1940, regals were the group's favorite type.

Regals were sometimes called "show geraniums" for their popularity in flower shows, for which they were grown as greenhouse plants or houseplants. However, in Southern California and coastal Northern California, gardeners also planted them in the ground. Temperatures under 30 degrees F may kill them, and frosts such as the one that struck the Bay Area in 1991 no doubt killed many of the old ones. Yet gardeners often tell me that their regal plants have been in their San Francisco gardens for forty years and more. These survivors may be particularly hardy varieties, or they may have been sheltered by their own branches or those of other plants. They may also have died to the ground and then regrew from still-living roots.

Where they are hardy enough for garden use, regals may form large, bushy accent plants. They can also provide a colorful edging along walks, steps, or fences, and they thrive in containers. The flowers are edible and nice for cake decoration, and they make excellent, long-lasting cut flowers.

Care and Reproduction

These plants are ideal near the coast, since they grow and bloom best where nights are cool: 55 to 65 degrees F. When nights are warmer, bloom ceases. While the main flush of bloom is in late spring, it will be prolonged in cool-night regions and may continue through the summer.

Regal geraniums survive in poor, dry soil; however, digging in organic amendment will help prevent root rot in clay soils and improve water retention in sandy ones. Fertilize plants in clay soil two or three times a year; in sandy soil, fertilize monthly while plants are growing, using a fertilizer with more phosphorous than nitrogen. Under- or overwatered plants develop yellow and dying lower leaves. Avoid sprinkling water on the leaves and blooms.

In pots, the plants bloom best when they are slightly rootbound. Roots may rot when the pot is too big, so never move a plant to a pot over 2 inches wider than the previous one. Water potted regals only when the soil surface has dried. While the plants are growing, fertilize with quarter-strength liquid fertilizer every time you water, shifting from a complete fertilizer to 0-10-10 during bud formation and bloom. Move containers to a protected location if frost threatens.

Regal geraniums will be much bushier and more compact if they are pinched and pruned properly. Prune after the spring flush of bloom and then again before the end of August, leaving at least half of the leaves and not cutting below the green part of the stem. Pinch during summer to shape plants and increase bushiness. Deadhead the plants, breaking off the stems of spent flower clusters where they join the main stem.

Regals can take heavy pruning, often even growing back after being cut to the ground, but before you try such drastic renovation measures, it is probably wise to also take cuttings. In late summer, take semimature cuttings (not freshly grown and not brown and woody) that include several nodes (places where leaves form). Remove any flower stems, and remove the leaves from the bottom inch or so of the cutting (including the stipules—the little green structures at the bases of the leaves). Rooting should occur within 2 or 3 weeks. (For more on growing plants from cuttings, see page 35). Pot them up, let them overwinter in a protected place, fertilizing as described earlier, and then set them in the ground when danger of frost is over.

Control and Removal

Digging regal geraniums out once is usually sufficient to remove them from the garden, though you may have to trace stems back as much as 10 feet to the main trunk to remove them. They rarely self-sow.

Varieties and Similar Species

In their heyday, regals included a vast selection of flowers. You'll still find white and shades of pink, purple, red, peach, or maroon, often marked with featherings or blotches of darker colors, or with extravagantly ruffled edges. New varieties of regals have been popular in recent years as potted gift plants. Named old varieties are also still available for purchase. Another good source is cuttings from plants in old gardens, since these plants show proof of long-term success. Some may be "sports," or mutations of old varieties, and so not identifiable but still worth growing.

The newer varieties called angel and pansy geraniums have some advantages over regals. The plants grow to only a foot or so tall and their smaller but equally elegant flowers bloom longer into summer. You may find them in your local nursery or from mail-order sources.

The Name

(See "The Name" under the next entry, *Pelargonium* x *hortorum*, for more information about the name "Pelargonium" and the "x" in the name.) The specific epithet *domesticum* derives from the Latin word *domus*, meaning "house." The common name regal geranium became popular because King Edward VII owned the estate where they first appeared. The common name Martha Washington geranium is the result of an American misunderstanding; the British sometimes called them Lady Washington, but they were referring to a British noblewoman, not our founding first lady.

Pelargonium x *hortorum*

Zonal geranium, common geranium, bedding geranium

PLANT TYPE: *Perennial* | HEIGHT AND SPREAD: *To 3 feet tall and 3 feet wide (often smaller)* | BLOOM TIME: *Spring, summer* | LIGHT NEEDS: *Full sun or light shade* | SOIL NEEDS: *Fertile, well drained* | WATER NEEDS: *Moderate* | OTHER TOLERANCES: *Cool coastal climates, seaside conditions, hot inland summers* | HARDINESS: *Zones 10 to 11*

onal geraniums are the traditional geraniums of window box fame, used as annuals in cold-winter areas or painstakingly overwintered indoors. Well cared for, zonal geraniums inspire cheeriness with their red, coral, pink, or white flower clusters and variegated leaves that are often strikingly attractive in their own right. They may survive unattended in protected Northern California locations, but

Ivy geranium (P. peltatum) *offers a less disease-prone alternative to the more common Zonal geranium.*

'Vancouver Centennial' is one of the zonal geranium varieties grown primarily for its variegated leaves.

without care they are often spindly and nearly leafless, and struggle against disease.

Source and Uses

The principle parents of zonal geraniums are two South African species: *Pelargonium zonale* (which has a faint brownish band on each leaf) and *P. inquinans;* both were sent to Europe from the South African Dutch colony in the early 1700s. By 1860 there were varieties with bicolor or tricolor leaves, including white, yellow, chartreuse, red, and maroon. Victorian "carpet bedders" often removed the flowers so the leaves alone would provide color in their formal planting patterns. Breeders also created double and other fancy flower forms, including "stellars," with starry flowers and distinctive pointy leaves.

In 1786, Thomas Jefferson sent zonal geraniums to the United States from France, and throughout his presidency he kept a potted plant in Washington. Zonal geraniums were among the first plants available in San Francisco nurseries as early as 1850.

While zonal geraniums are classic choices for window boxes and other containers, they can also be used in the ground, where they can fit into a number of themes, including cottage, Victorian, mediterranean, or tropical.

Care and Reproduction

Zonal geraniums, like regals, will be damaged at temperatures below 30 degrees F. Soil, water, and fertilizer needs are also about the same, but pruning is a little different. Prune in spring, starting by removing canes that are dead, damaged, or very spindly. Then cut 25 to 30 percent of the stems (choose the least leafy ones) to just above their two lowest leaves. If the plant is still ugly, wait until the cut stems show new growth and then cut more back until the shape of the plant improves. Pinch tips at any time up to the end of August to increase bushiness. Spent flower clusters often fall off; they can be cut to the base of the flower stem if they don't.

Any seed that is produced is not likely to develop into plants with the same features as the parents, so these plants are best grown from cuttings. Follow the same directions as for regals, but you can take cuttings in spring as well as in late summer without losing the main flush of bloom, since zonals bloom more continuously over the summer.

Zonals are more likely than regals to suffer from diseases such as virus or rust. Avoid watering the plants from above, especially late in the day. If diseases appear, it is best to remove the affected plants.

Control and Removal

Zonal geraniums rarely self-sow. If you want to eliminate a plant, you will find it easy to dig out.

Varieties and Similar Species

There are many new cultivars with bicolored and tricolored leaves, and you can also still find older ones, such as 'Crystal Palace Gem' (light green, chartreuse edges), 'Happy Thought' (green, cream center splash), and 'Mrs. Henry Cox' (multicolored). Single flowers are probably a better bet where summer fog is heavy, as doubles are more likely to rot in damp weather. You may find seed for zonal geraniums. It is generally for hybrids that have been bred to make uniform, compact bedding plants, such as those used as annuals in cold-winter regions.

Stellar geraniums, which have pointy leaf and flower shapes due to a single different gene, have become very popular in recent years as novelty foliage plants. They keep their dramatic leaf coloring even in relatively shady places, though they may not flower there. Examples are bicolored 'Vancouver Centennial' and 'Golden Ears' and the more recently introduced tricolors.

Ivy geraniums are *Pelargonium peltatum*, a species with shiny, ivy-shaped leaves and a trailing or clambering habit. While they are at their best in milder climates, and generally look terrible in Northern California winters, on average neglected ivy geraniums look better than neglected zonals, perhaps because they are less likely to become diseased.

They can climb fences or other plants for a spectactular show of pink, coral, red, or bicolored flowers all summer long.

THE NAME

European geraniums, or cranesbills, are frost-hardy perennials with flowers having five identical petals and seedheads that reminded people of bird's bills. The name *Geranium* derives from the Greek word *geranos,* meaning "crane." When plant explorers brought *Pelargonium* species from South Africa beginning in the 1600s, most botanists looked at the similar seedpods and dubbed them *Geranium* species. Carl Linnaeus classified them as such, and so they remained until 1789, when the French botanist Charles Louis L'Heretier (1746–1800) created the separate genus *Pelargonium* for them. The new name derived from the Greek word *pelargos,* meaning "stork." Among the significant differences between the two genera are that most *Pelargonium* species are tender to frost, and their flowers usually have unequal petals—that is, the top two are different in shape, and often different in color, than the bottom petals. Despite the new classification, most gardeners still call these plants geraniums.

Pelargonium x *hortorum* means "the storksbill of gardens." The "x" refers to the fact that the plants are the product of parents that were of two or more species. You can hear the Latin word *hortus,* meaning "garden," not only in the name of this plant, but also in the English word "horticulture," which refers to the practice of gardening.

Pelargonium (various species)

⬛ Scented geranium

PLANT TYPE: **Perennial** | HEIGHT AND SPREAD: **Varies by species (1 to 7 feet tall and 2 to 8 feet wide)** | BLOOM TIME: **Spring to fall** | LIGHT NEEDS: **Full sun or light shade** | SOIL NEEDS: **Moderately fertile, well drained** | WATER NEEDS: **Moderate** | OTHER TOLERANCES: **Low fertility, cool coastal climates, seaside conditions, hot inland climates** | HARDINESS: **Zones 9b to 11**

*T*he classification "scented geranium" is not a botanical one but really a catchall term for a group of *Pelargonium* species and varieties that are grown primarily for the fact that the leaves, when rubbed gently, produce an aroma. Even this designation is not quite correct, since one group, called the oakleaf pelargoniums, has little scent. Still, a number of wonderful plants are generally placed in this group. They are easy to grow and fit well into many garden plans.

A common heirloom scented geranium in Northern California gardens, 'Brilliant' is an excellent performer as a low hedge or draping over a retaining wall.

Peppermint-scented 'Chocolate Mint' scented geranium has chocolate-brown splotched leaves and delicate pink blossoms.

Source and Uses

All of these plants originated in South Africa. Some, such as *Pelargonium crispum* (with small, crinkly, lemon-scented leaves) and *P. tomentosum* (which has large, furry, peppermint-scented leaves), are species. Many others are the result of crosses between or among species.

Historically, gardeners have been most interested in these plants either for use in cooking and sachets or as novelties to be grown in cold climates as annuals or houseplants. But in milder parts of Northern California, many of these plants are proving to be handsome additions to the landscape as well. The flowers are generally small but may be quite pretty, the foliage remains attractive most of the year, and the scent is a bonus.

In scouting local gardens for naturalized pelargoniums, I have discovered that a number of them are scented types. One of them, 'Brilliant' (or 'California Brilliant'), is quite common in older Bay Area gardens, where it makes a handsome low border or, given a chance, will climb several feet up a fence or drape over a retaining wall. It is rose scented with 1-inch cerise-pink–centered red flowers in clusters 3 inches across. Other rose- or lemon-scented varieties with small pink or lavender flowers are also common.

Many varieties of scented geraniums make excellent container plants. Some are upright, while others drape nicely over the edges of the pots. If frost threatens, move them to a somewhat protected spot during the coldest months. In the ground, scented geraniums are useful in rock gardens, make good fillers among shrubs or bold-textured plants such as gingers and phormiums, and can also mix with any succulents that tolerate some summer water. The edible flowers can be used to scent baked goods. They also make long-lasting cut flowers.

Care and Reproduction

Like other pelargoniums, scented species tolerate low fertility, but they perform better if fertilized. Because these species are mainly from eastern South Africa, which has little rain and dry winters, good drainage is particularly important. While hardiness varies among species, scented geraniums typically tolerate temperatures to 25 degrees F.

Trim scented geraniums to shape them and keep them in bounds. Remove any brown leaves to keep plants looking good. If you need to prune to reduce size, do so in late summer but before the end of August, so the plants won't go into winter with tender new growth that may be damaged by frost.

Grow more plants by means of cuttings, as described for regal geraniums (page 160).

CONTROL AND REMOVAL

Once dug out, scented geraniums are not likely to return, and they do not typically self-sow.

VARIETIES AND SIMILAR SPECIES

Out of the vast numbers of scented geranium species and cultivars that had become quite confused by mid-twentieth century, horticulturists have drawn some semblance of order. They have classified the plants first by scent, then by leaf shape and color, and finally by flower color and form. The nose is not always objective, so you may not agree with the experts. If scent is an important criterion for you in selecting a plant, brush the leaves gently to smell them before you buy.

If you are looking for plants to use in the landscape, the following are a few of the many good choices:

✸ *P*. 'Brilliant': Rose scented (described earlier).

✸ *P*. 'Chocolate Mint': Mint-scented, large, lobed, furry leaves with brown central blotches; small, rose-veined pink flowers. A sprawling plant that can reach 4 feet tall and 8 feet wide if watered well in summer, but usually smaller. Takes partial shade.

✸ *P*. 'Grey Lady Plymouth': Rose-scented, silvery-green leaves with a narrow cream edge, and small pink-lavender flowers.

✸ *P*. 'Mrs. Taylor': Musk-scented, small, dark green leaves and bright red flowers. Long blooming. (Shown on page 11.)

✳ *P.* 'Prince Rupert Variegated': Lemon-scented, pale green leaves with small, crinkled, cream edges on long, upright stems, and lavender flowers.

The Name

For more on *Pelargonium,* see "The Name" under *Pelargonium* x *hortorum.* Unlike most of the entries in this book, scented geraniums comprise a group of several species and their many hybrids. Some of the main species involved are lemon-scented *P. crispum,* rose-scented *P. graveolens* (grah-vee-oh'-lens), apple-scented *P. odoratissimum* (oh-door-uh-tiss'-sih-mum), and peppermint-scented *P. tomentosum* (tow-men-tow'-sum). Some of the angel-type pelargoniums have some lemon scent because *P. crispum* was used in some of the breeding that created them; however, they are not classified as scented pelargoniums.

Mosquito Geraniums

Pelargoniums sold as mosquito-repellent plants are bioengineered to contain a gene that produces the scent of citronella, which is found naturally in a grass, *Cymbopogan nardus.* While the chemical citronella does repel mosquitoes, no research has been done to confirm the claim that the pelargonium plant containing the gene repels them also.

Pericallis × hybrida
(Senecio × hybridus, Senecio cruentus, Cineraria stellata)

Cineraria

PLANT TYPE: *Perennial* | HEIGHT AND SPREAD: *1 to 4 feet tall and 1 to 3 feet wide* | BLOOM TIME: *Mainly spring* | LIGHT NEEDS: *Full sun to shade* | SOIL NEEDS: *Moderately fertile, organic, well drained* | WATER NEEDS: *Moderate* | OTHER TOLERANCES: *Poor soil, clay soil, cool coastal summers, seaside conditions, deer resistant* | HARDINESS: *Zones 9b to 11*

The tall, spring-blooming, purple daisies that have naturalized in near-coastal Central and Northern California gardens are varieties of florist's cineraria. In cold-winter regions, short, squat types with broad masses of flowers are sold as houseplants, but here the species shows its perennial nature. Many of the ones in gardens are an older, taller variety, but when houseplant types are grown nearby, they interbreed. Houseplant forms often add

A palm-like cycad (left) creates a tropical effect in this partly shady border. Bright purple cineraria blossoms add color.

A picket fence adorned with various shades of cineraria flowers makes one think of a country cottage.

more flower colors to the mix but usually do not alter the tall, open habit of the naturalized plants.

Source and Uses

All of the ancestors of our domestic cinerarias grow wild only on the Canary Islands. They inhabit the "cloud zone" at middle elevations on the north sides of several of the islands. Though this zone gets only about 10 inches of rain each winter, winter fog adds enough moisture that oak and laurel forests cover the slopes. *Pericallis* species grow in the forest and on rocky cliffs, sprouting in the autumn and dying back in the warm, dry summers.

Modern *Pericallis* hybrids were created in the early 1800s by English plant breeders. The original crosses were not recorded, but evidence points to *P. heritieri*, *P. tussilaginis*, and *P. cruentus* as the main parents. Additional species may have been involved in those early hybrids or in more recent ones.

Left to its own in untended gardens, naturalized *Pericallis* x *hybrida* grows as it would in the wild. Seeds germinate in the fall, and flowers appear in spring. Some plants die in summer, while others regrow each fall from surviving roots. Even when grown in watered gardens, the main bloom period is still in spring, though occasional plants may bloom at other times.

The brilliant magenta, purple, blue-purple, pink, lavender, white, and two-tone flowers of naturalized *Pericallis* light up shady areas. They are most often used in less formal gardens, allowed to form drifts under trees or flowery skirts under shrubbery. In formal gardens, the gardener will need to keep a firm hand to avoid unwanted volunteer plants. Having said that, they look very nice in beds that are surrounded by low formal hedges, either massed alone or in combination with callas, foxgloves, or other naturalizing spring bloomers. They can reach full size in containers 12 inches or more in diameter, but plants grown in smaller pots are still quite attractive.

Care and Reproduction

Collect ripe seedheads in late spring and keep them in a paper bag so they can dry. Scatter seed on prepared soil in the fall. Let rain water it, then thin the seedlings to stand 6 to 8 inches apart. Nurseries sometimes sell plants in six-packs in the spring—ask for the tall variety of cineraria or for *Cineraria stellata*.

These plants don't do well in temperatures over 68 degrees F, and they sustain some damage in any frost. They do, however, recover quickly from moderate frost damage and can be protected from light frosts by being grown under architectural overhangs or trees. While the plants survive summer drought in a dormant state, they need regular water while blooming, to keep the leaves from dying prematurely.

Some gardeners pull all of the plants out every year and let them reproduce from fallen seeds. Others cut them to near the ground in summer and let them regrow in the fall. If the plants are allowed to grow from year to year, they become taller and have more flowering stems.

Chrysanthemum leafminer, a fly larva that tunnels in the leaves, creating trails, is often a problem. In informal settings, gardeners usually ignore these, but summer oil spray can be used to limit their reproduction.

Control and Removal

To completely prevent seeding, you would have to cut blooms when the tiny flowers that form in the centers of the daisies first fade, since the seeds are about to mature at that point. If any have formed fluffy seedheads, use flower shears to cut the stems, and drop your prunings into a wide paper bag to prevent the seeds from blowing away as you remove them. However, even if most of the seeds have blown from the plants, it is still worthwhile to cut off the stems of brown nubs, since they will still enclose a few seeds.

To control color, pull out plants with flower colors you don't like before they can make seed. Save plants with flower colors you do like by tagging their stems near the ground so you won't accidentally pull them.

Seedlings will pop up in profusion where *Pericallis* x *hybrida* has gone to seed—throughout summer where soil is moist, or with fall rains and into winter in unwatered gardens. When they are small, with only a few leaves, they are easy to pull out by hand, but once they are a few inches tall, the tops will break off, leaving the roots. To remove larger plants, hook a finger under the base of the plants, or use a trowel or shovel. Plants that are several years old will develop hefty root masses and will be rather difficult to dig, but once out, they will not return.

Varieties and Similar Species

Check out florist's cinerarias for new colors, such as red tones and bicolored flowers. Let them go to seed to add their colors to the mix in your garden.

The Name

This plant was once included in the plant genus *Cineraria*, and that genus name stuck as its common name. Since then, it was reclassified into the genus *Senecio*, and botanists have most recently recommended separating it into the genus *Pericallis*. The word *Pericallis* (pear-ih-cal'-liss) derives from the Greek prefix *peri* ("around") and the word *calli* ("beautiful"), referring to the beauty of the ray flowers (what we call the petals of a daisy). The "x" in the middle of the scientific name means that more than one species was used to create the hybrid, and the specific epithet *hybrida* derives from the Latin word meaning "of mixed parentage."

Persicaria capitata *(Polygonum capitatum)*

🌸 Pink fleece flower, rose carpet knotweed

PLANT TYPE: *Perennial* | **HEIGHT AND SPREAD:** *3 to 6 inches tall and 20 inches or more wide, spreading* | **BLOOM TIME:** *Spring, summer, fall* | **LIGHT NEEDS:** *Full sun or partial shade* | **SOIL NEEDS:** *Poor to moderately fertile, well drained* | **WATER NEEDS:** *Little to moderate* | **OTHER TOLERANCES:** *Sandy soil, cool coastal summers* | **HARDINESS:** *Zones 8 to 11*

*P*lants in this genus have been known as knotweeds or smartweeds or fleece flowers, but this particular species has never had a well-known common name of its own. Though I have seen the names "pink fleece flower" and "rose carpet knotweed" in books, most people seem to know it as "that little pink-flowered thing that crawls around," which is sort of like having a dog that answers to "Hey, you." Creep

The delicate pink flowers and chevron-marked leaves of Persicaria capitata *are especially handsome with gray stone and blue-green companion plants, such as this blue fescue grass.*

P. capitata *and Mexican daisy have both seeded themselves in this stone wall and have mingled prettily.*

around it does, anonymously or not, making a dainty ground cover or growing charmingly through pavement cracks. It has the distinction of being a plant that looks rather nice in small quantities but tends to cover large areas rather quickly, and of being a plant that survives in the absence of care but looks much better with a little attention.

Source and Uses

Persicaria capitata has a broad native range in the lower elevations of the Himalayan Mountains, from Pakistan to southwestern China, growing at 1,800 to 7,200 feet. It is common there in cultivated areas, on embankments, and among rocks. It was brought to Europe in the 1800s, a rather unassuming and unsung contribution to our gardens from a region that brought us many more fashionable plants, including rhododendrons, primroses, and blue poppies.

Where a tough ground cover is called for, such as around a street tree or on sloping ground, this plant fits the bill. It is sometimes used with Mexican daisy, letting them fight it out for the territory. It will grow in cracks in vertical walls or cascade over a retaining wall, and can take light foot traffic. If kept under control—that is, pruned often enough that rocks and other plants can also be seen—it can make a very nice small-scale rock garden plant. Even when the plant is growing well, a few leaves will become brick red, and when it is stressed, more will do so. Because of this, it is more handsome when growing against contrasting gray rock, concrete, or weathered wood than with brick or concrete painted brick red.

Care and Reproduction

To create a ground cover, plant *Persicaria capitata* plugs 12 inches apart. Once it is growing well, it will survive with little or no water, but without occasional irrigation some leaves will turn red and then lower leaves will shrivel. Leaves also turn redder in winter. They are damaged by frost, and temperatures below 25 degrees F will generally kill the aboveground part of the plant. The roots will survive to about 15 degrees F. However, even if cold kills the roots, the plant is likely to regrow in spring from seed. Groom plants throughout the year, removing any frost-damaged or weak, unattractive branches.

Persicaria capitata forms roots along the creeping stems where they touch moist soil, so you can start new plantings by replanting rooted sections of stem. It is also easy to root new plants from cuttings. In summer or fall, cut off stem tips that include several leaf nodes. Remove the lower leaves and plant the cuttings by burying several nodes in moist garden soil, or root them in cutting mix (see pages 35–37).

CONTROL AND REMOVAL

To be sure that *Persicaria capitata* won't spread into areas where it isn't wanted, use it in confined areas, such as in beds surrounded by concrete. When thus contained, it may still grow unrooted stems several feet long over bare pavement that you will sometimes need to cut back. Where it shares a space with other plants, or with garden features such as rocks, trim it frequently to keep it from engulfing everything. Do not plant it where it can get into low, dense shrubbery, or it will grow under the shrubs and poke up through them, becoming very difficult to remove.

Should you wish to be rid of *Persicaria capitata*, as long as it is in an accessible location (and not under creeping junipers, for example), you will find it rather easy to remove. The roots, which form along the stem as the plant grows, are shallow, so you can simply scrape the plant away with a hoe. If it grows back, scrape again, or, if the roots are in pavement cracks, you may need to use an herbicide. The plant is not on any California weed lists, but it is considered an unwanted invader in New Zealand and parts of Australia.

VARIETIES AND SIMILAR SPECIES

Persicaria capitata is sold under several variety names, including 'Magic Carpet', 'Afghan', and 'Pink Bubbles', but the descriptions of these plants do not say how they vary from the species, and indeed it is likely that they do not.

Several larger *Persicaria* species with narrow upright spikes of small pink, red, or white flowers are sometimes grown in gardens. Also worth looking for are ones with variegated leaves, such as *P. virginiana* 'Painter's Palette' (variegated green, off-white, brown, and pink), or *P. microcephala* 'Red Dragon' (purple with silver and green markings). A tall annual with dangling flower heads is *P. orientale*, known as kiss-me-over-the-garden-gate. Some species are terribly weedy and best avoided, notably *P. cuspidatum* (Japanese knotweed or Mexican bamboo).

THE NAME

Botanists do not agree whether this plant should be called *Polygonum* or *Persicaria*. In either case, it is still a member of the plant family *Polygonaceae*, the name of which derives from the Greek words *polys* ("many") and *gony* ("knee"), for the kneelike thickenings where the leaves join the stems. The new genus name *Persicaria* (per-sih-kahr'-ee-uh) means "peachlike" and derives from the Latin word *persicum*, which means "peach." What botanists found peachy about the former *Polygonum* species is not clear. Perhaps the shape of the leaves in one of the species reminded someone of peach leaves. The specific epithet *capitata* is from the Latin word *caput*, meaning "head," a name chosen to describe the little round flowerheads.

Salvia leucantha

Mexican sage, velvet sage

PLANT TYPE: *Perennial* | HEIGHT AND SPREAD: *2 to 4 feet tall and 3 to 6 feet wide* | BLOOM TIME: *Spring through fall* | LIGHT NEEDS: *Sun, light shade* | SOIL NEEDS: *Moderately fertile, well drained* | WATER NEEDS: *Little to moderate* | OTHER TOLERANCES: *Poor soil, acid or alkaline soil, clay soil, drought tolerant, cool coastal climate, hot inland climate, snail resistant, deer resistant* | HARDINESS: *Zones 9 to 11*

*I*f you look closely at this plant, you will see some of the features that place it in the mint family: square stems, opposite pairs of leaves, and whorls of tubular, two-lipped flowers. Although many mint family plants have fragrant leaves, including many *Salvia* species, this one has little scent. It is grown instead for its handsome gray-green foliage and arching stems of flowers. The velvety

The Mexican sage that European botanists first carried to Europe was a white-petaled variety shown here.

Mexican sage adds to the cottage garden charm of a border that also includes society garlic (Tulbaghia violacea), *a blue-flowered* Salvia, *and white centranthus.*

purple part of the flower is the calyx, or bud cover. The petals, which can be either purple or white, form a tube that extends from the calyx.

SOURCE AND USES

Salvia leucantha grows wild in the tropical and subtropical pine forests of central and eastern Mexico. White-flowered plants were first collected by Europeans in the late 1700s and were introduced in England in 1846. They were being grown in Santa Cruz, California, by as early as 1896, most likely imported from Europe. The first purple-petaled forms were collected in the wild at the end of the 1800s or early in the 1900s. Both forms are now grown in gardens around the world, where they are valued for their beauty and adaptability.

Although it is generally considered a perennial, Mexican sage gives the impression of a shrub and can fill a place in a low shrub border most of the year. It has a long bloom period, sometimes starting in spring, other

Mexican sage with purple petals was brought into cultivation about a century after the white-petaled kind. This unnamed variety has red-purple flowers and calyces.

years looking best from midsummer on, but always blooming into fall. It is a good plant for a drought-tolerant, mediterranean-style garden, and it arches nicely out of a container or over a retaining wall. Hummingbirds will hover to sip nectar from the flowers. In bouquets, the petals may fall rather quickly, but the fuzzy purple calyces remain on the stems.

CARE AND REPRODUCTION

These plants are not fussy about the soil, as long as it is not kept too wet. Give infrequent deep watering during the summer, and make sure the soil provides good drainage. When the plants are young, pinch off the branch tips. Each branch you pinch will form two branches, and more branches will result in more flower stems. Later, deadhead the faded flower stems, making the cut down into the leafy part of the branch, to encourage new ones to form. The plant looks best as an informal specimen, rather than a formally sheared one, so do not "give it a haircut" with hedge shears.

For the best appearance, cut this plant back hard every year and allow it to regrow. Some gardeners cut it to the ground in December; others wait and then cut last year's growth to the ground in late winter just as new growth emerges. Cutting the plant back once a year keeps it fresh and compact and removes any winter-damaged branches. If a plant was not cut back, you can still improve its summer appearance somewhat by cutting out last year's dead flower stems in spring or summer, along with any lanky, poorly leafed out, or frost-damaged branches.

To divide overgrown clumps, dig them in late winter just as they begin to grow, separating sections by hand or with a shovel or machete. The plant will also grow easily from tip cuttings taken in late summer. In spring, it can be ground layered. (Gently bend a branch to the ground, strip the leaves from its middle, and bury the bare part in soil. Stake the leafy branch tip to keep it upright. By fall the buried branch should have roots. Cut the branch from the plant, dig it, and replant.)

Control and Removal

Mexican sage rarely reseeds, and the plants are not difficult to remove by using a spading fork to dig around the rootball.

Varieties and Similar Species

There is some variation in the purple of the calyces and, in purple-petaled forms, of the petals, from blue-violet through red-violet. The different color forms don't seem to have uniform names. 'Midnight' is a named all-purple variety. A genetic sport of 'Midnight' named 'Eder' has leaves with an uneven creamy-white edge. 'Santa Barbara' is purple-petaled and about 60 percent of the size of the species, 2 to 3 feet tall by 4 to 6 feet wide. Hybrids with *S. leucantha* as one parent are also appearing on the market.

Of the many perennial *Salvia* species, until the past 20 years three were mainly grown in Northern California gardens: *S. leucantha*, *S. officinalis* (culinary sage, pink or purple flowers), and *S. elegans* (pineapple-scented sage, red flowers in fall). All are good choices, but many more are available, ranging widely in size, flower color, and climatic adaptation—far too many to list here. For help in choosing the best ones for your garden's style and microclimate, refer to the books listed in Suggested Reading (page 295). You may find a wider selection of these plants at specialty nurseries and at sales sponsored by nonprofit groups. For help in locating these, see Resources (page 299).

The Name

In 1753 Carl Linnaeus named a plant known in the Mediterranean region since ancient times *Salvia officinalis*. The genus name is the ancient Latin name for this plant, which derives from the Latin word *salvus*, meaning "safe," "well," or "sound." Linnaeus doubly emphasized the medicinal value of the plant by choosing the species name *officinalis*, which means it was the official sage of pharmacists. (Today we use this plant mainly as a seasoning for meat dishes.) At the time he named this plant, Linnaeus knew of only 28 sage species. The vast majority of the

900 or more species were growing, unknown to him, in the New World and East Asia. By 1791, samples of Mexican sage reached Antonio José Cavanilles (1745–1804), the leading Spanish botanist of that century. He placed it in the genus *Salvia* and gave it the specific epithet *leucantha* (lew-kan'-thuh). This word derives from the Greek words *leuco* ("white") and *anthos* ("flower"), reminding us that the plants he first described were the white-flowered ones.

Soleirolia soleirolii *(Helxine soleirolii)*

 Baby's tears, angel's tears, mind-your-own-business, Soleirol's curse

PLANT TYPE: *Perennial* | HEIGHT AND SPREAD: *3 inches tall and indefinite spread* | BLOOM TIME: *Summer* | LIGHT NEEDS: *Shade, partial shade* | SOIL NEEDS: *Not particular* | WATER NEEDS: *Moderate to ample* | OTHER TOLERANCES: *Low soil fertility, shallow soil, cool coastal climates, more sun near the coast* | HARDINESS: *Zones 9 to 11*

When Joseph Francois Soleirol, a French botanist and military officer who lived from 1781 to 1863, discovered baby's tears growing on the island of Corsica, the plant was unknown outside of its native areas. Europeans were soon charmed by its carpet of tiny, bright green leaves. It became a popular houseplant and, where winters are mild, a garden plant, though it occasionally horrifies gardeners by its rapid spread and its tenacity in the face of eradication efforts.

Baby's tears spill down the edge of a shady stairway. Growing through the baby's tears are a groundcover campanula, cineraria, and young centranthus plants.

A fern and the leaves of an out-of-bloom azalea create a green-on-green pattern with baby's tears in a shady corner.

Source and Uses

Baby's tears is native only to the islands of Corsica, Sardinia, and Majorca, in the Mediterranean Sea, where it grows in moist, shady places, mainly in the cooler mountain areas. In Corsica, it is found growing on rocks in olive groves. High in the Corsican mountains, it is found in habitats like the walls of the Restonica River gorge, where it clings to rocky cliffs while, far below, the river roars over falls and swirls in whirlpools.

Baby's tears has been valued since the Victorian era as a ground cover in garden areas so shady that little else may grow. It has also proven a handsome filler between paving stones and in cracks of shady walls, or as a ground cover under single-trunked plants in containers. Victorians used baby's tears as a houseplant in terrariums, in shallow trays, and to cover topiaries.

Because it creeps in shady places, because the leaves are so small, and because the flowers are barely visible, many people think that baby's tears is a nonflowering plant, maybe a sort of moss. However, flower it does. There are, in fact, two kinds of flowers, male and female, both lacking petals, and both so tiny that you will see them only when peering at the plants at close range.

Like its relatives, nettles and the common California weed pellitory (*Parietaria*), baby's tears is a larval food plant for red admiral butterflies (black wings with reddish markings). While I haven't noticed any chewed-up leaves, I have noticed red admirals lingering on the plants—probably planning to lay eggs there.

Care and Reproduction

Establish baby's tears from small clumps. You can buy these or dig your own from an existing planting. In late spring, dig sections of the plant with an inch or so of soil attached, and then cut them into 1- to 2-inch-diameter plugs. Set the plugs 10 to 12 inches apart in open ground, or 6 inches apart in cracks among paving stones, and keep the soil moist while the plants become established. Although the plants are from places with no summer rain, they require regular summer water to look their best in our gardens. They will die back after a frost, but the roots usually survive and allow the plant to grow back if temperatures don't drop below 23 degrees F.

CONTROL AND REMOVAL

When baby's tears is grown in an unmortared wall or between stepping-stones, it may need to be cut or torn back periodically to keep some stone exposed. (Parts of the plant growing too far from the soil may also be yellowish and thin.) When it is used as a ground cover in shady beds, it can engulf shorter plants, such as primroses, and cover the base of taller ones. Only experience will tell you which other plants will be able to hold their own in a particular patch of baby's tears and how often you will need to tear it back from (or out of) other plants to let them survive in it. It will tend to grow taller in deep shade than in lighter shade.

Baby's tears often spreads into adjacent shaded areas where it is not wanted. If it adjoins a lawn that is thin due to shade, it may grow into the lawn (where it will at least be greener than the struggling lawn). The best plan, if you are designing a garden, would be to put baby's tears where it can spread to the edge of a shaded, moist area with little foot traffic, in hopes that when it reaches that edge, its spread will be halted by bright sunlight, drier soil, foot traffic, or a combination of these. Or grow it where it will be stopped by a paved area.

You can probably get rid of this plant if you remove it persistently. You will need to grub it out at least once, taking the top inch or so of soil to prevent regrowth from the fragile roots and from seeds. (Don't leave the plants you removed where they can grow again, either.) Gardeners used to kill baby's tears by wetting it and then sprinkling it with iron sulfate. Treated areas will turn black and die, but it tends to grow back eventually, so the process must usually be repeated. If you try this, take care not to burn other plants growing with it (watering it off of their leaves will help), and avoid getting iron sulfate on pavement, as it will stain badly.

Varieties and Similar Species

The variety 'Aurea' has gold-colored leaves that look their best in light shade. 'Variegata' or 'Silver Queen' has leaves edged with white. This variegated form is probably better left to containers or houseplant use, since it tends to revert to all green, and it is a big nuisance to pick out the green-leaved parts to keep it looking good.

The Name

Both the tongue-twisting genus name and specific epithets of this plant name commemorate Joseph Francois Soleirol. The genus name *Soleirolia* (so-lee-ih-row'-lee-uh) is a noun, while the second *soleirolii* (so-lee-ih-row'-lee-eye) is an adjective. You may see other names for this plant. It was classified as a *Parietaria* for a while, and you may find it in books or nursery lists under the former name *Helxine soleirolii*.

Tanacetum parthenium
(Chrysanthemum parthenium, Matricaria parthenium)

 Feverfew

PLANT TYPE: *Short-lived perennial* | HEIGHT AND SPREAD: *1 to 3 feet tall and 1 to 2 feet wide* | BLOOM TIME: *Spring, summer* | LIGHT NEEDS: *Full sun, partial shade* | SOIL NEEDS: *Moderately fertile, well drained* | WATER NEEDS: *Moderate* | OTHER TOLERANCES: *Poor soil, cool coastal climate, hot inland climate, snail resistant, deer resistant* | HARDINESS: *Zones 4 to 11*

Though its feathery leaves and small white flowers are unassuming, feverfew is a wonderful plant to nestle among cottage garden flowers or among bolder forms such as canna or grasses. It is equally successful as a filler in bouquets, adding needed white accents among bigger and more colorful flowers. It has been used for centuries all over Europe and Great Britain

Under a blooming feverfew is a golden feverfew with columbines and johnny-jump-ups.

Feathery, chartreuse, golden feverfew with (clockwise from bottom) Stachys byzantina *'Silver Carpet',* Artemisia *'Powis Castle', white pyrethrum daisy,* TROPICANNA *canna, columbine,* Bidens *'Goldmarie', and alpine strawberry.*

as both an ornamental plant and a medicinal herb. Its name suggests it could reduce fever, which it probably can't do, but it has shown promise in scientific studies as a possible preventive for migraine headaches.

SOURCE AND USES

Feverfew is native to mountain scrub and rocky places in southeastern Europe. Its inclusion in English gardens dates from at least the 1400s, when it was included in an early "how-to" book, *The Feate of Gardening* by Master Ion Gardener. A form with double flowers was available by the next century, and by the 1700s there were varieties like our modern 'Silver Ball'. Victorians loved the chartreuse-leaved variety for bedding schemes. Modern gardeners also find this variety particularly useful, especially in combination with other plants that depend on unusual leaf color for impact. The plant has the added benefit of attracting hoverflies, the larvae of which will eat aphids in your garden.

CARE AND REPRODUCTION

Feverfew is easy to grow from seed, best sown in February or March, or you can start with nursery plants. Set plants a foot or so apart, dwarf varieties 8 to 10 inches apart. If you are growing the chartreuse-leaved form for its foliage, you may want to pinch off any flower stems that form. If you do let feverfew bloom, you can extend the bloom period by cutting out sections of flowers that are fading (look for brown centers). When most blooms have faded, cut all of the remaining flower stems. By late summer, feverfew plants often lose leaves and become rather unsightly, so most gardeners cut them nearly to the ground at that time. If cut back then, they may regrow attractive foliage as they head into fall.

Feverfew is a short-lived perennial that often lives only 3 or 4 years, though the tender growth of the first year may be the most attractive, so some gardeners don't keep it after that. If seeds mature, seedlings often appear the next spring, and you can select seedlings then for transplant to desirable locations. Or you can make cuttings in the spring by removing stems from the outside of overwintering plants, cutting as close to the roots as possible, since it is the bottommost part of the stems that are most likely to root. Cut the tops back to make 4- to 5-inch cuttings, remove several lower leaves, and insert the bottoms in moist rooting mix.

CONTROL AND REMOVAL

Be warned that some gardeners avoid this plant, and some who have planted it consider it a pest due to its prolific reseeding. Still, I have found it rather easy to control in my gardens. Deadheading reduces seeding considerably, and the seedlings that do come up are easy to recognize and very easy to pull along with other spring weeds. Mature plants can be pulled from soft soil, but if you try to pull them in dry or clay soil, the stems may break off, leaving the stem bases to regrow. In this case, digging with a shovel will easily remove the roots.

Feverfew does escape from gardens, mainly to areas with disturbed soil, such as agricultural fields, and it may also survive in moist meadows.

VARIETIES AND SIMILAR SPECIES

Feverfew is a composite, like a daisy, meaning that it has heads of many tiny flowers. Single-flowered forms have a single row of white ray flowers around a central pad made up of tubular yellow disk flowers. Double varieties (such as 'Sissinghurst' and 'Snowball') have many rows of white ray flowers. Other varieties have no ray flowers, so they are just balls of white ('Silver Ball') or yellow ('Golden Ball') tubular flowers. Both of the ball types are also dwarf plants, under a foot tall, as is 'Santana', a double variety with white ruffled flowers.

The feverfew with chartreuse leaves is *Tanacetum parthenium* 'Aureum', which is sometimes sold as golden feverfew or golden feather. Some golden feverfew plants have leaves that are more yellow, are more deeply lobed or "ferny" in appearance, or that form very dwarf plants, maybe only 6 inches tall. They often come true from seed, but if you don't let them go to seed, you'll need to buy them each year or take cuttings from favorite plants.

A similar species, *Tanacetum niveum,* from the Mediterranean region, is a hardy perennial, easy to grow from seed, with attractive gray-green leaves, that makes a 30-inch mound covered with 1-inch white, feverfew-like flowers. The most common cultivar is 'Jackpot'.

The Name

Feverfew is newly arrived in the genus *Tanacetum* (tan-uh-see'-tum), having been reclassified from the genus *Chrysanthemum*. When Carl Linnaeus named the genus *Tanacetum,* he was naming it for the herb tansy. The words "tansy" and *Tanacetum* both derive from the Greek word *athanatos,* which means "without death" or "immortal." Tansy itself probably got this name because it was used, until only a couple of centuries ago, as an embalming agent and also as a meat preservative. Feverfew came to this etymological association rather undeservedly, since it is not used as a preservative, though it does share a strong scent and bitter flavor. The specific epithet *parthenium* (par-then'-ee-um) refers to the Parthenon of ancient Greece and was probably chosen because of an ancient (and unlikely) story of a workman who fell from the Parthenon and was cured of his resulting dizziness by feverfew.

Vinca major

Periwinkle, greater periwinkle

PLANT TYPE: *Perennial, ground cover* | HEIGHT AND SPREAD: *1 to 2 feet tall and variable spread (spreads rapidly)* | BLOOM TIME: *Spring, sometimes fall as well* | LIGHT NEEDS: *Full sun to shade* | SOIL NEEDS: *Poor to fertile, well drained* | WATER NEEDS: *Little to moderate* | OTHER TOLERANCES: *Cool coastal climates, full sun near the coast, inland climates in shade, deer resistant* | HARDINESS: *Zones 7 to 11*

My first encounter with *Vinca major* was along a trail through native woodlands in a California park, causing me to exclaim that I didn't know it was native here. I have long since realized with chagrin that this plant is a good indicator that there was once a house and garden near a

Contained by a cobblestone wall in an urban garden, where it can't spread through the garden or escape to the wild, this Vinca major *is an attractive, low-care ground cover.*

Vinca minor should also be kept away from wild settings. In a garden, it provides a low, spring-flowering cover through which bulbs like this daffodil can grow.

wildland or park trail. These tough and invasive plants with their pretty blue flowers are welcomed into some gardens, but we need to take care to avoid further spread into the wild.

Source and Uses

Vinca major grows wild in the European Mediterranean across into Turkey, as well as in Morocco and Algeria. It is found in *garrigue* (analogous to California's coastal sage scrub habitat), as well as in wooded areas or near waterways where the soil can retain a bit of moisture through the dry Mediterranean summers. Having been brought to England by the Romans, it has also escaped to woodlands there.

Grow periwinkle to reduce erosion on slopes, to cascade over an embankment or over the edge of a container. It often survives in dry shade, even under trees, because its roots compete well with tree roots for water and nutrients.

Care and Reproduction

This plant will grow in just about any soil as long as it is well drained. It survives on little water but will look better with regular water. (If they need water, periwinkle leaves lose their shine and then wilt alarmingly.) Periwinkle blooms better in sun but is easier to keep moist in partial shade or even in full shade. Cut periwinkle back to a few inches tall in early spring to keep it from becoming overgrown and untidy looking.

To enlarge a planting of *Vinca major,* peg the arching stems down to the ground at the edge of a planting, so they can root from their tips. Do this at the end of summer, using a stone or forked stick. To obtain more plants, dig and divide them in early spring or in mid to late fall. Set nursery plants or small divisions 2 feet apart.

Control and Removal

While periwinkle doesn't climb walls or trees, it will grow through low shrubbery, resulting in a confused tangle, so it is a poor choice to combine with such plants. To prevent spread, cut back arching stems at the edge of a patch, as these will root at the tips.

Digging and cutting can be a successful way to remove the plant. Work from the edge of the patch, being sure to remove all stems and roots as you go. Check the patch at 3-month intervals during the year for regrowth from missed fragments. Glyphosate weed killer is effective if you have first used a weed whip to break stems and leaf surfaces, but be careful not to get the chemical on other plants, as it will kill whatever it touches. After using glyphosate, check the area for regrowth in the next early fall and late spring.

Vinca major has been on the California Exotic Pest Plants Council list of wildland pests of lesser invasiveness, but could be upgraded to the "Medium" impact list. It rarely produces seeds that will grow, but its rooting stems allow it to spread vigorously into wild areas, especially ones that are wooded or near streams, crowding out native plants. Avoid growing it adjacent to these areas, or discarding the plants or roots in wild areas. In one area of Northern California, near the town of Canyon in the East Bay, *Vinca major* has been found to produce seed that grows into new plants, so it would be best for wild habitats if the plants that are doing this could be eradicated from that area.

Varieties and Similar Species

Vinca major variety *alba* has white flowers, while *V. major* var. *variegata* (sometimes sold as 'Elegantissima') has white-edged leaves. The variegated form is somewhat less vigorous and is handsome in container plantings. A form with yellow-veined leaves is a novelty, but it often loses this trait as it grows.

Vinca minor, the lesser periwinkle, has smaller leaves and flowers and grows only about 9 inches tall, making it useful under spring bulbs. Because it is hardy to Zone 4, it is more common than *V. major*, both in gardens and as a wildland invader in the eastern United States. It tolerates more shade and roots at every leaf node, eventually making a dense mat that is rather difficult to remove. *V. minor* is available with single or double flowers of white or various shades of blue and purple, and with white- or yellow-edged leaves.

A warm-weather annual with similar pink or white flowers is known by the common name of vinca or Madagascar periwinkle. While it is related to the blue periwinkle, and was once classified as *Vinca rosea*, it has now been reclassified as *Catharanthus roseus*.

THE NAME

The genus name *Vinca* (ving'-kuh) was taken from the ancient Latin name for these plants. The Romans called it *pervinca*, probably from *vincire*, meaning to twine or bind. There are several theories about why the Romans chose that name. The plant doesn't twine as it grows, but some think the name refers to the use of it, or possibly of *Vinca minor*, in garlands and wreaths. Herbalists have referred to its use to stop bleeding as being a "binding quality," or they say that it was used to bind legs with cramps, and one even spoke of its use in a charm to induce love between a man and his wife—a sort of symbolic binding. The common name periwinkle also derives from the Roman name *pervinca*. The specific epithet *major* means "larger," distinguishing it from the smaller species, *V. minor*.

Incidentally, if you are more familiar with periwinkle as the name of a snail, you will be interested to know that the snails called periwinkles derive their name from an entirely different source, a combination of the Latin *pina*, a kind of mussel, and the Old English *wincel*, meaning a snail shell.

Chapter Five

BULBS

hen gardeners say the word "bulb," they are referring to a plant that stores food from year to year in one of several kinds of thickened underground structures. It might be a true bulb, which is layered like an onion. Or it might be a corm, which has roots on the bottom and buds on top, like a true bulb, but no internal layers. It might also be a rhizome, with buds along the side. Rhizomes often grow horizontally, like those of ginger or rhizomatous iris.

In Northern California, the bulbs that grow most easily, and that rebloom year after year, are not, for the most part, the ones that fill the pages of most bulb catalogs. If we see our best-adapted bulbs at all, we see them as specialties offered in the back, after the tulips, hyacinths, and other cold-winter bulbs have had their flashy say. Our best bulbs are often the ones that are difficult to grow in cold-winter climates, where they must be dug up and kept indoors for the winter or protected from summer rainfall. But their problem bulbs are our glorious successes.

The six bulb plants featured in this chapter are all old garden favorites that have been grown in California for at least a hundred years. Two, agapanthus and calla lily, have enjoyed continuous popularity, though some think they are overused. Two, *Watsonia borbonica* and *Chasmanthe floribunda*, have drifted into

A cottage-style garden uses montbretia to good advantage. Also shown, left to right, red-and-white flowered hybrid penstemon, lavender canterberry bells (Campanula medium), *and white foxglove.*

Hybrid spring-blooming watsonias offer a wider range of colors than the pink or white of wild Watsonia borbonica, *such as these coral blossoms.*

such obscurity that experienced gardeners are often not certain what they are. All six offer considerable charm with little work.

Five of the six of the bulbs featured in this chapter, as well as many other bulb plants, are dormant for part of the year. As they go dormant, they store food underground for the following year's bloom, so don't cut the leaves until they are nearly all brown. (And never tie them in knots!) Plant summer-dormant bulbs in an unwatered part of the garden, which will then simply be bare all summer. Or group them with plants that need little summer water. However, if the soil is well drained, many seasonally dormant bulbs can tolerate moderate water in their dormant season. This means that you can grow them mixed with plants that remain green while the bulbs are dormant, letting the green plants mask the bulbs' yellowing leaves. Another way to mask dying leaves or, in the case of naked ladies, bare stems, is to plant taller bulb plants behind shorter flowering plants or low hedges.

If bulbs are well adapted to our climate, it is usually best to decide where you want them and leave them for several years at a time. This lets them enlarge and multiply so they can bloom more profusely. Digging them to divide overcrowded clumps, or moving clumps, often reduces bloom for a year or longer. However, dividing is advisable when the number of blooms declines or when a clump has used up too much space. If the bulbs are in a large, compact clump, you may need a digging bar to pry them out. This tool is 4 to 6 feet long, with a knob at the top and a flattened business end. It will save you broken shovels or spades. (See page 27 for information on checking soil moisture before you dig.)

Whenever you move bulbs or soil from one part of a garden to another, you have to be careful that you do not overlook tiny bulblets, cormlets, and so forth in the soil. These are one way the plant reproduces itself. They take a year or two to grow to blooming size. If you want more plants, that's fine, but if not, be careful to remove these propagules as you remove the larger bulbs, and be careful about moving soil that could contain them around the garden. Some bulb plants also produce viable seed that may germinate under the parent plants, but this is not as common as reproduction by making offsets.

Weedy Bulbs

Four bulb-forming plants stand out among plants that are nasty weeds in Northern California gardens:

- Yellow nutsedge *(Cyperus esculentus)* looks like a short papyrus plant.
- False garlic *(Nothoscardum inodorum)* has no onion scent, surprisingly deep bulbs surrounded many ricelike minibulbs, and is not edible despite the name.
- Cape oxalis *(Oxalis pes-caprae)* has cloverlike leaves and yellow flowers in winter.
- Wild onion *(Allium triquetrum)* is onion scented, has nodding white flowers, and is edible.

The first two of these weeds are classified by the California Department of Food and Agriculture as noxious weeds; the second two are not. Cape oxalis is the subject of local wildland weed eradication projects and is under consideration by the California Exotic Pest Plant Council for

Cape oxalis, shown here blanketing the ground on a road-cut, is a disaster in the garden, where it crowds out other small plants, and is also beginning to spread in wildlands.

addition to the wildland invasives list, as it is beginning to escape into wild areas, especially those with sandy soil. Wild onion is used as food by some, but spreads quickly in gardens by both seed and bulbs.

Among the six featured bulbs, some, or relatives of some, have made pests of themselves in disturbed areas outside of gardens. Take care to keep garden bulbs inside gardens. Never dump soil that could contain bulblets, or plants with seeds or attached bulbs, in wild areas or by roadsides. Avoid planting these plants at the edges of waterways that could carry bulbs or seeds downstream. With a little care, you should be able to enjoy these naturalizing garden bulbs while keeping them from running away from home.

OTHER BULBS THAT NATURALIZE IN MILD-WINTER CALIFORNIA GARDENS

Alstroemeria spp.
Babiana stricta
Bulbinella floribunda
Canna hybrids
Clivia miniata
Hyacinthoides hispanica
Lycorus squamigera

Muscari spp. and hybrids
Narcissus spp. and hybrids
Nerine hybrids
Schizostylus coccinea
Scilla peruviana
Sparaxis tricolor
Tigridia pavonia

Perennial Weeds Among Bulbs

Because bulb plants are often not disturbed for several years, they are sitting ducks for invasions by weedy perennials. When you are moving or dividing bulb plants, be sure to go through the bulbs carefully and remove the underground runners of perennial weeds such as Bermuda grass, quack grass, or bindweed that may be growing among them. Also take the opportunity to remove such roots from the soil in the old and new sites. In particularly infested gardens, you may want to plant your bulbs in containers for a while until you have solved perennial weed problems among them and in their intended growing site.

Agapanthus praecox subsp. orientalis (A. umbellatus)

Agapanthus, lily of the Nile

PLANT TYPE: *Bulb (rhizome with fleshy roots)* | HEIGHT: *1 to 6 feet tall, varies by type* | BLOOM TIME: *Early summer to midsummer* | LIGHT NEEDS: *Full sun, light shade* | SOIL NEEDS: *Fertile, well-drained* | WATER NEEDS: *Moderate* | OTHER TOLERANCES: *Poor soil, clay soil, cool coastal summers, inland summers with light shade* | HARDINESS: *Zones 9 to 11*

When an agapanthus first bloomed in Europe, in 1679, it was dubbed the African hyacinth and hailed as a "remarkable wonder . . . crowned with flowers each of which is singularly beautiful." While it is still treasured in cold climates as a container plant to overwinter indoors, most Californians have seen so many agapanthus plants that

The drooping, midnight blue flowers of Agapanthus inapertus are a refreshing variation from ordinary agapanthus blossoms.

White-flowered agapanthus is less common than the medium-blue. It was chosen here to create a restrained color scheme in front of a warm-colored house.

they have become jaded to their charms. Still, you may find your appreciation of these dramatic plants reawakened by good placement, good care, and choice of a less common species or variety.

Source and Uses

Agapanthus species are not native to the region of the Nile (as implied by their common name, lily of the Nile), but to South Africa, where they are often grown in gardens. The plant that so amazed a European observer in 1679 was *A. africanus,* a Western Cape native with loose heads of blue flowers on 2½-foot stems. Some of these plants are certainly growing in California gardens; however, our most common species is *A. praecox* subsp. *orientalis.* This species bears dense heads of blue or white flowers on stems to 4 feet tall. It is native to the central part of the South African coast, which has both summer and winter rain. Both species are evergreen, keeping their broad, straplike leaves year round. Early records are quite confused, but it seems that *A. praecox* was not known in Europe before 1800.

Try a clump of agapanthus as a dramatic single specimen, or use it in formal rows. Leaves and flowers arch dramatically from containers, blooming best when the roots have become crowded. Cut flower stems as the blooms start to open for use in long-lasting bouquets, or leave them to provide nectar for butterflies.

Care and Reproduction

Agapanthus blooms best in full sun, except where summers are hot, in which case it appreciates light or afternoon shade. Too little sun will result in few blooms. Although it will survive in rather poor soil, it will look better with added compost or if given a slow-release fertilizer rich in phosphorous and potassium in the spring. Fertilizer is critical for plants growing in containers. All of the evergreen species look better with moderate summer water, though overwatering results in pale leaves and few blooms. Underwatered plants also bloom little and may be reduced to only a few short leaves. Evergreen agapanthus survives temperatures to 15 degrees F, but the leaves are damaged at 20 degrees F.

Some like the appearance of the seedpods that form after flowering, but most gardeners cut spent flower stems near their base. Pull dead, brown flower stems from plants, and cut yellowing or brown leaves out at the base. Hunt through the plants for snails and apply an iron phosphate snail bait in spring and summer.

Divide agapanthus only every 3 or 4 years, in the fall. Lift the clumps with a digging fork, a spade, or, if the clump is large, a digging bar. Go in from the side, to avoid damaging the delicate buds at the top. Separate the clumps into sections, using an axe if they are tight. Cut the leaves and stems back by half and replant immediately in well-amended, well-drained soil, leaving 1½ feet between full-sized types.

Agapanthus is not a reliable seeder, and plants that do grow from seed are likely to differ from their parent plants in unpredictable ways. Should you want to try, plant seeds as soon as they are ripe. Covered lightly with mix, the seeds will germinate in 3 to 8 weeks. Grow them in place for 1 year before transplanting. They are likely to bloom in the third year.

CONTROL AND REMOVAL

If you want less agapanthus, use a digging bar to remove the rhizomes. While this can be tedious and difficult, it usually needs to be done only once. Take care to keep the discarded plants out of wild areas. Dumped rhizomes are considered the source of escaped *Agapanthus praecox* subsp. *orientalis* along some southwestern Australian roadsides.

VARIETIES AND SIMILAR SPECIES

Many newer options offer gardeners fresh choices. There are dwarfs that produce 1½- to 2-foot stems of either blue or white flowers. 'Peter Pan' was the first blue-flowered dwarf, and a deeper blue selection is sold as 'Queen Anne'. The white-edged leaves of *Agapanthus* 'Tinkerbell' or the yellow-edged leaves of *A. africanus* 'Hinag' (SUMMER GOLD) are spectacular even before their blue flowers open. For different flower colors, try the lavender 'Gayles Lilac' or the excellent deep blue-violet 'Storm Cloud' from the Saratoga Horticulture Foundation.

The species *Agapanthus inapertus* has tubular, drooping, midnight blue flowers on 4-foot stems. This species, from eastern South Africa, becomes dormant in winter. Other winter-dormant, or deciduous, agapanthus plants include *A. campanulatus* and the Headbourne hybrids. Most deciduous types are hardy to 0 degrees F (learn the hardiness ratings of plants before you buy them). Water deciduous agapanthus well in spring and summer and grow it in a well-drained location to avoid overwatering by rain in winter. Remove dead leaves in the fall. Divide no more often than once in 6 years, in early spring before growth has begun, replanting immediately.

The Name

In 1788, the French botanist Charles Louis L'Heretier named this genus *Agapanthus* (a-guh-pan'-thus) from the Greek words *agape* ("love") and *anthus* ("flower"). *Praecox* (pray'-kox) is Latin for "precocious" or "early to mature." *Africanus* and *orientalis* mean "African" and "Eastern."

Agapanthus plants are often mislabeled in nurseries. In addition, plants bearing cultivar names are sometimes seedlings with similar traits rather than being identical to the original cultivar. So, to be sure what you are getting, buy plants from a trusted source or see the plant in bloom before you buy it.

Amaryllis belladonna
(Amaryllis rosea, Brunsvigia rosea)

🌼 Naked lady, belladonna lily, March lily

PLANT TYPE: *Bulb* | HEIGHT: *To 2½ feet* | BLOOM TIME: *Late summer, early autumn* | LIGHT NEEDS: *Full sun, light shade* | SOIL NEEDS: *Poor or fertile, well drained* | WATER NEEDS: *Ample when growing, none when dormant* | OTHER TOLERANCES: *Cool coastal summers, hot inland summers, deer resistant, gopher resistant* | HARDINESS: *Zones 7 to 11*

*A*maryllis belladonna seems to break the rules of green plant life when its leafless, reddish flower stems burst forth from apparently vacant earth in late summer. In only a few days, the dramatic spears grow to over 2 feet tall. When 12 to 20 large pink lilies open atop each bare stem, the plants do seem truly naked.

Naked of leaves, flower stems of Amaryllis belladonna *spring from its large bulbs in July through September.*

In winter and early spring, naked lady's strap-like leaves provide foliage to complement early-blooming spring bulbs such as these cyclamens and 'Quail' daffodils.

After the flower dies, the agapanthus-like leaves that emerge make this plant all skirt and no lady during the winter and early spring. The leaves turn yellow and die back in mid to late spring, and from then until bloom time the lady hides underground, leaving only the tips of large brown bulbs showing at the surface.

Source and Uses

Amaryllis belladonna is native to the coastal hills in the South African Western Cape Province, in the chaparral-like shrubland known as *fynbos* (fine'-boss). It blooms there in March, at the end of the Southern Hemisphere summer. The plant was introduced to Europe in 1700, reaching the eastern United States by 1812 and California by 1850. Widely offered by plant nurseries from the 1850s on, it has naturalized around many a California homestead.

In South Africa the plants are typically grown with deciduous agapanthus or with chasmanthe, combinations that give two seasons of bloom. When deciding where to plant, be aware that the flower stems will lean toward sunlight, and more of the flowers will face on the side toward the most light. Stems of sweetly scented naked lady blooms are excellent cut flowers, and the plants are easily grown in containers.

Care and Reproduction

Naked lady bulbs, which are up to 4 inches across, should be planted in a sunny location. In Zone 10, plant them with the tops just at the soil surface. Bury the bulbs progressively deeper where winters are colder, up to 6 inches deep in Zone 7. Plant in groups of three or more, with a foot between the groups. Good drainage is important, so sandy soil is best. While the plants will grow in relatively infertile soil, amendment with compost will give them a boost, as will some slow-release fertilizer added each year when the leaves appear.

In its native habitat, this plant blooms only after the wildfires that occur every 5 to 40 years, probably because the wildfires burn away shading brush. In sunny gardens, they bloom every year, but they may refuse to bloom if they are shaded in winter and spring. The leaves grow and die back with the normal rainfall of Northern California, benefiting from a watering or two only in a very dry winter. The plants will cheerfully brighten sites with no summer water; however, in well-drained soil, they can tolerate moderate spring and summer irrigation.

Remove the leaves when they are brown and papery. The bulbs are best left in place for years to multiply and produce large clumps, but they can be divided while dormant and replanted immediately. This is best done just after the plants bloom, or even during bloom, but even so, the transplanted bulbs may not bloom until the second year.

Naked lady flowers are pollinated by night-flying moths. The fleshy $\frac{1}{4}$- to $\frac{3}{8}$-inch seeds, which resemble white or pink pearls, form in papery pods and then fall to the ground near the plants. Collect seeds as soon as the pods split open, and plant them immediately, barely covering them with seeding mix. They should germinate in 2 weeks and will produce blooming plants in 3 to 6 years or longer.

Removal and Control

Few naked lady seeds germinate in dry sites, probably because they do not become dormant as most seeds do, and they die before our California rains provide enough moisture. This probably saves us from invasion by this plant, constraining it to widening its clumps rather than forming new colonies. Worldwide, invasion by seed is not common, though it occurs in part of Australia.

The bulbs are relatively easy to dig if you want to remove the plant, though small bulbs could be missed and regrow. Do take care not to discard bulbs or bulblets in wild areas, where they are likely to grow.

Varieties and Similar Species

In South Africa, the plant is described as blooming in various shades of pink and sometimes in white. The two types most commonly seen in the Bay Area are a light pink one that blooms as early as the last week of July and one with darker pink stripes, blooming in mid-September. If you are purchasing naked lady bulbs, you will find pale pink ones to be the most common.

You will also find hybrids with various species of *Brunsvigia*, sold as *Amarygia*. These bloom in late summer on naked stems, have flowers that radiate in all directions evenly, and can tolerate more summer water than *Amaryllis belladonna*. One naked lady variety, 'Hathor' or 'Haythor', which is white with a yellow throat, is probably a hybrid with a *Brunsvigia*.

Other intergeneric hybrids, called *Amarcrinum*, resulted from crosses between *Amaryllis belladonna* and *Crinum* species. One, *Amarcrinum memoria-corsii*, is from a cross with *Crinum moorei*. These plants have leaves all or most of the year, though they may look a bit mussy at bloom time.

The Name

Amaryllis (am-uh-rill'-luss) is a Roman proper name, made famous because the Roman poet Virgil chose it as the name of a pretty shepherd girl in a story poem. *Belladonna* means "pretty lady." Unfortunately, two different plants got connected to the name *Amaryllis*, due to errors made by Carl Linnaeus and later botanists, leading to centuries of discord among botanists and confusion among gardeners. And although the naked lady is the plant that was finally awarded the right to the genus name *Amaryllis*, the word has attached itself, as a common name, to the other plant in the dispute, thus perpetuating confusion. The "florists' amaryllis," which botanists now put in the genus *Hippeastrum*, is native to South America, bears large white, pink, red, or red-striped flowers in winter and spring, and is usually sold as a container or houseplant.

Chasmanthe floribunda

![icon] Chasmanthe, Adam's rib

PLANT TYPE: *Bulb (corm)* | HEIGHT: *2 to 7 feet* | BLOOM TIME: *Late autumn to mid-spring* | LIGHT NEEDS: *Full sun* | SOIL NEEDS: *Poor or fertile, well drained* | WATER NEEDS: *Moderate when growing, none when dormant* | OTHER TOLERANCES: *Partial shade, summer water, wind, cool coastal summers, hot inland summers* | HARDINESS: *Zones 9 to 11*

To the casual observer, *Chasmanthe floribunda*, ornamenting winter gardens with its fine flashes of orange or yellow, appears to be a sort of crocosmia on steroids. Though it is indeed a close relative of crocosmia, a fellow member of the iris plant family, close inspection reveals that it is a quite different plant. The flat sprays of 2- to 5-foot-tall leaves appear with fall rains, when crocosmia is dormant. In mid to late winter, the flower stems emerge. The

The curve in Chasmanthe floribunda's *3-inch long flowers matches the curve of the beak of the South African sunbird that pollinates them.*

Chasmanthe flori-bunda *is a good choice to provide a dramatic winter show as it does in front of this tall wooden fence.*

3-inch-long flowers consist of a curved tube ending in six petal lobes, the top one longer than the others. The flat flower heads open from the bottom, making a handsome, arrow-shaped form. The plants die back in mid-spring, before crocosmia begins to bloom.

Source and Uses

In its native area, the Western Cape Province of South Africa, *Chasmanthe floribunda* grows in dampish spots on rocky outcrops. South Africans plant it in large, informal gardens or, as at the Kirstenbosch National Botanical Garden, interplant it with deciduous agapanthus, which produces leaves and flowers in the opposite season. In addition to low-maintenance winter garden color, chasmanthe provides a good cut flower in a season when few are available, and it also attracts hummingbirds to California gardens. It looks good planted in clumps or drifts behind informal plantings that include large succulents such as century plant or *Aloe arborescens*.

Care and Reproduction

This plant will survive in Northern California gardens with no care at all, though in drought years, occasional fall and winter water may be needed to ensure the best growth. It is ideal for unirrigated areas, since it needs no water from mid-spring through fall, but it can tolerate summer water if the soil is well drained.

To keep the garden tidy, you will probably want to cut back the flowering stems after the flowers fade (and before seeds form) and remove the leaves as they turn brown in late spring. You will need sharp pruning shears to cut the dead leaves almost to ground level. Don't put this task off until fall, or you will be forced to work around the tender new shoots that are growing up through the tough dead leaves. In areas where winter will bring more than light frosts, dig and store the corms, replanting them in early spring when heavy frost danger is past.

Chasmanthe will eventually form a raised mass of corms up to a yard across and will continue to bloom for years without being divided, but dividing the clumps every 3 or 4 years will lead to heavier flowering. Dig when dormant, and cut apart sections of corms or pry out individual ones, discarding the small offsets and the flattened, dead corms that are stacked under each mature one. Replant right away. While chasmanthe will grow in infertile soil, an addition of compost will give the plants a boost and will also improve drainage in heavier soils. If you are using individual corms, plant them in well-drained soil, 2 to 3 inches deep and 6 to 10 inches apart. Corms may not bloom in the first year after transplanting.

You can also grow chasmanthe from the ¼-inch orange seeds, collected when pods start to split open in late spring or early summer, and planted in autumn. Plants grown from seed usually bloom in their third year.

Control and Removal

To be rid of the plant, dig the corms out at any time, using a digging bar if necessary. Small plants may sprout from missed offsets for a couple of seasons, so it would be advisable not to plant any fall-sprouting iris family plant, such as watsonia, in the area during that time, or you will confuse it with the chasmanthe that you may be pulling out.

Chasmanthe floribunda could escape cultivation into adjacent wild areas—and it has done so in some mediterranean-climate areas, including some locations in Australia and in some Central California coastal counties—but it is not listed as an invasive plant. Care is advised in disposing of extra corms and flower stems with mature seeds so they do not become established in wild areas.

Varieties and Similar Species

For those who prefer pastel colors, there is a form of *Chasmanthe floribunda* with flowers of a clear, soft yellow. It is often sold as *C. floribunda* var. *duckittii,* named after the Duckitt family, on whose South African farm it appeared, though some think the color is determined by a single recessive gene and so is not different enough to be considered a separate variety (see photo on page 43).

Chasmanthe floribunda and two other species survive in old California gardens or may be found at specialty nurseries. Flowers of *C. bicolor* are deep orange marked with yellow and green, the plants growing to about 4 feet tall. *C. aethiopica* grows to only 3 feet tall and is hardy to Zone 8. Its bright orange blooms are all turned to one side of the flower stems (see photo on page 1). *C. aethiopica* has somewhat more tendency toward weediness and escape from cultivation in California, so plant other species in preference.

The Name

Chasmanthe (kaz-man'-thee) was apparently named for the way the petal tips spread widely, from the Greek *chasma* ("yawning" or "gaping") and *anthos* ("flower"). The botanist who created this name was probably influenced by the fact that *Chasmanthe* was formerly classified in the genus *Antholyza* (an-thow-lies'-uh). The flowers remaining in that genus have petals spread wide, like the mouth of a raging beast, so their name derives from the Greek *anthos* ("flower") and lyssa ("rabies"). The gape of *Chasmanthe* is a minor echo of that major roar. The specific epithet *floribunda* is from the Latin word meaning "having many flowers."

Crocosmia x crocosmiiflora *(Montbretia x crocosmiiflora)*

Montbretia, crocosmia, firecrackers

PLANT TYPE: *Bulb (corm)* | HEIGHT: *2 to 4 feet* | BLOOM TIME: *Summer* | LIGHT NEEDS: *Full sun or partial shade* | SOIL NEEDS: *Fertile or poor, well drained* | WATER NEEDS: *Moderate* | OTHER TOLERANCES: *Clay soil, cool coastal summers, hot inland summers, deer resistant* | HARDINESS: *Zones 6 to 11*

he vibrant two-tone orange blooms of the plant we call montbretia brighten many a Northern California park or garden in summer. It is a survivor from the late nineteenth and early twentieth century, when gardeners in Europe and America were wild for the new crocosmia varieties that were being bred every year. Many of these cultivars had larger flowers or more interesting coloration, but our common flower is the oldest of them, and it is also one of the sturdiest.

Montbretia flowers are much smaller than those of chasmanthe, and they appear in summer.

A modern hybrid, 'Lucifer' has vibrant red flowers. It counts in its ancestry the species Crocosmia masoniorum, to which it owes the upright angle of its flowers on the stems.

Source and Uses

In 1880, the French nurseryman Victor Lemoine crossed two South African plants to create our garden montbretia. One was *Crocosmia aurea*, which in 1847 was the first of the species to reach Europe. The other was *C. pottsii*, a species that arrived about 20 years later. Like most crocosmias, these parent plants were from the woods and stream banks of South Africa's eastern dry-winter/wet-summer region.

In gardens, montbretias produce dependable bloom for about 2 months. Most bloom from early June into August, and all are in bloom around the Fourth of July, earning them the local common name firecrackers. For a vivid combination, try them with *Canna* 'Phaison' (TROPICANNA) and golden feverfew. Cut the stems when the lowest blossoms have just opened for long-lasting cut flowers, but leave some for hummingbirds, which will visit often.

Care and Reproduction

While montbretias and other *Crocosmia* varieties may survive a relatively dry summer, they will look and bloom much better with moderate summer water. When the leaves die back in late summer, cut them an inch or two from the ground, using sharp pruning shears. Although the plants are dormant until leaves sprout in spring, they tolerate our winter rainfall. Winter mulch is advisable in Zones 6 and 7, and summer mulch is a good idea where summers are very hot.

Divide crowded clumps in early spring, but no more often than once in 3 years. Crocosmia corms multiply by forming cormlets at the end of short runners. When dividing the plants, leave the parent corm attached to each group of cormlets, as it remains alive and provides some nutrition to the cormlets for the next year or longer. Plant crocosmia corms 2 to 3 inches deep and 6 to 8 inches apart in well-drained soil that has been amended with organic matter. Because montbretia is a hybrid between two species, it sets few seeds, and those that form may not grow. In any case, reproduction by cormlets is so successful that most gardeners are glad not to have seedlings as well.

CONTROL AND REMOVAL

Gardeners often don't remember planting montbretia, and it is quite possible that they introduced the plant by accidentally bringing corms in the soil on a gift plant. Once established, a clump is long-lived. It will enlarge, but if the soil near the edges of the clump is cultivated lightly each summer, and if any adjacent lawn is mowed, the plants will not spread rampantly.

To get rid of it, you need to dig out all of the corms and cormlets, and pull the small gladiolus-like plants that sprout in subsequent springs from cormlets that you missed. Montbretia has naturalized widely in England, as well as in Western Europe, Hawaii, and Australia. In California it has been a plant considered, but not listed, by the California Exotic Pest Plant Council as a wildland weed, and could appear on the future "Low" impact list. It will naturalize in areas with disturbed soil, like roadsides, so it is important not to discard soil containing corms or cormlets outside of the garden.

VARIETIES AND SIMILAR SPECIES

Of the hundreds of *Crocosmia* varieties created before the 1920s, three-quarters were lost by the end of World War II. This was due partly to a fall from fashion and partly to the upheavals of war. Many cultivars were lost in Great Britain through the "Dig for Victory" campaign, in which flower gardens were dug up to produce vegetables.

Some older varieties still available are 'Solfatare', sometimes misspelled as 'Solfaterre' (bred by Lemoine, smoky-brown leaves, deep yellow flowers, 2 feet tall, late summer); 'George Davison' (green leaves, orange-yellow flowers); and 'Emily McKenzie' (2 inch flowers, deep yellow with maroon markings). In the latter part of the twentieth century, English plant breeder Alan Bloom created a number of new cultivars. One important parent of his varieties is *Crocosmia masoniorum*, a species that bears its flowers upright on the stems. This trait is evident in the popular 'Lucifer' (scarlet red, 3 feet tall).

THE NAME

The genus name *Crocosmia* (krow-koz'-mee-uh) derives from the Greek words *krokos* ("saffron") and *osmea* ("a smell"), chosen because when the botanist who named it soaked the dried flowers of *Crocosmia aurea* in hot water, he found that the water turned yellow and smelled like saffron crocus. While the plant is sometimes used as a dye source, no one seems to have picked up the idea of using it as a saffron substitute.

But why is it called montbretia? There are two parts to the answer. First, when Victor Lemoine made his famous cross, *Crocosmia pottsii* was classified as *Montbretia pottsii*, so he named the hybrid *Montbretia x crocosmiiflora*. When the classification of the genus *Crocosmia* and the related *Tritonia* and *Gladiolus* was finally settled, the genus *Montbretia* disappeared, all of its members having been transferred to different genera. Our garden plant became *Crocosmia x crocosmiiflora*. Gardeners disliked this tongue twister and so opted for just plain montbretia (mont-bree'-she-uh). The name is now sometimes also used for other *Crocosmia* species.

And the meaning of montbretia? It honors Antoine Francois Cocquebert de Montbret, a promising young French botanist who sailed to Egypt with Napoleon's army in 1798. He was to serve as a librarian, but he fell ill and died in Cairo in 1801, when he was only 20. In 1803, a French botanist who had been his friend created the now obsolete genus name in his honor.

Watsonia borbonica *(W. pyramidata, W. rosea)*

Watsonia, bugle lily

PLANT TYPE: *Bulb (corm)* | HEIGHT: *To 6 feet* | BLOOM TIME: *Late spring* |
LIGHT NEEDS: *Full sun, light shade* | SOIL NEEDS: *Poor to moderately fertile,*
well drained | WATER NEEDS: *Moderate when growing, none when dormant* |
OTHER TOLERANCES: *Most soils, summer water, cool coastal summers, partial*
shade near the coast, hot inland climates | HARDINESS: *Zones 8 to 11*

*L*ike crocosmias, watsonias rose in popularity in the
early decades of the twentieth century and then fell into
relative obscurity. Watsonias probably owe their decline to the
many new large, colorful, frilly gladiolus varieties that were being sold
to gardeners. But although gladiolus is lovely, watsonia is more relaxed

*The most common
color of* Watsonia
borbonica *blossoms
is a delicate lavender-
pink.*

White-flowered
Watsonia borbonica
*plants were origi-
nally discovered on
one South African
farm. Without stak-
ing, the species
often leans, but this
can result in grace-
ful patterns.*

and graceful. The faintly fragrant flowers, shaped like curved trumpets, are arranged in two rows along the branching flower stems. The kind that most commonly survives in old California gardens, *Watsonia borbonica*, is a tall, elegant plant with 2½-inch late-spring flowers that are usually pink or white.

SOURCE AND USES

Watsonia borbonica is native to poor, sandy soils in the extreme southwest of the Western Cape Province of South Africa. In its native habitat, it may bloom only after a wildfire, but it blooms reliably in gardens and is a favorite with South African gardeners and park landscapers. Its height makes it a good choice for the rear of a flower border. The blooms make excellent cut flowers. In addition to the common pale to deep pink or white, there are also light purple, coral, and red varieties.

CARE AND REPRODUCTION

The flattened leaf sprays of *Watsonia borbonica* emerge in the fall and grow to 3 to 4 feet tall by the time the flowers open on their 6-foot stems. Winter rain is usually sufficient, but a dry winter can result in stunted plants, so be ready to water once or twice in drought years. The plants become dormant after blooms fade. Use sharp pruning shears to cut spent flower stems and dying leaves before new growth begins in fall. The dormant plants tolerate moderate summer water in well-drained soil, but if the soil is too wet in summer, the plants may bloom less the following spring. In hot inland climates, provide light or afternoon shade.

After several years, overcrowding will reduce bloom. When this happens, dig the corms in the summer and replant them farther apart. Full-sized *Watsonia borbonica* corms, which reach 1¼ to 1¾ inches across, should bloom in the first year after planting. Plant them 4 inches deep and 4 to 6 inches apart. While the plants tolerate relatively poor soil, they will respond if you add compost before you replant. Amid the larger corms you will find many small cormlets. These can be interplanted with the respaced larger corms or planted in a growing area to mature for 2 or 3 years before moving them to a more prominent location. It is more likely that you will have plenty of full-sized corms to plant, share with friends, or discard, and you'll wish to discard the extra cormlets.

To prevent the tendency of these plants to lean over, you can plant them in groups of six corms and then support each group on three tall bamboo stakes tied round with twine as the plants grow. Where they are not hardy, *Watsonia borbonica* corms can be dug while dormant and replanted after the danger of 10 degree F temperatures has passed.

Control and Removal

To get rid of the plant, as with crocosmia or gladiolus, you need to dig out the corms and then remove any missed cormlets as they send up their flat spikes of leaves. Watsonia sprouts in the fall, which should differentiate it from spring-sprouting species; still, it would not be wise to immediately replant the area with another fall-sprouting plant in the iris family, such as chasmanthe.

Watsonia borbonica is not considered a wildland weed in California, though some potential is there, as the small cormlets could be overlooked in discarded soil. Other *Watsonia* species have become pests, notably *W. meriana*, a summer-dormant species that grows on roadsides and in fields in Mendocino and Sonoma Counties. It flowers at 20 to 48 inches tall, bearing its dull red-orange, purple, or white flowers in late spring. A variety of this plant, *W. meriana bulbilifera*, makes bulblets on its stems that can form new plants. This species and its variety gave watsonias a bad name in Australia for some time and are the subjects of an active eradication campaign there.

Varieties and Similar Species

In 1897, a Cape Town businessman, H. R. Arderne, found white-flowered *Watsonia borbonica* growing on his property. Botanists at first classified it as a separate species, *W. ardernei*. Now they have decided it is a subspecies, with slightly shorter-tubed flowers that may be white or pink. So if you have the white-flowered one, it is *W. borbonica* subspecies *ardernei*. Pink-flowered ones may be subspecies *ardernei* or may be *W. borbonica* subspecies *borbonica*. In addition to these botanical subspecies, you may find hybrid cultivars that bloom in other flower colors.

Besides *Watsonia borbonica* and its hybrids, the watsonias you are most likely to find in nurseries are hybrids of *W. pillansii*, which, until recently, was known as *W. beatricis*, though it is usually sold as plain *Watsonia*. This one is evergreen, blooming in late summer, hardy in Zones 9 to 11. It grows 18 to 48 inches tall, with 3-inch flowers. The species has apricot-colored blooms, but hybrids with pink, peach, and nearly red flowers are also available. Evergreen watsonias should be planted in late March or in April and given water year round. Evergreen species are not recommended outside of their hardiness range, as they can't be dug and stored in winter because they are never fully dormant.

THE NAME

Watsonia (what-sohn'-ee-uh) was named for the English scientist and physician Sir William Watson (1715–1787), who popularized in England the Linnaean system of naming plants. *Borbonica* refers to an island near Madagascar, now called Réunion but once called Isle de Bourbon, where the first plants of this species were collected by a botanist. Despite the name, the plants are native to South Africa, not Réunion Island.

Zantedeschia aethiopica

White calla, calla lily, arum lily

PLANT TYPE: *Bulb (rhizome)* | HEIGHT: *3 to 4 feet* | BLOOM TIME: *Mainly in January to July* | LIGHT NEEDS: *Sun to shade* | SOIL NEEDS: *Poor to fertile* | WATER NEEDS: *None to ample* | OTHER TOLERANCES: *Bog or water gardens, cool coastal summers, hot inland summers, deer resistant* | HARDINESS: *Zones 8b to 11*

The snowy, sensuous curves of white calla lilies have made them popular as cut flowers, subjects for paintings and photography, and motifs for the decorative arts. While gardeners often share an appreciation of these stately flowers, whoever has tried to get rid of the plant is sure to have a rather negative view of it. This dichotomy between beauty and weediness is observed wherever the plants are grown.

Elegant white callas add glory to any corner of the garden, but take care when moving soil, so that they stay where they are wanted.

Source and Uses

In its native South Africa, white calla is appreciated in many gardens, though, as in ours, it may have crept in uninvited. In the wild, the plant sometimes creates vast fields of white-specked green.

The trick to enjoying this plant in your garden is to place it well and to persist in eradicating it where it is not placed well. It makes a charming spring show in a border with cinerarias and foxgloves and fits equally well into tropical or mediterranean-themed gardens. It will thrive in a large container to make a handsome garden accent. The flowers are long-lived in bouquets. Cut them before the tiny yellow flowers (on the central column, called the spadix) have released their white pollen.

White calla can grow in boggy soil or even in water. To grow it in a pond, suspend it up to 12 inches deep in a plastic tub filled with heavy soil, lowering it gradually over a period of weeks, so it can adjust to aquatic conditions.

Look for other varieties of Zantedeschia aethiopica, *such as 'Hercules', which grows to 7 feet tall and has white-speckled leaves.*

Care and Reproduction

White callas survive neglect because they are unusually adaptable. In dry-summer western South Africa, they are dormant in summer. In dry-winter eastern South Africa, they are winter dormant. If the soil is moist all year, they never become dormant. Where frost bites the leaves, they die back but return in spring. This adaptability allows them to survive neglect in gardens, but with fewer blooms, poor leaf color overall, prematurely yellowing leaves, and smaller plants. For healthier plants, use organic soil amendment or mulch, and fertilize container plants monthly while in bloom. Keep the soil moist from fall to midsummer. To encourage an earlier and more vigorous winter bloom, withhold water after midsummer. Near the coast, white callas tolerate full sun, while inland they appreciate partial shade. In either region, they may be taller and greener in full shade.

When a flower begins to turn brown, pull the whole flower stem out of the plant. The fragile stem base usually breaks, leaving the rest of the plant undamaged, but if a leaf comes out with the flower stem, no great harm is done. As a plant nears dormancy, pull or cut yellowing leaves. Periodically hunt snails among the leaves and in the flowers, and bait around plants with an iron phosphate snail bait.

It is best to dig and replant rhizomes from July into fall, when the tops of the plants are dormant, but white callas will generally survive transplanting any time of year. (If the plant you are moving is actively growing, cut the leaves back to reduce water loss.) Plant dormant white calla rhizomes on their sides, 4 inches deep, leaving 12 to 18 inches between plants.

If seeds form, soft orange fruits mature along the spadix. Two varieties, 'Green Goddess' and 'Hercules', seem more likely to form seed in California than the species. However, their seedlings may not be as attractive as the parent; therefore, it is wiser to propagate using rhizomes.

Control and Removal

Prevent seed formation by removing spent flowers. When digging to move or divide plants, use a digging fork gently to avoid breaking up the rhizomes. Search for the easily detached yellowish rhizome buds as you dig. You will probably miss some and have to dig out the resulting small plants for several seasons. Avoid moving soil from areas in which white calla recently grew, as it is likely to contain these buds.

Zantedeschia aethiopica has naturalized in subtropical climates world-wide. In some of these areas, such as New Zealand and Australia, it sets seeds profusely and invades native areas. In northern California, it has escaped cultivation in limited areas of most coastal counties, probably from abandoned plantings or dumped rhizomes. It has been included by the California Exotic Pest Plant Council as a plant "considered but not listed," but could appear on the "Low" or "Medium" impact lists in the future. Prevent further spread by removing any flowers that are forming seeds and by using care to keep rhizomes or ripe seeds out of wild areas, especially areas that are constantly moist from seepage or nearby waterways.

Varieties and Similar Species

White calla's various cultivars wax and wane in availability. 'Minor' and 'Little Gem' are no more than 18 inches tall. 'Hercules' plants reach 7 feet tall, with white-flecked leaves and large white spathes (the white swirls we think of as petals). 'Crowborough' resembles the species but is somewhat hardier. The variety 'Red Desire' has a white spathe around a red spadix. Only two varieties of **Z. aethiopica** have colored spathes. 'Green Goddess' has extra-long spathes, green at the top, shading to white at the base. 'Pink Mist' has pale pink spathes.

Calla lilies of other species, and hybrids among them, are more difficult to grow in Northern California than is **Z. aethiopica**. We can all enjoy their yellow, pink, orange, or lavender blooms in their first summer, but because they are adapted to milder parts of the dry-winter region of eastern South Africa, they will survive winters only in frost-free sites

Caution

Sap of white calla will stain clothes. The brown stain will appear only after the clothes have been laundered.

with extremely well-drained soil. They are worth a try in sandy soil near the coast; otherwise it's best to grow them in containers, so they can be moved under an overhang, or even indoors, in winter.

The Name

White calla is not a lily at all but an arum, like Jack-in-the-pulpit. Carl Linnaeus saw this when he named it *Calla aethiopica,* grouping it with the smaller European arum *Calla palustris.* A later botanist created a new genus for it, which he named *Zantedeschia* (zan-tuh-deh'-she-uh) after a nineteenth-century Italian botanist named Zantedeschi. The species name, *aethiopica* (ay-thee-ohp'-ih-cuh), does not refer to the modern nation of Ethiopia but derives from the ancient Greek term used to refer to places south of Libya and Egypt—in other words, "the lands south of the known world."

Chapter Six

SUCCULENTS
& CACTI

❋

$\mathcal{S}$ucculent plants, ones that store water in thickened stems or leaves, are adapted to climates that are dry all or part of the year. Many grow well in our Northern California gardens, offering striking forms and bright flowers while needing little water. Frost-tender succulents thrive only in milder-winter parts of the region, but there are a few hardier types that gardeners in colder locations can enjoy.

Because frost-tender succulents have been grown more often as houseplants or in greenhouses in cold climates than out-of-doors, the majority of reference books assume you will be growing them indoors. These books lack information on how much cold the plants can take, how they respond to rainfall in different seasons, and what their eventual size will be in the ground. The instructions in this chapter refer to outdoor growing. Suggested Reading, on page 295, directs you to books, and Resources, on page 299, will help you locate public gardens where you can expand your knowledge of outdoor succulent gardening.

Of the seven succulents and one cactus discussed in this chapter, cactus and agave are solely New World plants, while aloes are native only to the Old World. The other four plants are from the family *Crassulaceae,*

Echeveria elegans *blooms in a garden of mostly succulents. A steep rocky bed has been built to improve drainage.*

Masses of bright yellow stars bloom atop Sedum praealtum *early in spring.*

227

which has representatives in both worlds. While the origins are clear, the distinctions have often become blurred, since people have been moving between continents and carrying plants (and the names for them) around for several hundred years. We find the European hen and chicks plants (genus *Sempervivum*) in Mexican gardens, along with the similar Mexican native *Echeveria*. Mexicans are likely to call them both *siempreviva,* the word the Spanish brought to Mexico with their European language and plants. And American visitors to classical ruins in Greece are startled to see escaped prickly pear cactus growing around them. We think it gives a flavor of our Wild West to the scene, but they are a familiar feature to the Greeks, having been part of the Greek landscape for several centuries.

We tend to think of succulents, in a general way, as being from desert areas where the weather is unremittingly dry, sunny, and hot, and so we assume they all need no water, full sun, and high temperatures day and night. This is not the case. They may like warm days but can often survive cooler ones, and whatever the temperature of the days, they require cooler nights. The need for cool nights is due to the fact that most succulents and cacti, including all seven featured in this chapter, use a different type of photosynthesis than other plants. Other plants have open leaf pores (stomates) in the daytime, while they use water, carbon dioxide, and the sun's energy to make sugar. The plants in this chapter open their stomates at night and convert carbon dioxide into malic acid. Then, in the daytime, when the stomates close to conserve water, they use the sun's energy to convert the acid into sugar. The shift to the daytime process is stimulated by an increase in temperature.

Many succulents grow well in partial shade. The ones that do are often from mountainous areas, where the uneven terrain puts them in shade for part to most of every day. And not all are from regions with year-round drought. Some, including aeoniums, are from regions with a mediterranean climate, and so they are familiar with our pattern of rainy winter and dry summer. Others, such as jade plant, echeveria, and *Sedum praealtum,* have adapted to the opposite pattern—wet summer and dry winter—but are adaptable enough to handle our winter rainfall, as long as the soil has good drainage. These three are among the succulents that gladly share summer beds with plants that need summer water, though even aeoniums can tolerate summer water if drainage is good.

The succulents and cactus (and cactus is really just one kind of succulent) described in this chapter are not extremely fussy about soil. However, if your soil is very heavy clay, or if it seems to stay soggy in rainy parts of the winter, it may not let these plants thrive. You can improve clay soil's drainage by adding organic matter (see also Chapter One on soil improvement). It may also help to add some builder's sand. Planting on a slope or in a raised bed framed with rocks or timbers are other ways to improve drainage. Many succulents will also thrive with their roots in an unmortared rock wall.

While it is true for all plants that it is best to water well (deeply) and then let the soil drain well (for several days or longer, depending on the situation) before you water again, this is especially true for succulents, because they are adapted to such a pattern. These plants tend to be shallow rooted, but deep watering will encourage the roots to go as deep as possible, aiding stability. Drier soil between waterings lets the roots get plenty of air, reducing the chance that they will rot.

All of these plants reproduce well from parts that break off. This ability is often an adaptation to feeding and damage by animals, as is the case with jade plant, which is part of the diet of large South African tortoises. In addition, stems may lean over to root, and plantlets with roots may even form on larger plants and then fall to the ground and grow. You can make more plants by encouraging these processes—removing pieces of the plant and putting them in soil. Directions in the following entries will tell you how to do this for each featured plant. These instructions often include directions to "heal" the cutting, which means to keep it in a warm shady place for a short while so the cut end can form a scar. Healed cuttings are less likely to decay. Succulents do form seeds, but reproduction via cuttings is usually so much faster that it is the preferred method.

Either method of reproduction can let a plant escape from gardens. Seeds have made a pest of at least one cactus (prickly pear spread in Australia when birds ate the fruit), but reproduction by discarded prunings or whole plants left where they can root and grow is probably a greater hazard here, and this is a problem over which gardeners have more control.

Escape by succulents is more common in areas that never get frost, so this is more likely to happen in Southern California. Still, at least two kinds are considered pests in Northern California. There was recently quite a brouhaha over a U.S. postage stamp featuring a photo of the ice plant *Carpobrotus* carpeting the Pacific coastline. While we, like Europeans who are used to seeing prickly pear, have become quite accustomed to seeing this invader, native dune plants are destroyed by it, and it also has the less-than-charming habit of pulling down sandy embankments, causing landslides rather than stabilizing them. Another succulent that has escaped in Northern California is red apple *(Aptenia cordifolia)*. Its thick leaves and small, bright red flowers are often seen on irrigation waterway embankments in the Central Valley and at the edges of wetland near the coast. Hence, these particular succulents are poor choices for Northern California gardeners.

Aeonium (various species)

❋ Aeonium

PLANT TYPE: *Succulent* | HEIGHT AND SPREAD: *1 to 4 feet tall and 1 to 2 feet wide* | BLOOM TIME: *Late winter, spring* | LIGHT NEEDS: *Partial shade* | SOIL NEEDS: *Well drained* | WATER NEEDS: *Moderate, none in summer* | OTHER TOLERANCES: *Summer water, cool coastal summers, full sun near the coast, seaside conditions* | HARDINESS: *Zones 9b to 11*

*T*he science fiction forms and often vibrant flowers of the larger species of *Aeonium* are sure to attract attention. Aeoniums have leafy rosettes, similar to those of hen and chicks but often much bigger, usually carried atop bare, often branched, stems. The leaves may be green, deep purple, or striped. Flowers may be pink or white but are often a showy yellow.

Rosettes of the maroon-leaved 'Zwartkop' aeonium are borne on stems up to 3 feet tall.

The foot-wide whorls of leaves and bright yellow flower heads of Aeonium arborescens *are sure to get attention.*

Source and Uses

Most aeoniums are native to the Canary Islands, off the northwest coast of Africa, where they survived the last ice age and the development of the Sahara Desert. They continued to evolve, so that there are now more than 30 Canarian species. However, one of the most common species in Northern California, *Aeonium arboreum*, is from Morocco, dwelling on rocky cliffs high over the Atlantic Ocean.

Aeoniums look good with other succulents or can, if they are placed well, make a striking contrast to plants with very different forms. Try them with bulbs, palms, grassy plants, or even in a perennial border. They also look good in containers, which can then be moved to a protected area if severe frost is expected.

Care and Reproduction

Being from mediterranean climates, aeoniums grow in winter and are dormant in the summer. Our natural rainfall is generally sufficient for their survival. They do not need summer water—it doesn't make them grow in summer, but neither does it seem to harm them as long as the soil drains well. (Poorly drained soil can promote decay in any season.) If they are too dry, or if the weather gets hot, they may shrivel, the rosettes closing somewhat, but recovering with fall rains.

Prune aeonium to limit the size of clumps, to improve their shape, or just to get rid of heads that have become ugly. Remove whole stems to the ground or cut them to a joint with another stem. The best time to prune is just after they bloom, but you can also shape plants during the summer and early fall. If you want the plants to bloom, however, be sure that some heads reach full height for the species and that you don't remove too many each year.

You can grow new plants from any heads you've removed. Cut the stems to a few inches long (maybe two or three times as long as the diameter of the head) and let them heal for at least 3 days before planting them shallowly in well-drained soil. You can plant several of slightly different heights together, with the heads just touching, so they will grow into an instant clump. If aerial roots have formed on the stems, you can just leave them on.

Aeonium stems may die after blooming, especially in species that don't branch. If so, cut the dead stems out. In branching forms, the leaves below the flowers may fall off, but the plant will often branch and form new rosettes at that site. In this case, leave the spent flower stems where you want more branching to occur, and remove them where you don't. Another possibility is that rooted plantlets will form on the spent flower stem. Although aeonium will form dust-like seed after bloom, the seedlings that form from it may be hybrids that are different from, and maybe not as nice as, the parents. In any case, propagation is so easy from cuttings or plantlets that you will not need plants from seeds.

CONTROL AND REMOVAL

Aeonium arboreum and some other types will make a thicket that covers many square feet if left to grow. Stems will fall over, plantlets will break off, and roots will form. Some kinds grow by underground suckers. You may want to use a firm hand to limit this profusion, taking most of it out from time to time, and then replanting just a few heads. Removal, as with most succulents, is not difficult, but be careful that you don't discard plant parts where they will be able to grow. Some aeoniums spread readily from gardens to adjacent areas in sandy soil, so monitor them, especially near the coast. *A. arboreum* grows wild in several Southern California counties and around the Mediterranean.

VARIETIES AND SIMILAR SPECIES

Aeonium arboreum is a 3- to 4-foot-tall, branched plant with green leaves that are broader near their tips. Rosettes average 12 inches in diameter but can reach 20 inches. Cone-shaped heads of bright yellow flowers bloom in the spring. There are no hairs on the leaf surfaces or the flower stems. *A. arboreum* 'Atropurpureum' has leaves flushed with red. Other common tall, green-leaved aeoniums in our gardens and in nurseries may be actual species or named cultivars, or they may have grown from unnamed hybrid seedlings. There seems to be considerable confusion.

The hybrid *Aeonium* 'Zwartkop' (or 'Schwarzkopf') has deep maroon, almost black, leaves in rosettes to about 8 inches across. It has bare, branched stems up to 3 feet tall, and *A. arboreum*-like yellow flowers. Plants sold as 'Zwartkop' seem to show some variation in depth of color and in whether they hold their color over winter. They are generally damaged by temperatures under 28 degrees F. Other purple-leaf hybrids include 'Cyclops' (large, solitary rosettes), 'Garnet', and 'Zwartkin'. Other aeonium varieties offer variegated leaves, most often green and yellow with some pink markings. Examples are *A. arboreum* 'Island Sunset', *A.* 'Sunburst', and *A.* 'Kiwi'. Size varies, so get information with the plants you buy.

Aeonium haworthii, another common species, is native to the Canary Island of Tenerife. The plants form rounded clumps a foot or so tall and 2 feet or more wide, with 3-inch-diameter, bluish green rosettes that are often edged in red, and slender, branched stems. The clusters of pale yellow to pinkish-white flowers are up to 6 inches tall (see photo page *x*).

The Name

The genus name *Aeonium* (aye-ohn'-ee-um) derives from the Latin word *aeon* ("an immeasurably long period of time," "forever"). The name is ancient and refers to the ongoing nature of these plants. It is similar in meaning to the genus name of a related succulent, *Sempervivum,* which is Latin for "forever-living." The specific epithet *arboreum* (ahr-bor'-ee-um) is Latin for "treelike."

Agave americana

⊞ Century plant

PLANT TYPE: *Succulent* | HEIGHT AND SPREAD: *5 to 7 feet tall and 8 to 12 feet wide (flower stem is 15 to 40 feet)* | BLOOM TIME: *Spring and summer* | LIGHT NEEDS: *Full sun, partial shade* | SOIL NEEDS: *Moderately fertile, well drained* | WATER NEEDS: *Little to moderate* | OTHER TOLERANCES: *Drought tolerant, cool coastal summers, hot inland summers, deer resistant* | HARDINESS: *Zones 9 to 11*

A century plant makes a strong visual statement—wonderfully bold and sculptural. But it does get very big. Like the cute puppy that grows up to be a huge dog, *Agave americana*

Each leaf of Agave Americana *'Medio Picta' sports a pale central stripe. Its relatively small size makes this variety a good choice for containers or narrow raised planters.*

Give full-sized varieties of A. americana *plenty of room to enjoy their sculptural beauty without painful encounters.*

just keeps growing. And this puppy can bite. It has sharp, recurved spines on the sides of the leaves and longer ones at the tips, all of which can really hurt if they stick you. The tip spines are easy to bump into. As garden writer Roger Swain says, because the leaves "taper rapidly to nothingness, it is easy to get too close."

Source and Uses

Century plant originated in the uplands of Mexico and is traditionally used in both Mexico and South America as a barrier plant to contain livestock. It was carried to Spain shortly after the Spanish conquistadors discovered it and is now widely grown in mediterranean and desert climates worldwide. (In case you are wondering, tequila is made from a similar species, but generally not this one.)

These plants give a desert or tropical look to a garden. They are fine on embankments (where they aid in erosion control) or in large borders. They can also be maintained in containers for some time. Be careful to place these plants, as garden designers say, "away from frequented areas." Unfortunately, it is difficult for many gardeners to imagine century plant at its typical 8- to 12-foot-wide glory, so it is often planted close to sidewalks, paths, or stairways and then whacked back when it gets too wide, resulting in an unattractive form and a weakened plant.

Care and Reproduction

Century plants can survive brief temperature plunges to as low as 15 degrees F, but injury is likely after longer periods below 20 degrees F, and they are slow to recover from frost damage. They are tolerant of a wide range of soils. While they can survive on rainfall in Northern California, they will do better with deep monthly watering in cool summers, or as often as every 10 days in really hot weather.

It is normal for the lower leaves of growing agaves to turn brown and die and for an occasional leaf tip to die. If you mind these, they can be removed with very sharp pruning shears. If only part of the leaf is dead, cut it just outside of the dead part, as cutting into the living leaf opens it to disease.

The name century plant refers to the legendary age of the plant at blooming, but in truth, it blooms when it is only 10 to 35 years old, taking longer to do so where summers are cool or winters cold. The yellow flowers, on stalks at least 15 feet tall, produce copious nectar appreciated by insects and birds, including hummingbirds. (Wild agaves are pollinated mainly by bats.) The plant dies slowly after it blooms, its tough leaves collapsing and both leaves and flower stalk turning dark brown. While the dead stalk is a dramatic vertical accent, it should not be left indefinitely, since the plants sometimes fall over as they decay, and could hurt someone. Use a pruning saw to remove the dead flower stem. Leaving several feet of the flowering stem when you cut it is a good idea, as it will give you something to hang onto when you are removing the whole plant.

Century plants are most often propagated by offshoots known as pups that form at the ends of short, horizontal underground stems. Some plants will form few pups, others may form a solid ring of them. They can be removed, in soft or recently watered soil, by lifting and tugging or, if they are rooted, by digging and tugging. To grow them, remove them in spring or fall. If a pup has roots, plant it; if it is unrooted, root it first in cutting mix.

Control and Removal

Removing a century plant is hard work, and untended clumps may form a thicket of plants that will be harder to master later. To avoid this, you may want to remove many of the pups while they are young and discard them, or replant them farther from the parent plant.

To remove larger plants, living or dead, for disposal, start by cutting off most of the leaves with very sharp pruning or hedge shears. Then use a digging fork or shovel to loosen the roots all the way around the plant. If the plant has a flower stem stub, a second person can try to wiggle it at the same time.

Varieties and Similar Species

Century plant varieties have green, blue-green, or variegated leaves. Some variegated types stay smaller than others, and some have leaves that curve and flop over charmingly, belying their tough nature. If you want a smaller plant, or one with curved leaves, obtain a pup from a plant you have seen at maturity, or buy your plant at a reliable nursery. 'Marginata' or 'Variegata' both have white or yellow leaf edges. These may be big plants or smaller ones, and they may have pinkish tints in the light part of the leaves. The cultivar 'Striata' is large and upright, with several milky-white vertical stripes on pale blue-gray leaves. 'Medio Picta' is a stable and predictable variety with a single broad yellow or white stripe down the leaf centers. It grows to only 3 feet tall, so it is good for pots and small gardens.

There are more than two hundred species of agave, many of them grown in European gardens before they became available to U.S. gardeners. Among your many interesting options are *Agave parryi*, *A. victoriae-reginae*, and the spineless *A. attenuata* and *A. vilmoriniana*.

The Name

The genus name *Agave* (uh-gahv'-ay) derives from the Greek *agauos* ("admirable"), referring to the dramatic flowering stalk. Although agaves are New World plants, they were carried to Europe so early that some Europeans have mistaken them for natives. Others recognize their similarity to aloes by calling them "American aloe."

Protect Yourself

Whenever you are working on or around a century plant, be sure you wear thick leather gloves and long sleeves. You may also want to use chunks of florist's foam or recycled wine corks to cover the leaf tip spines while you are near a plant. In addition to the hazard of the spines, the sap of these plants causes an allergic reaction in some people, resulting in an itchy dermatitis.

Aloe arborescens

Tree aloe, candelabra plant, Krantz aloe

PLANT TYPE: *Succulent* | HEIGHT AND SPREAD: *6 to 12 feet tall and 6 feet wide* | BLOOM TIME: *Winter* | LIGHT NEEDS: *Full sun, partial shade* | SOIL NEEDS: *Neutral, poor to fertile, well drained* | WATER NEEDS: *Little to moderate* | OTHER TOLERANCES: *Drought tolerant, cool coastal summers, hot inland summers, deer resistant* | HARDINESS: *Zones 9 to 11*

South African aloes vary from tiny "grass aloes," under a foot tall, to astonishing 60-foot single-trunked aloe trees. Several of these handsome plants are common in California, one of the most common being *Aloe arborescens*. It's an eye-stopper, with its dramatic midwinter spikes of scarlet flowers atop tall masses of pinwheel leaf whorls.

Most tree aloe plants bear scarlet flowers but there is also a yellow-flowered variety. Flowers of the similar species A. mutabilis are two-toned— orange fading to yellow.

Tree aloe, which attracts hummingbirds to gardens in winter, can be kept at a smaller size but is glorious when allowed to grow tall.

Source and Uses

Aloe arborescens grows from the Eastern Cape Province around the east side of South Africa and up into Zimbabwe. Native South Africans have long planted it atop tall earthen walls to make effective *kraals,* or corrals, for livestock, and starts are still sold in *muthi,* or herbal shops, for this purpose. This and many other kinds of aloe are also now popular South African landscape plants, with tall aloe plants appearing in median strips, along driveways, and on either side of front doorways.

Europeans carried *Aloe arborescens* home in the early 1700s, and it became common in coastal Mediterranean gardens. Since its arrival in California with early Spanish settlers, its popularity here has fluctuated. There are dramatic, old plantings, such as the ones along the Recreation Trail in Monterey. Others, such as the ones that once graced Sutro Park in San Francisco, have been summarily removed. The plants enhance gardens with mediterranean, desert, or tropical themes, and they invite hummingbirds to enjoy a winter meal.

In nature, *Aloe arborescens* often grows with its roots wedged between rocks. While it doesn't need rocks in a garden, it looks good among large ones. The plant grows well in containers and is even a fairly successful houseplant if given reasonably bright light, though of course container plants won't reach full size.

Care and Reproduction

Like many of the plants in this book, *Aloe arborescens* can survive without any attention at all, but it will look better if given care. For survival, it asks only good drainage, but it does best in organically amended soil. Without summer water the leaves will become reddish and shriveled; periodic summer water will let them remain plump and green. In most of its native range it gets no winter rain, but its westernmost region gets rain all year, so it can tolerate our winter rainfall. It can take some frost, showing leaf damage at 29 degrees F, and it may survive temperatures to 17 degrees F. The plants will be more attractive if you cut out dead flower stems in the spring.

Cuttings of *Aloe arborescens* are easy to root. Prune off a foot or so of stem, remove any dead or dying lower leaves, and trim the stem to 6 inches below the last remaining leaf. Place the cutting in a warm, shady place for 1 week to heal the cut, and then plant it in well-drained soil.

California plants don't often form seeds, because most of them originated as cuttings taken from a single clone. When cross-pollination occurs, seeds form, and you can collect these by tying a stocking over the seedhead when the lower capsules begin to split. When most of them have opened, cut the stem and dry the seeds in a warm, dry place. Sow seeds on moistened cactus mix, barely covering them with coarse sand. After a year, some will be big enough to plant in the garden; others will need longer.

CONTROL AND REMOVAL

This is a plant best set where it can grow freely into the large, rather unruly plant that it is. If branches do grow where they are not welcome, they can be pruned off at any time. Try to cut them to the joint formed with another branch, or at least cut the stem low enough so that the bare stub doesn't stick out of the plant.

Removing a large plant will take time, but if it is cut down and then dug out, *Aloe arborescens* is not likely to come back. The spines can hurt if you encounter them while you are moving fast while cutting a plant, though they are not nearly as sharp as those of century plant.

VARIETIES AND SIMILAR SPECIES

Yellow-flowered plants of *Aloe arborescens* are available. These plants tend to remain smaller than the scarlet-flowered ones. (Flowerheads of a similar species *A. Mutabilis* are two-toned, with yellow flowers at the bottom, orange at the top.) You may also find *A. arborescens* 'Variegata', with longitudinal white-striped leaves. *A. x spinosissima*, a plant assumed to be a hybrid between *A. arborescens* and *A. humilis*, mounds to only 2½ to 3 feet tall with scarlet flowers, good for a smaller garden. You may also see large aloe plants with candelabra branched flower stems and fewer whorls of larger leaves. These may be a hybrid between *A. arborescens* and *A. ferox*. You might also come across *A. ferox* itself, each plant of which has only one tall, broad whorl of leaves with a branched flower stem on top.

Little known but dramatic *Aloe polyphylla* forms a handsome, low, gray-green spiral to 3 feet wide and likes cool, misty weather, making it ideal for near-coastal gardens.

Also popular in California gardens are small species such as *Aloe saponaria*, which makes low, single whorls of white-spotted leaves and 2½-foot stems of red, pink, peach, or yellow flowers, most commonly in summer.

The Name

Although most species of *Aloe* are native to Southern Africa, the genus name *Aloe* (al'-low or al-low'-ee) was the Latin name for a North African species known since antiquity for the ability of the gel in its leaves to soothe burns, bruises, and abrasions. We now call that plant *Aloe vera*. Despite being an Old World plant, *Aloe vera* was carried to the Caribbean by the Spanish so early in their colonization that it also became known as *A. barbadensis*, meaning "from Barbados." *A. vera* is common in local gardens, usually in small pots, and is often stunted by having its leaves cut for use in skin care. If allowed to mature, it will form 3-foot-tall stems of yellow flowers in summer. *A. arborescens* has some of the same soothing chemicals and is used in South Africa for skin injuries. Its specific epithet *arborescens* is Latin for "treelike."

Crassula ovata (*C. arborescens, C. argentea, C. portulaca*)

Jade plant, jade tree, money plant, Chinese rubber plant

PLANT TYPE: *Succulent* | HEIGHT AND SPREAD: *3 to 6 feet or more tall and 3 to 4 feet or more wide* | BLOOM TIME: *Winter* | LIGHT NEEDS: *Full sun, partial shade* | SOIL NEEDS: *Moderately fertile, well drained* | WATER NEEDS: *None to moderate* | OTHER TOLERANCES: *Cool coastal summers, hot inland summers, deer resistant* | HARDINESS: *Zones 9b to 10*

his accommodating succulent lives in many a cozy living room in colder climates, with winter wind blowing at the windows. The tidy little fat-leaved houseplants tolerate small pots, low light, and low humidity, giving little evidence that they can grow to 10 feet or taller in their native South Africa. In Northern California gardens the plants may reach

While the main show is the handsome leaves, mature jade plants grown in sun produce starry white or pink flowers in winter.

A houseplant in cold climates, jade plant is common in Northern California gardens wherever frosts are rare.

6 feet tall. The shiny mid-green leaves may develop red shadings in sunlight, and mature plants growing in a sunny place may be covered with white or pink blooms in the winter months.

Source and Uses

Jade plant grows mainly on dry, rocky slopes along the eastern coast of South Africa, a region of mild, dry winters and summer rains. It has adapted to the dry winters by having not only thickened leaves, but also special openings, called hydathodes, on the upper surfaces of the leaves, which are able to absorb moisture from humid air or dew.

In South Africa it is not a highly favored garden plant, but indigenous plant champions encourage gardeners to plant it, especially in butterfly gardens, since it attracts South African species of butterflies. In mild-winter coastal Northern California, we see it in settings ranging from pots on the patio to raised beds by the front door, as well as growing in the ground to form short or tall hedges.

Care and Reproduction

Jade plant growing in the ground doesn't require very fertile soil, but the soil must be well drained, to avoid root decay in our winter rainy season. In our summers it survives with little or no water, but being from a region with summer rain, it appreciates periodic deep watering, with care to let the soil dry somewhat in between. Poor drainage and overwatering in either season will cause the lower roots to rot. The tall, heavy plants may then topple over, pulling the remaining roots, which are close to the surface where they can find oxygen, from the ground.

The plant thrives in a container outdoors, not minding if its roots have filled the pot. Water jade plants in containers whenever the soil is moderately dry. In regions with hard frosts, container plants can be moved indoors in winter.

The plants are stimulated to bloom by winter's shorter days, but they may not do so when they are still young or when they are growing in shade. If a plant is going to bloom, it may do so as early as November or not until January.

Although the plants are evergreen, as they begin to grow in the spring they drop a few old leaves. This is a good time to prune any unsightly branches or to prune to improve the shape of your plants, though it is best to leave them in a rather informal shape. It is also a good time to take cuttings so you will have new plants in reserve to replace old ones. Cut off an attractive branch a few inches long, let it heal in a dry place for at least a day, and then set it 1 to 2 inches deep in well-drained soil. Water very infrequently until roots begin to form, which could happen in as little as a month. Single leaves will also grow, but this takes much longer and is not necessary in most cases, as you will generally have plenty of stem cuttings.

CONTROL OR REMOVAL

Plants that are too big can be reduced in size, though cuts into thicker branches or the trunk are slow to heal, and pruning that is too severe may result in unattractive plants. Do institute an annual checkup to remove unwanted rooted starts beneath established plants.

The shallow roots of jade plants make them relatively easy to remove, although because they are heavy with water, you will want to cut up larger plants before you try to dig them out. There is definitely a hazard that discarded leaves or stems could grow where they are not wanted, so be careful where you discard them.

VARIETIES AND SIMILAR SPECIES

Gardeners will find green-leaved compact forms such as 'Cosby's Dwarf' useful, as well as varieties that have flowers of a superior pink color. Nurseries also sell variegated or twisted-leaf forms that are most useful as houseplants. (Variegated leaf types can burn in sunny locations but may tolerate full sun in a foggy garden very near the coast.)

Crassula arborescens, or silver jade plant, is a similar species native to the dry-summer Western Cape region. Its gray-green leaves have conspicuous dots on their surfaces and often have red edges. The plants grow slowly to 3 to 6 feet tall, and mature ones bear white flowers in summer that fade to pink. This plant would be better adapted to our winter rainfall climate than *C. ovata,* but it is not very commonly grown.

Portulacaria afra, or elephant food, is a smaller-leaved but otherwise similar plant that is so frost-tender that it survives, looking not very happy at that, only in the mildest parts of the Bay Area.

THE NAME

The genus name *Crassula* derives from the Latin word *crassus,* which means "thick," referring to the thick leaves that are common in the members of the genus. The same root is used in the name *Crassulaceae,* the name of the plant family to which this genus belongs, along with *Echeveria, Sedum,* and *Aeonium.* The specific epithet *ovata* (oh-vah'-tuh) means "egg-shaped," referring to the leaves.

Echeveria x imbricata (Echeveria elegans)

Hen and chicks, echeveria

PLANT TYPE: *Succulent* | HEIGHT AND SPREAD: *Mounds to 6 inches and flowers to 1 foot, spreading* | BLOOM TIME: *Spring and summer* | LIGHT NEEDS: *Full sun, partial shade* | SOIL NEEDS: *Moderately fertile, well drained* | WATER NEEDS: *Moderate to ample (none in winter)* | OTHER TOLERANCES: *Shallow soil, winter water in well-drained soil, cool coastal summers* | HARDINESS: *Zones 9b to 11*

These fat little whorls of leaves get the common name "hen and chicks" from the way they form smaller plants around the large ones. They share the name with similar plants in the genus *Sempervivum*. But while *Sempervivum* species are hardy European natives, *Echeveria* species are New World plants, most of which are relatively frost-tender. Of the hundreds of species and

Echeveria flowers, such as these showy, two-toned Echeveria x imbricata *blossoms, attract hummingbirds.*

Grown in California for more than 100 years, E. x imbricata *is a common sight. It has whorls of blue-green leaves with gracefully curved tips.*

varieties of *Echeveria*, two kinds, *E.* x *imbricata* and *E. elegans*, are especially common in Northern California gardens.

E. elegans is commonly sold as Mexican snowball. Its leaves are gray-green and fatter than those of E. x imbricata.

Source and Uses

Most *Echeveria* species are native to rocky, mountainous habitats in Mexico, though there are native species from southwestern Texas to northwestern Argentina. Spanish botanists first carried Mexican *Echeveria* specimens to Europe in the late 1700s. Victorian gardeners used these tidy little plants in formal bedding schemes, and the first ones to reach the United States were European hybrids.

Echeveria x *imbricata* was an early hybrid first sold in 1873 by J. B. A. Deleuil, of Marseilles, France. It is still found in California gardens today, though many have been lost in our periodic freezes, since it is only hardy to 20 to 25 degrees F. *E. elegans*, which is common in gardens and nurseries, may be able to take temperatures that are a few degrees colder than those *E.* x *imbricata* can withstand.

Several species of *Echeveria* are grown in Mexican gardens, where they are sometimes used to completely cover vertical garden walls. Dramatic as this may be, more intriguing garden compositions are possible if *Echeveria* colonies are limited in size so that other plants or rocks can add interest to the composition. They are great edging plants, and they lend themselves to use in both formal and informal designs. They thrive in containers and have also been used in floral arrangements, such as table centerpieces and living wreaths.

Care and Reproduction

Mexican *Echeveria* species are tropical highland plants accustomed to having dry winters and rainy summers. They survive California's winter rains if the soil is well drained, and they need regular summer water, though they tolerate some drying between waterings. In the wild they often live on rocks where there is little soil, depending on pockets of decayed organic matter for nutrients, so they don't mind shallow or rocky soil, but they do appreciate amendment with organic matter and perhaps light fertilization in the summer months. They are more successful near the coast, where frost is less common and summers are cooler. Inland, shade helps somewhat with summer heat, but it cannot make conditions ideal. (The similar plants of the genus *Sempervivum* would be a better choice in inland gardens.)

Echeveria flowers are bell shaped, usually hanging on curving flower stems up to about a foot tall. Hummingbirds visit them to sip their ample nectar. Groom plants by removing spent flower stems. Then, every 2 or 3 years, as growth begins in March, inspect the clumps to see if they are looking messy because of dead leaves under the rosettes, or if they have mounded up on long stems. If the problem is minor, remove unsightly rosettes and dead leaves. In serious cases, remove the clump and replant the best rosettes on shorter stems with the dead leaves removed. Unrooted rosette stems, which should be allowed to heal for a few days before planting, will root in 3 to 4 weeks.

In addition to starting plants by rooting whole rosettes, you can grow plants from single leaves. Pull leaves off in March and lay them on moist soil mix, placing them in a warm, dry place out of the sun. Keep them quite dry until new plantlets have formed. After roots form, in about a month, move the plants to a brighter place and begin to water them. Echeverias do form seed, but it is not a preferred propagation method, since seedlings grow slowly and the plants hybridize readily, so seedlings may not resemble parents—and may not be as nice.

CONTROL AND REMOVAL

Control the slow spread of echeverias by removing the side rosettes from clumps. Because of their shallow roots, echeveria clumps are easy to remove permanently. Do avoid discarding rosettes or even spent flower stems where they could regrow, as even the flower stem bracts of some kinds can grow new plants.

VARIETIES AND SIMILAR SPECIES

Echeveria x *imbricata* has rosettes of blue-green leaves 4 to 6 inches in diameter. The ⅝-inch flowers are pink with yellow tips. *E. elegans*, often sold as Mexican gem or Mexican snowball, has 3- to 5-inch rosettes that are pale gray-green, with leaves a bit thicker than those of *E*. x. *imbricata*. They bear flowers similar to those of *E*. x *imbricata*, but only ½ inch long. Leaves of both may take a lavender tinge, especially in winter.

From the many available kinds, here is a short list of other easy echeverias:

✱ *E. elegans* 'Super Clone' is similar to *E. elegans* but hardy to 10 to 15 degrees F.

✱ *E. agavoides* has apple-green rosettes up to 12 inches across and is an easy houseplant, but is also hardy to 15 to 20 degrees F. *E. agavoides* 'Red Edge' has deep red margins near its leaf tips.

✱ *E.* 'Doris Taylor', or woolly rose, is one of the easiest to grow of the many furry echeverias.

THE NAME

Anastasio Echeverria (etch-uh-veh'-ree-uh) was a botanical artist who traveled to Mexico in 1798 with a Spanish plant-hunting expedition. After 15 years of hard work under harsh conditions, the team returned to find a new Spanish king who didn't care a bit about plants. Echeverria's beautiful drawings languished unpublished for years. When Napoleon's army overran Spain, one of the expedition botanists fled, carrying the drawings to the Swiss botanist Alphonse de Candolle in an oxcart. Later, the Spanish botanist asked for them back, but de Candolle had doubts about their safety and so had them copied, using 120 draftsmen for 10 days. His fears proved right, since the originals were lost in the confusion of war. De Candolle later honored the artist Echeverria by naming a genus after him (but dropping one of the "r"s in his name). The specific epithet *imbricata* (im-brih-cah'-tuh) means overlapping, like roof shingles, and the "x" between *Echeveria* and *imbricata* indicates that two different species were crossed to make the hybrid.

Opuntia ficus-indica

✳ Prickly pear cactus, Indian fig

PLANT TYPE: *Succulent (cactus)* | HEIGHT AND SPREAD: *15 feet tall and 15 feet wide* | BLOOM TIME: *Late spring into summer* | LIGHT NEEDS: *Full sun best* | SOIL NEEDS: *Not particular, well drained* | WATER NEEDS: *None to little* | OTHER TOLERANCES: *Cool coastal summers, hot inland summers, usually deer resistant* | HARDINESS: *Zones 9b to 11*

*T*here is a craziness to the form of a prickly pear cactus, with its broad pads angling out in wild disarray. The yellow or orange flowers perch on the edges of the pads and then develop into colorful fruits that are, in some varieties, quite tasty. If you have room in your garden for this big plant, it is a striking feature. If your garden is smaller, you will need to give careful attention to pruning to keep it

Prickly pear flowers are luminous when sunlight shines through them.

The fruit is highly ornamental but can be quite tasty. If you want to harvest fruit or pads, don't let a plant grow so large that you can't reach the top to harvest.

attractive and in bounds, or you may want to consider smaller *Opuntia* species or other cacti.

Source and Uses

Opuntia ficus-indica is one of many kinds of cactus that have been eaten by native peoples of the American Southwest and Mexico for thousands of years. In fact, although it is assumed to be native to Mexico, it has hybridized in cultivation for so long that its original appearance and exact place of origin are not known. The pads *(nopales)* and fruit *(tunas)* are still eaten in Mexico, and the fruit is also popular in South Africa, the Middle East, and the Mediterranean (especially Italy).

Prickly pear cactus in California gardens is likely to be an offspring of the "mission cactus" brought from Mexico by Spanish padres. In the missions, it was grown for its fruit and was also used as a living fence around food gardens and orchards and as a source of mucilage for the plaster applied to adobe structures.

Prickly pear can be a fine sculptural element in a garden, working well with Southwest or mediterranean design themes. Planted a foot apart and allowed to fill in, it makes a wickedly effective barrier hedge, though this is probably more prickly pear than most of us want to contemplate.

Care and Reproduction

Prickly pear cactus grows slowly and lives at least 20 years. It can survive unwatered in Northern California but will have plumper, smoother pads and juicier fruits if watered occasionally in the summer. If you plan to eat the fruit or pads, water it regularly, and also fertilize the plant.

The plants can often use a bit of pruning. Prune to shape the plant, to keep it from growing into paths or other plants or from leaning on garden walls, and to keep it from becoming too tall to reach. While its maximum height and spread are 15 feet, it is possible to maintain it at 6 feet tall and wide. The best method is to remove young pads (6 to 12 inches long) with a knife in mid to late spring. Thin out areas with too many pads and remove ones growing in unwanted directions. (The young pads, with the spines and short spinelettes—glochids—cut off, can be cooked and eaten, using recipes for *nopales* in Mexican cookbooks. They taste a little like green beans.) If necessary, use a pruning saw to remove mature pads (it will leave scars). Avoid the chopped look of a bare, brown trunk with green pads only at the top by allowing some branches to form lower on the plant.

To grow prickly pear, the best start is a rooted pad. Choose one from a plant with few spines, and if you plan to eat the fruit, get a start from a plant whose fruit you liked, or from a named variety. (The fruit varies from bland to reminiscent of honeydew melon and can be red, yellow, white, purple, or green when ripe.) Mature pads root easily if they are left to heal for a few days in a warm, shady place and are then propped upright with their bottom inch in the soil. They will grow slowly at first, but in a few years you will have a large plant.

Control and Removal

This plant certainly has the ability to spread on its own. It does so in Southern California and in Texas rangeland, and it has been a major problem in both Australia and South Africa. Birds can spread the seed when they eat the fruits, and broken-off pads or even pieces of pads can grow. Plowing this plant under results in many new plants. Having said that, I must also say that it is not on statewide weed lists, I have never seen a seedling in a garden, nor a bird eating the fruit, and it is not difficult to keep prickly pear from spreading in a garden environment. Just don't leave cut pads where they can grow, in gardens or in wild areas.

To remove a plant, a good plan is to impale small sections with a pitchfork while a second person removes them with a pruning saw. Be sure to wear gloves, as the spines (though usually sparse) and the shorter glochids are a hazard. Remove any spines or glochids from your skin with tweezers.

Varieties and Similar Species

The species varies in flower and fruit color, fruit flavor, and number of spines. A number of other *Opuntia* species have a similar flat-padded form and showy, though not always edible, fruit. Some offer smaller plants, hardier plants, or colorful pads. Several you might consider are *O. violacea (O. macrocentra)* (purple-padded prickly pear, to 4 feet), *O. basilaris* (beavertail cactus, to 3 feet, pinkish pads), and *O. microdasys* (bunny ears, to 3 feet, tufts of yellow glochids).

THE NAME

Prickly pear was the first cactus ever seen by Europeans. It caused quite a stir in sixteenth-century Spain when conquistadors brought it from Mexico. The Spanish first grew it for its dramatic form, but it was soon being grown across Europe for its fruit, which reminded Europeans of figs because of its many seeds. Both the genus and the species name refer to the fig. The genus *Opuntia* (oh-pun'-she-uh) is named after an ancient Greek town known for its figs. The town was Opus, and it was occupied by a tribe known as the Locri Opuntii. The specific epithet, *ficus-indica*, is Latin for "Indian fig." This name refers to the East Indies, which is what Columbus called the Caribbean islands he discovered while seeking India.

Sedum praealtum

 Yellow sedum

PLANT TYPE: *Succulent* | HEIGHT AND SPREAD: *2 to 3 feet tall and 2 to 3 feet wide* | BLOOM TIME: *Late winter, spring* | LIGHT NEEDS: *Full sun or partial shade* | SOIL NEEDS: *Not particular, well drained* | WATER NEEDS: *Little to moderate, none in winter* | OTHER TOLERANCES: *Cool coastal summers, hot inland summers, seaside conditions* | HARDINESS: *Zones 9 to 11*

A retaining wall provides a home for blooming Sedum praealtum *as well as white and pink-flowered centranthus.*

*T*his is the "stealth succulent." It is common in California gardens and parks, but few people notice or can identify it. It is true that this plant is not striking in form, being a rather nondescript, sprawling subshrub with thick, mid-green, 3-inch leaves, but it nicely decorates out-of-the-way parts of a garden in sun or shade, and when it blooms its masses of brilliant yellow flowers are a harbinger of spring as cheerful as those of daffodils.

Source and Uses

The original habitat of *Sedum praealtum* is not clear, since it has been cultivated for so long in Mexico and Central America for medicinal purposes, but it is presumed to have originated in Mexico. (The plant is still sold in Mexican herb shops, or *yerbarias.*) Neither is the course of the plant into our gardens well recorded. It had reached Switzerland by 1847. That's when the botanist Alphonse de Candolle obtained a specimen that had been growing in a local garden and gave it a name. It became quite common in British cottage gardens, though it had fallen out of fashion by the mid-twentieth century.

Sedum praealtum is rarely mentioned in California gardening books, though it probably has been growing here for at least a century. A photo of it appears in the 1908 book *Gardening in California* by John McLaren, who planted much of San Francisco's Golden Gate Park. Perhaps some of the specimens that survive in various urban parks were planted in that era.

Be all this as it may, the plant, though unassuming when not in flower, is easy to grow and serves equally well in a succulent planting or in a flower border, in a rock garden, or in large containers, serving as a foil to plants with more dramatic forms. It is able to survive on rocky slopes or in dry shade, though it may bloom less in shade. When it does bloom, the flowers can be cut and used in arrangements.

Care and Reproduction

Sedum praealtum is not particular about soil as long as the drainage is good. It can share a bed with plants that need summer water, or it can survive with no summer water, though the leaves will shrivel if the soil becomes too dry in summer. To prevent this, watch plants in unwatered sites for leaf surfaces that have lost their luster, and water well if you see this sign of water stress. Leaves may also acquire a reddish tinge in summer or while flowering. This is normal, and their green color will return in winter.

Groom plants of *Sedum praealtum* by removing spent flower stems. Prune only if the plant is growing larger than the space you have for it or if certain branches are reaching out in unattractive ways. The plant is likely to be more compact and less in need of shaping when grown in sun than in shade. If snails damage the leaves, remove any you see and scatter iron phosphate snail bait.

Sedum praealtum spreads by forming roots either on branches that lean to the ground or on branch pieces that break off of the plant. You can hasten and control this process by taking cuttings in early spring and setting them shallowly in well-drained soil.

CONTROL AND REMOVAL

While it is not an aggressive spreader, if left to its own *Sedum praealtum* will gradually colonize an area. To control its spread, check the edges of a planting for rooting stems, either attached or not, and remove them. Like other succulents, *S. praealtum* is shallow rooted, so it is not difficult to dig out. If you want to eliminate the plant, digging out all of its parts will probably do the job, since it doesn't seem to make seedlings. However, as with any succulent, do not discard the plants in wild places where they can root and grow. It grows wild on the Islands of Madeira and Jersey, and in other locations around the Mediterranean Sea, and it has escaped to some disturbed sites in the Bay Area.

VARIETIES AND SIMILAR SPECIES

The most common *Sedum praealtum* in Northern California is probably the subspecies *praealtum*. Two other subspecies, *parvifolia* and *monticola*, that might be in local gardens or nurseries are so similar that only a botanist would see the difference. It is interesting to note, however, that the subspecies *monticola* grows not only in the ground, on mountain slopes in Mexico, but also as a "pendulous epiphyte" on oak trees.

A very similar species, *Sedum dendroideum*, is much less commonly grown. This plant is somewhat more upright and compact than *S. praealtum;* in fact, the young plants look like little trees. It grows to a rather dense 2-foot-tall by 2- to 3-foot-wide shrub. Another difference is that there is a clearly visible row of glands along the leaf edges, and these are often red in summer. *S. dendroidium* is less hardy than

S. praealtum, being somewhat damaged by light frosts. (Older books will speak of *S. dendroidium* subspecies *praealtum,* but *S. praealtum* has since been designated a separate species.)

THE NAME

Although this sedum is from the New World, there are also sedums from the Old World, so the genus name *Sedum* dates back to ancient times in the Mediterranean region. It is from the Latin word *sedo* ("to sit"). This name was originally given to several of what we now call sedums and sempervivums, for the way in which they grew on rocks and walls. The species name *praealtum* (pray-all'-tum) is Latin for "very tall," while that of the similar species *dendroidium* (den-droy'-dee-um) means "treelike."

Chapter Seven

SHRUBS & WOODY VINES

A shrub is usually defined as a woody plant that has more than one trunk and branches to the ground, though some single-trunked woody plants, such as rhododendrons, are also called shrubs. Shrubs are rarely over 15 feet tall. Within this definition are many forms, from tall and narrow to low and wide. Vines climb and clamber, softening hard surfaces. Shrubs and woody vines give continuity to the garden by remaining in place through the seasons and over the years.

While shrubs can be wonderfully useful plants, many with colorful flowers and attractive leaves, they can also be ugly when they are poorly grown. Many of the unattractive shrubs in Northern California gardens would look quite handsome if they were only properly watered and pruned.

Identify your shrubs and determine their water needs. Although many of the region's garden shrubs get by on moderate summer water, few look good without any. If they will need to be watered, start paying attention to soil moisture as rains taper off in spring. Also, keep the soil under them moist as fall begins, since the plants will be more frost-sensitive if they are dry when cold weather comes. Use an organic

Poor man's rhododendron blooms profusely during much of the year.

Mirror plant has the surprising habit of growing in trees. This one drapes out of the crown of a Canary Island palm (Phoenix canariensis).

mulch under shrubs to retain water in the soil and provide nutrients for the plants.

Both lack of pruning and poor pruning can cause shrubs to be unattractive. Many kinds of shrubs, if never pruned, eventually become lanky with bare trunks. In this case, you can go with the flow, thinning out a few stems and informally shaping the top but leaving the shrub tall with bare trunks. Sometimes this works. Your other options are removing the shrub and starting over or renovating it to try to return it to a short, bushy form.

Shrubs that can be renovated when they have become overgrown and unattractive are ones that can regrow after you have cut into bare (leafless) wood and ones that produce many stems from the ground. (To see if renovation will work on a shrub that isn't listed here, you can cut one stem back to a bud below the leafy part, just before the year's active growth period, and see if it resprouts and grows.)

Many multistemmed shrubs will resprout if all of the stems are cut back at once, to a couple of feet tall or even to the ground. If you don't know whether this will work for a specific multistemmed shrub, you can renovate more cautiously by cutting a third to half of them to the ground each year, waiting until new stems start to grow before removing more. Shrubs with only one stem (trunk) need to be renovated by careful, selective pruning of the branches, sometimes over several years. For more details on pruning and renovation, see regionally appropriate books in the Suggested Reading (page 295).

The most common reason that shrubs in gardens are unattractive is they have been sheared without attention to design. Shearing is the use of hedge pruners to give a shrub a "haircut," resulting in a solid, opaque, often geometrical form. Such a form has its place in gardens, but not as a means of keeping a shrub from becoming too large. Sheared shrubs should serve a purpose, such as to accent a design or to create a screen or barrier. Too many sheared shrubs will give a garden a rigid, uninteresting look. (If you do shear shrubs, remember to keep their tops narrower than their bottoms so that light can get to the base of the shrub.)

Sheared shrubs can sometimes be renovated, returning them to a less formal, more open appearance. This is done by reaching down into the plant and cutting out some of the branches with hand pruners so that light can enter the plant. Start with the most tangled messes of twigs, cutting them at the point where they join another branch. A sheared shrub consists of a flat, leafy surface covering an interior mass of leafless branches. When light can enter, the bare stems may regrow leaves.

If your informally shaped shrub is becoming too large, avoid shearing. Instead, thin it by reaching into it and using hand shears to cut overlong branches at the point where they join another branch. This will make the plant a bit smaller and preserve its irregular, informal shape. If a shrub forms many canes, as poor man's rhododendron does, thinning will entail cutting some whole branches to the ground, starting with ones that are spindly, leafless, or otherwise inferior.

Pinching involves taking off just the tips of some of the branches. It is a way to make small changes in the branching pattern and shape of a shrub as it grows. Pinching stimulates the plant to form more than one branch on the tip, resulting in a fuller look. If it is a flowering shrub, more branches will mean more flowers—but you have to time your pinching so that it doesn't prevent the plants from blooming.

To decide when to pinch or otherwise prune a flowering shrub, you need to know whether it blooms on one-year-old wood or on new growth. Shrubs that bloom on old wood should be pruned right after bloom. Ones that bloom on new wood should be pruned in late winter, after danger of frost is past. If you have any doubt, look up the plant.

In selecting new shrubs, ask about eventual size to avoid having ones that are too large. Ask also about varieties or cultivars that are dwarf or more compact, since they may let you grow the shrub species you want in less room. For example, *Abelia x grandiflora* grows to 8 feet tall, but the cultivar 'Sherwoodii' is only 3 to 4 feet tall.

I have chosen not to write about roses, as there is simply too much to cover. Your best source of information is the meetings and publications of local rose societies.

Vines

Vines may be perennials, either woody or nonwoody, or they may be annuals. The ones listed in this chapter are woody perennial vines. As with shrubs, lack of water and poor pruning make them less attractive. Check the water needs of your plants to avoid unattractive leaf loss. Vines are, by their nature, rampant growers, good for covering vertical or horizontal space fast and often requiring frequent pruning to keep them in bounds. Sometimes you want a vine to completely cover what it is growing on. Then the shape of that surface—such as an entire wall—becomes the shape of the vine plant. But often the design of a garden is improved if the vine is pruned to prevent it from completely covering whatever it is that it is clambering over, such as a brick wall or the rocks in a rock garden. The decision to let a vine have its way should be a design decision, not a decision made by default because the vine took over.

Weedy Shrubs and Woody Vines

A number of shrubs and vines have become wildland invaders in Northern California, and they pose a particular problem because it is substantial work to dig or chop and carry them away. Some of the worst are most kinds of brooms (in the genera *Genista*, *Cytisus*, and *Spartium*), gorse *(Ulex europaea)*, Himalayan blackberry *(Rubus discolor)*, English ivy *(Hedera helix)*, and the perennial vine Cape ivy *(Delairea odorata)*. Nurseries may still sell some kinds of broom, but the current thinking is that any of them could become garden escapees. English ivy is common in gardens, as is Algerian ivy, which is escaping in some areas, but both should be grown with great care.

In addition to the plants just listed, birds eat berries and then distribute seeds, sowing berries from a few garden shrubs in wildlands. The following berried ornamental plants are becoming problems in wildlands near the coast, and particularly in the San Francisco Bay Area:

✱ *Cotoneaster lacteus (C. parneyi)* (milky cotoneaster)

✱ *Cotoneaster pannosa* (silverleaf cotoneaster)

✱ *Cotoneaster microphyllus* (little-leaved cotoneaster)

✱ *Ilex aqufolium* (English holly)

✱ *Pyracantha angustifolia* (narrow-leaved firethorn)

✱ *Crataegus monogyna* (single-seed hawthorn)

If your goal is to feed birds, particularly if you live on the coastal side of the valley where these plants are escaping, consider growing some of the following native shrubs with berries or seeds that native birds enjoy. For more information on growing native shrubs, see Suggested Reading (page 295), and contact your local chapter of the California Native Plant Society. Good choices include:

✱ *Ceanothus* species (California lilac): small seeds

✱ *Heteromeles arbutifolia* (toyon): orange-red berries

✱ *Lonicera inrolucrata* (twinberry honeysuckle): black berries

✱ *Mahonia aquifolium* (Oregon grape): blue berries

✱ *Prunus ilicifolia* (holly-leaf cherry), *Prunus lyonii* (Catalina cherry): red-purple fruit

✱ *Rhamnus californica* (coffeeberry): dark purple berries

✱ *Ribes sanguineum* (pink- or red-flowering currant): blue-black berries

✱ *Sambucus mexicana* (blue elderberry): blue to black berries

✱ *Sambucus racemosa* (red elderberry): blue to black berries

The unusual foliage colors of Coprosma repens 'Pink Splendor' create a handsome color scheme with plants that include (top left to right): Fuchsia splendens, Parthenocissus quinquifolia 'Star Showers', Cordyline baurii, and a yellow-flowered Osteospermum.

Coprosma repens (*C. bauerii*)

❋ Mirror plant

PLANT TYPE: *Woody shrub* | HEIGHT AND SPREAD: *Variable, to 10 feet tall and 6 feet wide* | BLOOM TIME: *Late summer (insignificant)* | LIGHT NEEDS: *Full sun or partial shade* | SOIL NEEDS: *Average fertility, well drained* | WATER NEEDS: *Little to moderate* | OTHER TOLERANCES: *Poor soil, sandy soil, cool coastal climates, beach conditions, snail resistant, deer resistant* | HARDINESS: *Zones 9b to 11*

*T*first became aware of mirror plant when I looked up and saw a small shrub with the shiniest of leaves perched high in a tree. It was growing in a branch scar high on the trunk of the Monterey cypress at the front of the large lawn in Strybing Arboretum in San Francisco's Golden Gate Park. While that mirror plant has since died, I have seen the plants rooted in many other trees, most often among the fronds of Canary Island palms. It will also grow in pine, eucalyptus, and California pepper trees.

The white-speckled foliage of C. repens *'Marble Queen' creates striking, pale backdrop for blue-flowered navelwort (*Omphalodes cappodocica)*, a perennial relative of annual garden forget-me-not.*

Source and Uses

Coprosma repens grows wild on New Zealand's North Island, which has a moist, subtropical climate. North Island is firmly in mediterranean latitudes, being between 34.5 and 41.5 degrees south, and it does have less rainfall in summer than winter, but its climate is not quite a mediterranean one, since rain is possible there any day of the year. Mirror plant also inhabits the northern half of the closely adjacent South Island, but only near the coast and at lower elevations, since the rest of the island is too cold for it. In nature it often grows on windy seacoast sites or among rocks where there is very little soil.

Mirror plant was brought to England by the late 1700s. Victorians both there and here loved it. Birds distributed the seed of those Victorian mirror plants hither and yon, and now once you start looking for mirror plants in older Northern California neighborhoods in mild-winter areas, you will see it everywhere—in trees, sneaking through other shrubbery, in sidewalk cracks, around street trees. . . .

Because it is so malleable to shaping by pruning, mirror plant is a shrub that can be used in many ways. It can be sheared into formal hedges as low as 2 feet tall or as high as 8 to 10 feet. In addition, informally pruned mirror plants frame entrances nicely or, if pruned artistically, serve as specimen plants. The plant has been mostly ignored for some years, but recently introduced cultivars with strikingly variegated leaves are becoming more popular.

Care and Reproduction

Mirror plant is generally trouble free. It grows in our soils without added fertilizer but will look better with the addition of organic mulch or a bit of fertilizer in the spring, especially if it is growing in sandy soil. It can also survive for years in unwatered California gardens but will be more attractive if it is watered regularly, though not frequently, in the summer. It withstands winter cold to about 22 degrees F.

Many mirror plants go unpruned or, at best, get whacked back when they get in the way, so few existing plants have the handsome forms that would be possible if they were pruned carefully. The branches often arch downward, and this aspect can be emphasized in informally pruned shrubs or even used to create a bare-trunked plant with a cascading crown. At a minimum, prune and pinch to maintain a nice shape. Do any major pruning after July if the plant is as big as you want it, or in February if you want the plant to grow bigger.

The plants can be rooted from cuttings taken in late summer, and can also be rooted by ground layering a lower branch (see page 181).

CONTROL AND REMOVAL

Branches that are about to flower heavily are often more upright with smaller leaves. You can prune these out to prevent heavy crops of the small orange berries or, on male plants, to avoid the windborne, possibly allergy-aggravating pollen. Some mirror plants have grown from seeds spread by birds into wild areas near the coast, but the plant has not become a serious problem.

If errant seedlings appear in your garden, pull them or move them to a better location in the first year before they can make deep roots. To remove a mature plant, you will need to chop it down and then dig out the roots. Use a Pulaski, a tool with an adze on one side and an ax head on the other that is lighter and easier to use than a pick ax.

Mirror plants rooted in trees can be rather charming, and they do not take food from the tree, but they can contribute to decay, so some gardeners remove them.

VARIETIES AND SIMILAR SPECIES

Three older variegated cultivars frequently survive in gardens. 'Exotica' has a yellow splash in green leaves. 'Picturata' (England, 1876) is similar, but male (no berries). 'Beatson's Gold' (female) is a rounded shrub with leaves that have yellow centers and margins. Common among newer cultivars are 'Coppershine' (coppery tinged leaves), 'Marble Queen' (female, green centered leaves with green-speckled white edges), 'Pink Splendor' (male, leaves have green center, yellow edges, with a pink overcolor that is stronger in winter), and 'Rainbow Surprise' (cream and green leaves tinged gold and pink; then, in winter, hot pink and olive green).

Coprosma x *kirkii* is a low, mounded shrub with smaller, less shiny leaves that is used as a ground cover.

The Name

Winning the prize for least appealing name origin of the fifty plants, the genus name *Coprosma* (kohp-ros'-muh) derives from the Greek words *copra* ("dung") and *osma* ("smelling"), for the unpleasant odor of some members of the genus. Fortunately, the kinds we grow in gardens don't have a foul odor, even when you crush a leaf or berry. (The one that is most responsible for the name is *C. foetidissima,* a New Zealand plant that really stinks when you simply brush against it.)

The specific epithet *repens* (ree'-penz) is from the Latin word meaning "creeping," referring to the tendency of this plant to be low growing, with horizontal branches. The species takes this form most dramatically when it is growing in wind at the seaside, and it will also cascade downward out of a retaining wall or a palm tree.

Echium candicans *(E. fastuosum)*

Pride of Madeira, echium

PLANT TYPE: *Woody shrub* | HEIGHT AND SPREAD: *5 to 8 feet tall and 5 to 6 feet wide* | BLOOM TIME: *Mid to late spring* | LIGHT NEEDS: *Full sun* | SOIL NEEDS: *Poor to moderately fertile, well drained* | WATER NEEDS: *None to little* | OTHER TOLERANCES: *Low fertility, cool coastal summers, inland climates in protected sites, snail resistant, deer resistant* | HARDINESS: *Zones 9 to 11*

These big, bold, gray-green-leaved plants are covered with spikes of flowers that bloom for weeks in the spring. The buds are pink, but the bell-shaped flowers open to blue or blue-purple, with red stamens extending beyond the ends of the petals. Close examination reveals that each spike is made up of many expanding coils of flower buds, and that each coil has only a few open flowers at a time, while more buds unfurl beneath them.

These are the pink flowers of the biennial species Echium wildpretii. *Those of* E. candicans *are very similar, but most often blue with red stamens.*

Bold and beautiful, E. candicans *looks its best when allowed to take the space it needs to produce its typical mounded form.*

Source and Uses

This plant is native to the island of Madeira, located off the coast of Africa, north of the Canary Islands. It grows on cliffs in the laurel forest zone, which extends from 1,000 to 4,000 feet above sea level. Here neither frost nor hot summer weather is common. Rainfall, which is more frequent in winter, varies from 120 inches per year in the north to a Central California–like 21 inches in the south.

This large plant works best in the back of a border, or as an attention-getting specimen plant. It also grows well on slopes, on which it will reduce erosion. It attracts bees, primarily bumblebees, as well as hummingbirds.

Care and Reproduction

Pride of Madeira is fully hardy down to 20 degrees F and may survive 15 degrees F, but late frosts will kill the flower buds. It is best adapted to near-coastal areas that echo the narrow temperature range of its native Madeira, and in these cool-summer climates, it survives with little summer water. Inland, it is sometimes successful if watered weekly in summer and given a site that offers some protection from winter cold. It thrives in poor soil—in fact, highly fertile soil will reduce flowering. It is used to heavy winter rains but needs very good drainage and so is not well suited to heavy clay soil.

A plant in a 4-inch or gallon pot is the best buy. Once planted out, it will quickly catch up with plants in larger containers, especially if they have become rootbound. You can also dig and transplant small seedlings that sprout under larger plants in the fall. Water transplants regularly for a few weeks and lightly through the first summer. Plants will generally begin to bloom by the second year. *Echium candicans* can also be grown from cuttings taken in midsummer

Prune off spent flower spikes in summer, cutting into a part of the stem with healthy leaves. You can also thin the stems, removing some to bare stem joints, to create a more open shape and prevent wind damage to too-thick plants. Some people find the hairs on this plant to be a skin irritant. To reduce this hazard, prune on a damp day or the day after watering the plant, and wear gloves.

CONTROL AND REMOVAL

Be sure you have allowed enough space for this plant to reach its full size, since it looks best if allowed to reach natural size and form. It will grow back reasonably well if you need to remove some branches that have grown beyond the space allotted, and it may even grow back slowly if you cut it back to a stump, but good planning is your best option.

Each flower makes four nutlets, very similar to those of the related borage, and the plants reseed freely. Cut flower stems as soon as the last flowers fade to reduce seed fall and dig out any unwanted seedlings within a few months after you see them. This plant has invaded some wild habitats in urban areas, such as Twin Peaks in San Francisco and San Bruno Mountain in Daly City. Avoid growing it in or adjacent to wild areas and do not discard seedheads of any *Echium* species in wild places.

To remove a mature plant, cut it up and dig out the stump. The trunk may be several inches across, but it is sort of pithy, rather than solid wood, and not heavy to carry away.

VARIETIES AND SIMILAR SPECIES

Two other *Echium* species are sometimes found in old gardens or in nurseries. Both are from the Canary Islands and share a tolerance for poor soil and little water. *E. wildpretii,* known as the tower of jewels, forms a 6- to 10-foot-tall single stem of leaves topped with a spike of pink flowers, while *E. pininana* forms a single stem, to 18 feet tall, with a spike of blue flowers. Both of these species are biennials or short-lived perennials, meaning they flower in 2 to several years, and then die after blooming. They reseed themselves for future displays, but can be a bit of a problem in that they are large plants that seed themselves in unexpected places, and *E. pinanana* is a somewhat more aggressive invader of wild areas than *E. candicans*. Give these tall plants a site with deep soil, so deep roots can prevent toppling when they are mature.

Seed catalogs may also list viper's bugloss *(Echium vulgare)*, a 2- to 3-foot-tall European native biennial that's usually treated as an annual, sown in fall or late winter for bloom in spring and summer borders (see photo on page 63). Its vibrant blue, pink, or white flowers are borne in much more open heads than those of its taller relatives. Be cautious with this plant. California gardeners who have grown it say they got rid of it when they wanted to without too much trouble, but it has become quite a pest in Canada and in Washington State, and is considered a noxious weed in Australia. Avoid growing viper's bugloss in or near wild areas or disposing of spent plants in wild areas where seeds could fall and grow.

THE NAME

Carl Linnaeus, who named this genus, was quite familiar with viper's bugloss because it is native to Europe. He probably had this plant in mind when he chose the genus name *Echium* (eck'-ee-um). Ancient Greeks called the plant *echion*, derived from the word *echis*, meaning "viper" or "adder." They thought viper's bugloss would discourage snakes and, if that failed, that a concoction of the roots in wine would be good for the resulting snakebite. When later botanists studied pride of Madeira, they placed it in the same genus. The specific epithet *candicans* (kan'-dih-kanz) means "white or whitish gray," referring to the white hairs on the leaves.

Fuchsia (classic hybrids)

⊞ Fuchsia, ladies' eardrops

PLANT TYPE: *Woody shrub* | HEIGHT AND SPREAD: *Variable* | BLOOM TIME: *Late spring through fall* | LIGHT NEEDS: *Partial shade* | SOIL NEEDS: *Fertile, organic, well drained* | WATER NEEDS: *Moderate to ample* | OTHER TOLERANCES: *Cool coastal climates, full sun at the coast, inland climates with special care* | HARDINESS: *Zones 9 to 11*

*H*ybrid fuchsias, offering elegant, large blossoms in many color combinations, were once quite common in Northern California, especially near the coast, as favorite and easy garden shrubs. Then, in the early 1980s, most of the available hybrids fell prey to the fuchsia gall mite, a pest that turns leaves and flowers into twisted, lumpy masses. Faced with the choice of repeated spraying or removal, many gardeners took out their fuchsias. Of the

Blossoms of Fuchsia *'Rose of Castile Improved' have pale pink sepals and four petals that start out purple, but soon change to bright magenta.*

'Rose of Castile Improved' (created in 1869) is one of the oldest fuchsia hybrids that still thrive in our gardens.

hundreds of so-called "classic" hybrids once available, only a few remain common in California gardens. These few tough survivors are worth identifying, since they seem to have some resistance to the mite and have often survived with very little care.

Source and Uses

A couple of species of fuchsia reached Europe from Central and South America in the 1700s, but it was not until the 1800s that the number of available species and the interest of gardeners spurred the development of fancy hybrids. The main species used for breeding were *Fuchsia splendens* and *F. fulgens* from Mexico and *F. magellanica* from the southern end of South America, with a number of others playing minor roles. The fuchsia gall mite had not been brought to Europe with any fuchsia species.

By midcentury there were hundreds of hybrid fuchsia varieties in Europe, and those that reached California were enthusiastically received. In 1854, 24 varieties of fuchsia were already being displayed in a San Francisco flower show. Popularity continued both there and here, but European fuchsia breeding and growing were set back seriously by World War I and its aftermath, as gardeners concentrated on survival.

A big event in California fuchsia history was the trip to Europe by members of the American Fuchsia Society in 1930. They sent back 51 varieties by ocean liner, of which 48 made it to California alive. These plants, half of which were given to the UC Berkeley Botanical Garden and half to Berkeley Horticultural Nursery, were parents of many subsequent American-bred hybrids.

Hybrid fuchsias have often been, and still are, used as show plants, bred to make huge, showy flowers and grown in containers to compete for prizes. But in the ground, where adapted, they make handsome upright or trailing shrubs that bloom for a long season, attract hummingbirds, and can be used as cut flowers.

Care and Reproduction

Most fuchsias originated in various sorts of moist woodlands at middle elevations in tropical and subtropical climates. Because of these origins, they expect partial shade, a soil that is fertile and high in organic matter, and a cool, humid environment. They require soil that drains well but is never allowed to dry out completely. Mulch them with compost or manure in early spring, and, for maximum bloom, give them a fertilizer formulated to enhance bloom monthly until fall. Most are killed by frost, though ones that came from the southern part of South America, such as *Fuchsia magellanica*, can lose their leaves and recover or even regrow from the roots if frost kills the top. Some inland gardeners have managed to grow fuchsias by planting them in shadier spots, making sure the soil is moist at all times, covering plants when frost is expected, and perhaps using misters to increase summer humidity.

Prune fuchsias in March to shape them and keep them in bounds. Pinching branch tips as they grow out will increase bushiness and flowering, though you have to cease pinching so the new branch tips can develop flowers.

Hybrid fuchsias typically grow easily from cuttings, especially from March prunings, but California gardeners used to pass cuttings around throughout the year.

Control and Removal

Fucshias are, for the most part, easy to remove. Hybrid fuchsias have survived untended on Alcatraz Island but are not generally thought of as invasive or weedy.

Varieties and Similar Species

The main surviving Alcatraz fuchsia hybrids are 'Mrs. Lovell Swisher' (bred in Los Angeles in 1942) and 'Rose of Castile Improved' (from England, 1869). The first is described as having single flowers with pinkish white sepals and deep rosy corollas; the second has pale blush pink sepals and purple corollas. Both are vigorous, easy varieties. 'Rose of Castile Improved' is rather common in San Francisco gardens, where, if well cared for, it forms arching branches of flowers on plants that can reach 12 to 15 feet in a single season. Two varieties with similar flowers may also be found in the region's gardens. 'Lena' (England, 1862) is usually a lower, spreading plant, with flowers colored like 'Rose of Castile Improved' but semidouble—that is, having a few more than the standard four petals. 'Lena', though common, has been shown to be susceptible to the fuchsia gall mite, while the very similar but fully double 'Constance' (from Berkeley Horticultural Nursery, 1935) is semiresistant. 'Coralina' (England, 1844), a hybrid with flaring red sepals, purple petals, and big purple leaves, can still be found, as can 'Cardinal' (American, 1938) with its deep red sepals and petals of a slightly deeper red. Surveys of surviving old hybrids have only begun, so if you have one not described here, a nearby botanical garden would surely love to hear about it.

THE NAME

Gardeners are often stumped when they attempt to spell the genus name *Fuchsia*. Though it is usually pronounced "few'-shuh," we could probably spell it more easily if we said "fewk'-see-uh," which is more correct, since it was named for the German botanist and medical doctor Leonhart Fuchs (1501–1566). This name was chosen by Father Charles Plumier, a French Catholic priest who tried to carry the first fuchsia to Europe. His specimens of *F. triphylla* from the Dominican Republic were all lost in a shipwreck in 1695, but he did publish a drawing in a book, giving Europeans an early glimpse of these wonderful flowers.

If the Mite Strikes

Fuchsia gall mites are tiny creatures that burrow into plants and feed inside. They are spread by wind, insects, hummingbirds, and human handling of the plants. Once inside, they are immune to pesticides except for systemics, which enter every plant cell. Systemics are often toxic to hummingbirds, so if you use them, it is best to prune off all flowers for a few weeks. If you have only a little damage, prune it off and use oil spray in winter to kill the mite eggs that are hiding in leaf buds. If the damage becomes intolerable, your best option is to replace the affected plants with mite-resistant types.

Fuchsia (species and recent hybrids)

✦ Fuchsia (various)

PLANT TYPE: *Woody shrub or small tree* | BLOOM TIME: *Late spring through fall* | HEIGHT AND SPREAD: *Variable* | LIGHT NEEDS: *Partial shade* | SOIL NEEDS: *Fertile, organic, well drained* | WATER NEEDS: *Moderate to ample* | OTHER TOLERANCES: *Cool coastal climates, full sun at the coast, inland climate with special care* | HARDINESS: *Varies, mostly Zones 9 to 11*

*B*efore the accidental import of the gall mite to the West Coast, fuchsia hybrid breeders concentrated on creating large, usually wide-flaring flowers. While a few determined California fuchsia enthusiasts have continued to grow (and spray) mite-susceptible hybrids, other gardeners have set out to rediscover the beauty

Flowers of the fuchsia variety 'Campo Thilco' are similar to those of the species F. magellenica, but unlike the species, it resists the fuchsia gall mite.

of certain fuchsia species that are mite-resistant and have also begun to recross these with each other and with old hybrids to create flowers that resemble classic hybrids but resist the mite.

Source and Uses

Mite-resistant fuchsia species are found wild in Mexico, Central America, Peru, Bolivia, and Brazil. A number of them have long, narrow, tubular flowers of the sort that were popular in Europe before the 1840s, when the new hybrids began to appear. Some of these long-tubed species have been grown in California gardens for decades. (But long tubes do not necessarily denote mite resistance. The fairly common red-leaved *F. triphylla* 'Gartenmeister Bonstedt' is quite susceptible.)

Almost all of the pre-1980 fuchsia hybrids contained genetic material from *Fuchsia magellenica,* which is generally susceptible to fuchsia gall mite. Still, many uninfected plants of this species persist in old gardens, as well as on Alcatraz Island. *F. magellenica* has small leaves, and slender flowers. Flowers of the species most often have red sepals and purple petals, but on some plants the entire flowers are pale pink.

Care and Reproduction

Most fuchsia species can be grown in conditions similar to those needed for classic hybrids: fertile, moist, organic soil; partial shade; and cool, humid weather. Like hybrids, they can be pruned in spring. Some are treelike in the wild but rarely become more than tall shrubs in gardens. Others scramble up trees and so will drape on a trellis or fence. Some grow easily from cuttings, as the hybrids do, but most need more careful technique.

Control and Removal

Like the hybrids, most species fuchsias are not invasive or difficult to remove. If digging out a *Fuchsia fulgens,* you will need to remove tuberous roots. *F. campos-portoi* has rhizomes that can regrow if not removed, but it is not common in the market. *F. boliviana* sometimes self-sows in moist soil.

Varieties and Similar Species

Following are some of the mite-resistant species and new hybrids you will find. For more choices and for updates, contact the American Fuchsia Society.

✽ *F. boliviana*, a rather lanky, open shrub to 12 feet in the cool, mossy forests of Peru, Bolivia, and Argentina, which has large leaves and hanging bunches of flowers to 3 inches that are either all red or pink with long white tubes.

✽ *F. denticulata*, from Peru and Bolivia, is perhaps best known by the variety 'Fanfare', which was bred by San Francisco nurseryman Victor Reiter in 1940. This plant has long-tubed 3-inch flowers with a carmine red sepal tube and lobes and red-orange petals. It is more shrublike in sun, a scrambler or semivine in shade.

✽ *F. fulgens* has large leaves and hanging bunches of long-tubed 1½- to 2-inch flowers that have pink or orange green-tipped sepals and scarlet petals. In its native Mexican habitat, it may survive the dry winter, leafless, on water stored in its tuberous root, but in the Bay Area, with plenty of water and fertilizer, it blooms nearly all year.

✽ *F. splendens*, sometimes called the "chili pepper fuchsia," is native to Mexico and Costa Rica. It has a rather broad red- or peach-colored tube, with green sepals and petals. It will act as a climber if it has enough root room, or will shape up as a large shrub to 7 feet tall (photo on page 266).

✽ *F. campos-portoi*, a species native to the high mountains of Brazil, is strongly mite resistant and so has great potential as a parent of re-created classic hybrid flower forms. Examples of recent hybrids formed using it at Strybing Arboretum in San Francisco are *F.* 'Campo Thilco' and *F.* 'Albrae'.

✽ *F. glaznoviana* is an excellent garden plant with flowers similar to those of *F. magellanica*. This native of the rain forests and high mountains of Brazil is a dense shrub with small, shiny, pointed leaves and bright pink-and-purple flowers, held at an angle. It blooms from early spring to fall.

✳ *F. arborescens* has small mauve-pink flowers of the typical fuchsia form, with spreading sepals, borne in 6- to 8-inch-wide masses on large shrubs. With ample fertilizer and water, this large shrub blooms all year in frost-free gardens. A Dutch hybrid, *F.* 'Miep Aalhuizen' is a similar plant that grows to a 5- by 5-foot shrub.

New hybrids with classic hybrid flower form and mite resistance include the following:

✳ 'Angel's Earrings' and 'Dainty Angel's Earrings' are Japanese hybrids of unknown parentage usually sold as container plants. They have small but attractive flowers.

✳ *F.* 'Galfrey Lye' and *F.* 'Galfrey Blush' were created by Dr. Peter Baye at San Francisco's Strybing Arboretum. Both have as one parent the classic white-sepaled, red-petaled 'Lye's Unique', but the other parent has given them mite resistance.

The Name

For the source of the genus name Fuchsia, see page 278. *F. magellanica* was named for the Straits of Magellan, at the windy tip of South America, which define the southern end of the range of this species.

The Fuchsia Flower

The usually colorful tube of a fuchsia flower is formed of united sepals, and these typically separate and flare at their ends, creating the outer tier of flower color. The inner tier is made up of petals, which may be the same or a different color. The stamens and pistil usually extend beyond the petals and are often brightly colored. Behind each fuchsia flower is an ovary, which will develop into a green or purple berry containing seeds. These are edible, usually sweet but rather bland.

Hedera algeriensis *(Hedera canariensis)*

✳ Algerian ivy, Canary Island ivy, freeway ivy

PLANT TYPE: *Woody vine* | HEIGHT AND SPREAD: *1 to 2 feet tall and variable width to at least 10 feet (spreads rapidly)* | BLOOM TIME: *Late summer, fall (on mature plants only)* | LIGHT NEEDS: *Partial or full shade* | SOIL NEEDS: *Fertile, organic, well drained* | WATER NEEDS: *Moderate* | OTHER TOLERANCES: *Relatively poor soil, drought, air pollution, salt spray, cool coastal climates, full sun near the coast* | HARDINESS: *Zones 8 to 11 (variegated forms 9 to 11)*

This is the ivy that has become so popular in large-scale public uses in California that we call it "freeway ivy." Miles of its dark green leaves drape freeway embankments and public parks. It can, with assiduous pruning, be confined to small spaces, but unless you want to prune it weekly, is better left to large-scale

Do not let ivy bloom and form berries because birds will spread the ivy seeds into wildlands.

Using Algerian ivy as a restrained design element, such as covering this low fence, is definitely a high-maintenance proposal, requiring weekly nipping and pruning.

uses. Algerian ivy leaves are much farther apart on the stems than those of English ivy, and it has leaves up to 6 or even 8 inches long, while those of English ivy rarely exceed 4 inches.

Source and Uses

A purely Mediterranean relative of English ivy, Algerian ivy is native to Algeria and Tunisia in North Africa, to Portugal, and to the Azores, the Canary Islands, and Madeira.

Care and Reproduction

The needs of Algerian ivy are quite similar to those of English ivy (*Hedera helix;* see page 287), though it is more sensitive to environmental extremes. Temperatures below 10 to 20 degrees F damage or kill it, and strong winds will shred the leaves, giving them an unkempt appearance.

Use iron phosphate bait to reduce the snail and slug population under ivy used as a ground cover.

Control and Removal

Algerian ivy, if uncontrolled, will gallop over land much faster than English ivy and can form trunks up to 6 inches thick. To keep the plant in confined spaces professional gardeners prune out unwanted branches weekly, but the necessary work may well be more than a recreational gardener cares to do. Let it get overgrown and it will become discouraging to tackle; turn your back for too long and it will become the boss. Having said that, control and removal techniques are the same as for English ivy.

Algerian ivy makes a deeper cover than English ivy, and when it is climbing a vertical surface, it becomes a very attractive nesting site for rats. To discourage rats keep climbing ivy pruned to under a foot thick. (Neither ivy seems to attract rats when it is used as groundcover.)

Another difference is that Algerian ivy is more likely to bloom and set seed than English ivy. Plants in the genus *Hedera* can be kept in a non-flowering, juvenile form forever, but once they change to mature growth, they will bloom and form seeds every year thereafter. Prevent flowering by pruning off any flowering shoots. These upright shoots with unlobed leaves form clusters of petal-less greenish or yellow flowers in early fall, followed by purple-black berries. Ivy is more likely to flower when plants are climbing, but groundcover plants also occasionally form upright blooming branches. (In Europe, where *Hedera* is less of a wildland invasive, these upright shoots are rooted and grown as novelty shrubs, but this seems a poor idea here.)

While ivy flowers and fruits may seem attractive, they create a nuisance within the garden and in the wider environment. First, some people are allergic to the pollen, gagging when the wind blows it their way, and the berries themselves are poisonous to humans. Second, rats are fond of the berries, so berries will make your plants even more attractive to these unwelcome rodents. Third, birds, especially robins, love to eat ivy berries. From the lavender splashes that the birds will drop on nearby garden structures and vehicles, to the seedlings that result when seed falls on the ground, this feeding has unpleasant results. The seedcoats are etched and scratched by their passage through birds' digestive tract, making it more likely that the seeds will grow. Seedlings will appear wherever birds have perched—at the base of fences, under trees—both in the garden and in wildlands. This plant was apparently overlooked on past California Exotic Pest Plant Council lists, but it is likely to be given the same rating as English Ivy *(Hedera helix)* on future lists.

Varieties and Similar Species

Hedera canariensis has several cultivars with white- or cream-variegated leaves, most commonly sold as 'Variegata'. Check over variegated plants as they grow for branches that have reverted to a different variegation pattern, even all white or all green leaves, and prune these out to maintain the original leaf coloration.

The Name

For the meaning of *Hedera*, see The Name in the *Hedera helix* entry on page 290. The specific epithet for this plant, *algeriensis* (ahl-jir-ee-en'-sis), refers to the Algerian part of its native range.

Will Climbing Ivy Cause Damage?

If mortar in a brick or stone wall crumbles when scraped with a knife, then ivy will damage the wall. Such a wall must be remortared (also called pointing) before it can support ivy. On a wall with sound mortar, the short, clinging rootlets do no damage, but ivy should be kept away from window frames, roof tiles, and gutters. Ivy will damage any wooden structure, either by encouraging decay or by making it heavy and prone to wind damage.

Whether ivy should be allowed to climb garden trees is controversial. Ivy does not take any nutrients from the plants it climbs, and British studies have shown no hindrance to the growth of ivy-covered trees. But California arborists say that ivy on the lower trunk traps moisture, increasing the likelihood that disease will take hold, especially on more drought-tolerant trees. What gardeners don't often realize is that dead ivy leaves build up under the ivy, commonly to a foot or two deep, packing wet, decaying material around the trunk base or crown. Ivy higher in trees can block light from leaves and can make a tree top-heavy and thus more prone to storm damage. It can also flower and fruit high above a gardener's watchful eye and thus spread seed into wildlands.

Ivy climbing a tree may or may not harm it, but it will be difficult to remove if it climbs too high.

Hedera helix

❋ English ivy

PLANT TYPE: *Woody vine* | HEIGHT AND SPREAD: *Under 1 foot tall and variable width (spreads rapidly)* | BLOOM TIME: *Autumn (rarely blooms)* | SOIL NEEDS: *Fertile, organic, well drained* | LIGHT NEEDS: *Partial or full shade* | WATER NEEDS: *Moderate to ample* | OTHER TOLERANCES: *Relatively poor soil, acidic soil, basic soil, drought, air pollution, cool coastal climates, full sun near the coast, deer resistant* | HARDINESS: *Zones 5 to 11*

Ivy comes to us with a long history of cheerful associations, beginning with its connection to the Greek god Dionysius or Bacchus, the god of wine, and continuing after the medieval Catholic Church took it over, along with holly (a former Roman symbol of friendship), to symbolize Christmas. It also comes with a long history of garden uses, from covering brick walls to

Cool temperatures deepen the gold of the edges of 'Gold Child' English ivy leaves. If ivy climbs over rocks, keep it pruned so rocks can peek through.

Like Algerian ivy, English ivy needs frequent nipping to keep it pruned this formally, but its smaller size makes it easier to control.

forming topiaries. More recently, it has been viewed from the other end of the telescope as an invasive weed of wildlands. Although it will probably never be banned, we will hear more and more about the importance of keeping it within garden confines.

Source and Uses

English ivy is native to Great Britain and much of Europe—north into Scandinavia, east to western Russia, and south to the Caucasus. The ancient Romans used it in gardens as well as in garlands and crowns. Its popularity in European and American gardens peaked in the Victorian era, fell in about 1914, and then rose again starting in the 1920s with the proliferation of new, more interesting cultivars.

Ivy can be used in gardens as an informal ground cover, to cover masonry buildings, walls, metal fences, or freestanding topiaries, or as a formally pruned accent on walls or stairs. It drapes nicely from containers, where it can be used under upright plants.

Care and Reproduction

Ivy is extremely tolerant of different soils, except those that are poorly drained and therefore constantly soggy. It will withstand full sun where days are cool and often foggy, but in full sun on a very hot day, water on the leaves may cause damage that leads to decayed spots.

Ivy is not a low-maintenance plant because it is so vigorous. The more formal its use, the more attention to pruning and grooming is needed to keep it attractive and in bounds. Since it will strive to climb whatever upright structure it encounters, it is best not to plant it near anything you don't want it to climb unless you plan to prune it very frequently.

To reproduce a type of ivy that you particularly like, make semihardwood cuttings of the trailing stems from spring to autumn. To do so, cut just below a node (where the leaves attach), remove the leaves from the bottom inch or two, and put it into cutting mix (a rooting hormone is optional). Cover with a plastic bag held up with short stakes until it roots (see Chapter One).

Control and Removal

To keep ivy in a confined area, nip and trim it frequently while it is actively growing. Do not shear it, but cut out individual branches that stick out where they aren't needed, cutting them back just below the point where they began to grow. Constant pruning is impractical on a house wall or other taller structure, so prune once in May or June, after the flush of spring growth has slowed. Don't let the ivy at the top of a wall or fence flare out and become overgrown, as this not only looks unattractive but also can catch in the wind and pull the wall over or can mature and produce berries.

To remove unwanted ivy coming from an adjacent yard, you will need to cut it back and dig out rooted stems several times a year. Where other plants aren't present, ivy used as a ground cover can be killed by first using a string weed trimmer or hedge shears to break the stems and the protective waxy covering on the leaves and then applying a glyphosate herbicide. To remove ivy from walls or trees, cut each stem at its base and then use a claw hammer and a flat screwdriver to pry it off, working from bottom to top. Do not cut stems for later removal, since the dead stems will stiffen and become much more difficult to remove. After you have severed a stem, immediately paint the cut base with a glyphosate herbicide, being careful not to get it on a tree you are cleaning or on any other plants.

Hedera helix often forms vast "ivy deserts" under American forests, crowding out native plants. In California, it is a common sight under stands of Australian blue gum *(Eucalyptus globulus)*, its only competitor there being Himalaya blackberry *(Rubus discolor)*. In its native Great Britain, ivy does a better job of sharing space with other forest natives, because it has more animal foragers there. In any case, in California, *Hedera helix* has been on the "B" list of the California Exotic Plant Pest Council and could be on the list of plants with "High" impact in wildlands when the lists have been revised. To keep it out of still more stretches of wildlands, do not plant it in them or adjacent to them. Do not dump prunings in wildlands or near waterways, because they are likely to take root. And, in addition, prevent the plants from forming berries, lest birds eat them and deposit the seeds in wildlands. For more on preventing seed formation, see the *Hedera algeriensis* entry starting on page 283.

VARIETIES AND SIMILAR SPECIES

For ground cover or small-scale uses, small-leaved, self-branching forms such as 'Hahn's', 'Pittsburgh', or 'Needlepoint' will be least rampant. Nice choices to climb walls are 'Gold Heart' (yellow center splash) and 'Glacier' (gray-green and white). In rock gardens, variegated forms such as 'Glacier', 'Gold Child', or any particularly interesting small leaf can provide interesting accents if they are carefully pruned so that some rocks and other plants remain visible. There are hundreds of ivy varieties, all kept track of by the American Ivy Society (see Resources, page 299).

THE NAME

Hedera (head'-ur-uh) is what the ancient Romans called this plant. *Helix* is a Greek word meaning "spiraling," which, as is sometimes the case with plant names, doesn't really fit the plant, since the vine does not climb by twining but by rootlets that cling to a surface.

Caution

Though it is not common, some people get a skin rash similar to that caused by poison oak when they touch plants in the genus *Helix*. Also, all parts of the plants are moderately poisonous to humans, though not to other animals.

Impatiens sodenii *(I. oliveri, I. uguenensis)*

✷ Poor man's rhododendron, shrub impatiens

PLANT TYPE: *Cane-type shrub* | HEIGHT AND SPREAD: *3 to 10 feet tall and 2 to 4½ feet wide* | BLOOM TIME: *Spring to fall* | LIGHT NEEDS: *Partial to full shade* | SOIL NEEDS: *Moderately fertile, well drained* | WATER NEEDS: *Moderate* | OTHER TOLERANCES: *Relatively poor soil, little water, cool coastal climates, full sun near the coast, snail resistant, deer resistant* | HARDINESS: *Zones 10 to 11*

For some years after its introduction into Northern California gardens, *Impatiens sodenii* was started mainly by cuttings shared among gardeners, rather than being purchased at nurseries. It earned the common name poor man's rhododendron by quickly producing large flowering shrubs from these cuttings.

Well cared for, Impatiens sodenii *makes an exceptionally useful landscape shrub.*

The pink flowers of I. sodenii, *often called poor man's rhododendron, mingle here with lavender flowers of a true rhododendron (*R. ponticum) *on a neighboring shrub.*

This plant blooms much longer than rhododendron, opening new flowers during most of the year. The stems bear whorls of 6 to 10 rhododendronlike leaves, each whorl producing a succession of 2- to 2 ½-inch pale to mid-pink blossoms that fade to nearly white with age. Behind each flower is a long, elegant petal spur.

SOURCE AND USES

This is a plant of the East African tropical highlands, found in central Kenya and north central Tanzania at elevations from 3,000 to 8,100 feet, where it grows at forest margins and on rocky slopes. I like to picture it growing, as reported in one book on Kenyan wildflowers, "near waterfalls and streams and in misty situations." However, its somewhat succulent, moisture-storing stems also enable it to grow in drier, more exposed conditions, even in cliff crevices, where the plants are squat, with smaller leaves and flowers. It has also been transplanted into gardens in many parts of Kenya.

Rainfall in its native region varies from 20 to 40 inches a year, with a long spring rainy season and a shorter fall one. Temperatures at the elevations where this plant grows typically range from lows of 50 to 60 degrees F in the summer to late-winter highs in the 80s.

Impatiens sodenii was first grown in England's Kew Gardens in 1902. The first record of it in the Bay Area is in a 1913 Peninsula estate garden. By 1931 it was used in Golden Gate Park, and by the 1960s it was a rather common Bay Area plant. It is handsome in a tall mixed shrub border and can be kept shorter for a low border or trimmed to fit a narrow situation. Before the devastation caused by the fuchsia mite, *Impatiens sodenii* and fuchsias were a common garden combination.

CARE AND REPRODUCTION

This plant is adaptable to various soil types and can survive with little or no irrigation, though it will look best in moderately fertile soil with moderate summer water. The soil must not be constantly wet, so good drainage is essential. If the soil becomes too dry, the plant will have smaller leaves, and some of the leaves will fall off. Areas with coastal influence are ideal, replicating the moderate temperatures of its homeland. Plants will be damaged by light frost. Frost-damaged plants can regrow if the crown (the area at the soil level) is alive, but the plant doesn't survive long if that happens every year.

Prune lightly year-round to shape and groom plants, removing discolored leaves and shortening overlong branches, but don't prune too heavily at any one time, or you will reduce blooms. Cut the plants back hard in March to remove any frost damage and keep them compact. To keep plants at 5 feet tall, cut them back to 3 feet tall. If the canes are crowded, thin them at this time, cutting to the ground those that are most spindly or have few leaves. After 5 years or so, you may want to dig and divide the crowded clump of canes into two or more new plants.

Like other *Impatiens* species, the plant has seedpods that burst open at a touch when the seeds are ripe. To collect seeds, you need to identify a ripe pod and grasp it quickly so the seeds will pop into your hand. Ripe pods are bulging but still green and quite succulent. While seed is fun to collect and grows rather easily, stem cuttings are a much faster way to reproduce the plant. These will root at any time of year, but spring and summer are best.

Control and Removal

Impatiens sodenii will reseed in California, but usually not abundantly, and unwanted seedlings are easy to pull out. So long as all of the plants in California continue to have flowers of the same color, seedlings will bloom true, though if other colors are introduced and become common in gardens, we will only be able to be sure of the flower color of plants grown from cuttings.

Mature plants are not deeply rooted unless you purchased them in large nursery containers, which would have encouraged deeper roots. Once dug out, they do not regrow. Be aware that this plant has escaped cultivation in New Zealand and Costa Rica, although I found no evidence that it has done so to any significant extent in Northern California.

Varieties and Similar Species

You may find this plant in nurseries under its former names that include *Impatiens oliveri*, *I. uguenensis*, and *I. magnifica*. A form with red-marked white or nearly white flowers and 4-inch spurs has been marketed locally as *I. uguense* in recent years, and pure white-flowered forms have long been in cultivation in Britain. There are also lavender- and purple-flowered wild plants.

The Name

European plant explorers came upon this plant in the East African highlands several times between the early 1890s and 1935. They all placed it in the genus *Impatiens*, but several of them gave it different specific epithets. The International Botanical Congress decided that the first, and therefore valid, name was *Impatiens sodenii*, a name given to this plant in 1894. We know that the genus name *Impatiens* is simply the Latin word for "impatient" (see also page 78), but the authors (botanists Heinrich Engler and Otto Warburg) chose not to reveal the reason they selected the species name *sodenii* (so-den'-ee-eye). Although several botanists have recently puzzled over the question, and they suspect that Soden is the name of a person, it seems that the meaning has been lost to history.

SUGGESTED READING

Barton, Barbara and Ginny Hunt, eds. *Gardening by Mail: 5th Edition*. New York: Houghton Mifflin, 1997.

> *In this book, plants are grouped by types or by genus, followed by a list of nurseries and seed companies that carry them. Also includes horticultural societies, magazines, and libraries.*

Bossard, Carla C., Randall, John M., and Hoshovsky, Marc C. *Invasive Plants of California's Wildlands*. Berkeley: University of California Press, 2000.

> *This book provides full information on the identification and control of 78 California wildland weeds. In addition to its paper form, the entire book is now available on the CalEPPC website (www.caleppc.org); see also CalEPPC in Resources.*

Brenzel, Kathleen Norris, ed. *Sunset Western Garden Book*. Menlo Park, CA: Sunset Publishing Company, 2001.

> *A reference book for succinct information on growing most of the western garden plants you will encounter. Sunset's climate codes are more detailed than those of the USDA, though our pattern of microclimates is so complex that these codes still may not be able to tell you if a particular plant will thrive in your garden. The book includes a section containing basic gardening instructions.*

Bricknell, Christopher. *Pruning: Roses, Deciduous Shrubs, Evergreens, Hedges, Wall Shrubs, Fruit Bushes and Trees, Deciduous Trees*. New York: Simon and Schuster, 1979.

> *Many line drawings clearly illustrate the accompanying directions on pruning and renovating plants.*

Brown-Folsom, Debra. *Dry Climate Gardening with Succulents*. New York: Pantheon Books, 1995.

> *One of the few books that gives information about gardening with succulents that grow in the ground, it features photographs from the Huntington Botanical Gardens to illustrate some of the marvelous possibilities.*

Clarke, Graham and Toogood, Alan. *The Complete Book of Plant Propagation*. London: Seven Dials Press, 2001.

> *A good beginner's guide to the many ways of starting new plants, this book includes information about seeds, cuttings, and grafts. Line drawings and brief entries describe the best ways to reproduce hundreds of plant species.*

Clebsch, Betsy. *A Book of Salvias—Sages for Every Garden*. Portland: Timber Press, 1997.

> *This book will help you select from the multitude of new sage species and varieties in order to use them well in your garden. It includes ideas for combining the plants with other garden perennials, as well as lists of sage species for various garden situations.*

Dallman, Peter R. *Plant Life in the World's Mediterranean Climates: California, Chile, South Africa, Australia, and the Mediterranean Basin*. Sacramento: California Native Plant Society and Berkeley: University of California Press, 1998.

> *Dallman explored plant habitats in all five of the world's mediterranean regions; the book explains how the climate and soils of the five regions are similar, how they are different, and how plants have adapted to these very similar climates. The information is not only fascinating, but also extremely useful to gardeners who grow plants from any of these regions.*

Duffield, Mary Rose, and Jones, Warren. *Plants for Dry Climates: How to Select, Grow, and Enjoy*. Denver: Perseus Books Group, 2001.

> *Inland gardeners will particularly appreciate this book on plants that thrive in climates with hot, dry, windy summers. The authors also discuss how to improve the chances that plants will remain healthy in these conditions.*

Endicott, Katherine Grace. *Northern California Gardening: A Month-by-Month Guide*. San Francisco: Chronicle Books, 1996.

> *Endicott is responsible for many years of "when to do it" gardening columns for the* Chronicle *newspaper. This book is arranged by month, giving key garden tasks for each month for both coastal versus Central Valley gardeners, as well as hundreds of useful tips.*

Euser, Barbara J., ed. *Bay Area Gardening: Practical Essays by Master Gardeners*. San Rafael, CA: Writers Center of Marin, 2002.

> *This is a collection of helpful, inspiring essays on earth-friendly local gardening topics by Marin County Master Gardeners. They have been reprinted from the* Marin Independent Journal.

Gildemeister, Heidi. *Mediterranean Gardening: A Waterwise Approach*. Berkeley: University of California Press, 2002.

> *This book on mediterranean gardening (the author gardens in southern Spain) that emphasizes water conservation offers help with both design and plant choices to help you reduce or avoid the need for summer irrigation. It includes a plant encyclopedia.*

Gilmer, Maureen. *California Wildfire Landscaping*. Dallas: Taylor Publishing Co., 1994.

> *Gilmer tells what you need to know to incorporate fire safety into your California garden.*

Gilmer, Maureen. *Redwoods and Roses: The Gardening Heritage of California and the Old West*. Dallas: Taylor Publishing Co., 1995.

> *This is a history of the human uses of native and imported plants in California.*

Harbouri, Caroline, ed. *The Mediterranean Garden: A Journal for Gardeners in All the Mediterranean Climate Regions of the World*. Paenia, Greece: Mediterranean Garden Society.

> *The journal, which is a benefit for members in the Mediterranean Garden Society, features articles on plants and garden design in mediterranean regions. The Society's website shows the journal's table of contents, and also offers information about the mediterranean climate and plants that thrive in it (www.MediterraneanGardenSociety.org).*

Hart, John, et al. *The Gardens of Alcatraz*. San Francisco: Golden Gate National Park Association, 1996.

> *Learn about the history of the famous prison island and the 145 species of nonnative plants that survived from its military base and prison gardens.*

Hart, Rhonda Massingham. *Deer Proofing Your Yard and Garden*. Pownal, VT: Storey Communications, 1997.

Choosing plants, creating garden design, and constructing barriers to prevent deer from eating your garden are all explained in this book.

Isaacson, Richard T., ed. *Anderson Horticultural Library's Source List of Plants and Seeds, 5th Edition*. Chanhassen, MN: Anderson Horticultural Library, 2000.

Search this book by plant name to find a nationwide list of nurseries and seed companies that carry the plant or its seed. The Anderson Horticultural Library also offers an online plant-finding reference for those who pay a subscription fee.

Keator, Glenn. *Complete Garden Guide to the Native Perennials of California*. San Francisco: Chronicle Books, 1990.

———. *Complete Garden Guide to the Native Shrubs of California*. San Francisco: Chronicle Books, 1994.

A pair of books that list gardenworthy native plant species and offer suggestions for using them. Sections in each help you learn to grow, propagate, and design gardens with the plants; lists of California native plant and seed sources are also included.

Latymer, Hugo. *The Mediterranean Gardener*. London: Frances Lincoln, 2001.

The author, who gardens and owns a nursery on the Island of Majorca, describes garden design and care for mediterranean climates. The book includes inspiring photographs and a plant encyclopedia.

Lowry, Judith. *Gardening With a Wild Heart: Restoring California's Native Landscapes at Home*. Berkeley: University of California Press, 1999.

A lyrical guide to creating a California "restoration garden," where native plants encourage the survival of ecological complexity.

Nottle, Trevor. *Gardens of the Sun*. Portland: Timber Press, 1996.

A celebration of paying attention to where you are gardening and seeing clearly what works there, this book provides wonderful ideas for design, plant choice, and culture, with inspiring photos to help create a garden in a mediterranean climate. This book is especially suitable for those in hot summer microclimates, but all mediterranean gardeners will enjoy the fresh approach.

Peirce, Pam. *Golden Gate Gardening: The Complete Guide to Food Gardening in the San Francisco Bay Area and Coastal California, Revised Edition*. Seattle: Sasquatch Books, 1998.

This guide to growing vegetables, herbs, edible flowers, and fruit includes helpful information for all of the region's gardeners. You will find an explanation of the microclimates of Northern California's western side, as well as guides to improving soils, composting, watering, and managing weeds and other pests.

Reich, Lee. *The Pruning Book*. Newtown, CT: Taunton Press, 1997.

This book provides general pruning instructions, illustrated with line drawings and photos. Short instructions explain when and how to prune many specific plants.

Schmidt, Marjorie G. *Growing California Native Plants*. Berkeley: University of California Press, 1980.

Still a classic on growing natives, Schmidt's book includes information on growing and designing gardens with annuals, perennials, bulbs, shrubs, and trees.

Successful Plants for the Peninsula: A Selection. Palo Alto, CA: Western Horticulture Society, 1989.

> *A group of Western Horticulture Society members wrote entries on favorite perennials for peninsula gardens. Some are well-known plants, others are unusual selections. Each entry includes useful tips for growing and propagating the plant in our region.*

Stevens, Barbara and Conner, Nancy. *Where on Earth: A Guide to Specialty Nurseries and Other Resources for California Gardeners.* Berkeley: Heyday Books, 1997.

> *Currently out-of-print, and probably a bit out-of-date, but invaluable for finding specialty nurseries, botanical gardens, plant societies, colleges that offer classes in horticulture, and Coop Extension offices.*

Sullivan, Ron. *The Garden Lover's Guide: San Francisco Bay Area.* San Francisco, CA: Chronicle Books, 1998.

> *Lists nurseries, nonprofit plant sales, public gardens, garden tours, and plant societies in the Greater Bay Area. Nonprofit plant sales can be a very good source of plants that may be wonderful garden plants though they are hard to find in commercial nurseries.*

Sutton, John. *The Gardener's Guide to Growing Salvias.* Portland: Timber Press, 1999.

> *This author covers sages from the perspective of England and Europe. California gardeners will find information on many sages that are also available in the United States, and will find the explanation for how to grow and propagate sages particularly useful.*

Toogood, Alan. *Plant Propagation: The Fully Integrated Plant-by-Plant Manual of Practical Techniques.* New York: DK Publishing, 1999.

> *Extensive directions and many color photos guide the would-be propagator in reproducing many species of plants.*

Turner, Dick, ed. *Pacific Horticulture . . . The Magazine for West Coast Gardeners.* Berkeley: Pacific Horticultural Foundation.

> *Along with useful articles and color photographs,* Pacific Horticulture *includes a calendar of horticultural events for the region. Subscriptions are a benefit of membership in the California Horticultural Society, Strybing Arboretum Society, Western Horticultural Society, Southern California Horticultural Society, and the Northwest Horticultural Society, or may be obtained without joining these organizations. For more information and recent contents, visit their website (www.pacifichorticulture.org).*

Voget, Caroline, ed. *Veld and Flora: Journal of the Botanical Society of South Africa.* Claremont.

> *This magazine features South African native plants, or "indigenous plants" as they are called there, and includes information on their wild habitats and uses in gardens, as well as many color photographs. The website of the society (www.botanicalsociety.org.za) offers membership information and links to other sites about South African plants and gardening.*

RESOURCES

SOURCES OF INFORMATION ABOUT WEEDS AND WILDLAND INVASIVES

California Department of Food and Agriculture • pi.cdfa.ca.gov/weedinfo
This website provides a full list of the state's noxious weeds, with descriptions, photos, and maps, and a description of the CDFA noxious weed program.

California Noxious Weeds Control Project Inventory
For a web page that allows you to click on listed plant names and learn the location of local eradication projects, go to: endeavor.des.ucdavis.edu/weeds/specieslist.asp, or use the following web page to search the list using any of several categories: endeavor.des.ucdavis.edu/weeds/

California Exotic Pest Plant Council (CalEPPC) • 1442-A Walnut Street #462 • Berkeley, CA 94709 • 510/525-1502 • www.caleppc.org
On CalEPPC's website you can read their list of Invasive Nonnative Plants of Greatest Ecological Concern in California as well as an electronic version of their book, Invasive Plants of California's Wildlands. *Members receive a quarterly newsletter, the CalEPPC News.*

California Native Plant Society • 1722 J Street, Suite 17 • Sacramento, CA 95814 916/447-2677 • caleppc.org
By calling the California Native Plant Society or accessing their website, you can search for the local chapter nearest you and find out what it is doing to preserve wildlands and promote the use of native plants in gardens. The regional chapters often sponsor classes, events, and native plant sales. They can also tell you where you can see native habitats that have been preserved or re-created in botanical gardens in your area.

PLANT SOCIETIES FOR FEATURED PLANTS

American Fuchsia Society • www.american-fuchsia-soc.org
American Ivy Society • www.ivy.org
Cactus and Succulent Society of America • www.cssainc.org
International Geranium Society • www.geocities.com/RainForest/2822/

US DEPARTMENT OF AGRICULTURE, COOPERATIVE EXTENSION

The Cooperative Extension, a public information branch of U.C. Davis, offers many resources for gardeners. Find them in your white pages, in every county but San Francisco, in "County Government Offices," under "Cooperative Extension, University of California," or by email, using the formula "ce[name of county]@ucdavis.edu," (for example "cealameda@ucdavis.edu). Many county extensions offer gardening classes through Master Gardener programs. The extension also publishes many helpful books, slide shows, and videos, which you can obtain through print or online catalogs at:

University of California • Agriculture and Natural Resources • ANR Communication Services • 6701 San Pablo Avenue • Oakland, CA 94608-1239 • 510/643-5370 • 800/994-8849 • www.anrcatalog.ucdavis.edu

INDEX

navelwort *(Omphalodes cappodocica)*, 91
Nephrolepis cordifolia, 112
Nigella: N. damascena (love-in-a-mist), 92–95; *N. hispanica*, 94; *N. orientalis* (love-in-a-mist 'Transformer'), 94; *N. sativa*, 95
northern California: mediterranean climate of, 9–10; rainy season in, 10

O

Oenothera speciosa 'Rosea' (primrose), 47
Olmstead, Frederick Law, 7
Omphalodes cappodocica (navelwort), 91
Opuntia: O. basilaris, 255; *O. ficus-indica* (prickly pear cactus), 2, 229, 252–55; *O. macrocentra*, 255; *O. microdasys*, 255; *O. violacea*, 255
Oregon grape *(Mahonia aquifolium)*, 265
organic matter, 23–25
oriental poppies, 107
ornamental gardening, 4
Oxalis pes-caprae (cape oxalis), 199
ox-eye daisy *(Leucanthemum vulgare)*, 57, 109

P

palm *(Phoenix canariensis)*, 14
paludosum daisy *(Mauranthemum paludosum)*, 83–87
pampas grass *(Cortaderia selloana)*, 109
Parietaria (pellitory), 185
"partial shade," 28
Pelargonium, 108, 167–70; *P. angulosum*, 160; *P. crispum*, 168, 170; *P. cucculatum*, 160; *P. fulgidum*, 160; *P. grandiflorum*, 160; *P. graveolens*, 170; *P. odoratissimum*, 170; *P. peltatum*, 160; *P. tomentosum*,

168, 170; *P.* x *domesticum* (regal geranium), 159–62; *P.* x *hortorum*, 162–66
pellitory *(Parietaria)*, 185
Pennisetum setaceum (fountain grass), 109
pennyroyal *(Menta pulgeum)*, 109
perennials: acanthus *(Acanthus mollis)*, 110–14; bergenia *(Bergenia)*, 123–26; centranthus *(Centranthus ruber)*, 127–30; climate for, 108; columbine *(Aquilegia)*, 115–18; cutting back of, 106; description of, 105–07; *Digitalis purpurea* (foxglove), 135–38; English daisy *(Bellis perennis)*, 119–22; *Erigeron karvinskianus* (Mexican daisy), 128, 139–42; *Eschscholzia californica* (California poppy), 108, 143–46; Kenilworth ivy *(Cymbalaria muralis)*, 131–34; *Linaria purpurea* (purple toadflax), 134, 147–50; *Lychnis coronaria* (rose campion), 17, 68, 151–54; *Mirabilis jalapa* (four o'clock), 155–58; *Pelargonium* x *domesticum* (regal geranium), 159–62; *Pelargonium* x *hortorum* (zonal geranium), 162–66; *Pericallis* x *hybrida* (cineraria), 13, 108, 171–74; *Persicaria capitata* (pink fleece flower), 36, 175–78; *Salvia leucantha* (Mexican sage), 179–83; scented geraniums *(Pelargonium)*, 167–70; selecting of, 107–08; soil for, 106; *Soleirolia soleirolii* (baby's tears), 184–87; subtropical, 108; *Tanacetum parthenium* (feverfew), 188–91; *Vinca major* (periwinkle), 192–95; weedy, 108–09, 200
Pericallis: P. cruentus, 172; *P. heritieri*, 172; *P. tussilaginis*,

172; *P.* x *hybrida* (cineraria), 13, 108, 171–74
periwinkle *(Vinca major)*, 192–95
Persicaria: P. capitata (pink fleece flower), 36, 175–78; *P. cuspidatum*, 178; *P. microcephala*, 178; *P. orientale*, 178; *P. virginiana*, 178
Phoenix canariensis (palm), 14
pinching, 263
pine *(Pinus canariensis)*, 14
pink fleece flower *(Persicaria capitata)*, 36, 175–78
Pinus canariensis (pine), 14
plants: adaptability of, 14–17; caring for, 22; climate for, 11–14; cold temperature effects, 29–30; grooming of, 30–33; growing of, 54–56; hardiness of, 29–30; history of, 1–4; names of, 17–22; reproducing of, 34–37; scientific names of, 17–22; sexuality of, 3; shadow for, 28–29; soil requirements, 22–25; staking of, 30; succulent. *see* succulent plants; sunlight for, 28–29; variety of, 13–14, 43; water for, 25–28
poor man's orchid *(Impatiens balfourii)*, 63, 75–78
poor man's rhododendron *(Impatiens sodenii)*, 12, 291–94
Portulacaria afra (elephant food), 246
prickly pear cactus *(Opuntia ficus-indica)*, 2, 229, 252–55
pride of Madeira *(Echium candicans)*, 271–74
primrose *(Oenothera speciosa* 'Rosea'), 47
pruning, 33
Prunus: P. ilicifolia (holly-leaf cherry), 265; *P. lyonii* (Catalina cherry), 265
purple linaria. *see* purple toadflax *(Linaria purpurea)*
purple loosestrife *(Lythrum salicaria)*, 109

Photos by Pam Peirce: xi, 8, 11, 63, 83B, 92B, 96B, 123B, 143B, 171T, 171B, 227, 248, 291

Plant designers: Bob Clark: 87, 88B, 100 / Harland Hand: vii, 248 / Jonathan Plante: 119B / Candra Scott: 62